"I know of no more reliable gu[ide to this spiritual giant of Victorian Christianity as a touch]stone. Anything written by him is not to be missed. Ryle, who died in 1900, is still being used by God across the world today. *Ryle on the Christian Life* will be a key book for veteran readers of Ryle and newcomers alike."
    Iain H. Murray, author, *J. C. Ryle: Prepared to Stand Alone*

"This volume is deeply grounded not only in a robust and rich understanding of the era in which J. C. Ryle lived but also in a very meticulous and judicious reading of his written work, especially his tracts. They are rarely the subject of theological and historical reflection, and church history is the poorer for it. This neglected form of print media has had an enormous influence for good, and as Andrew Atherstone stresses, Ryle was, above all, the 'prince of tract writers.' This is an excellent study of Ryle and his theology, which is as pertinent for us today as it was in his Victorian world."
    Michael A. G. Azad Haykin, Professor of Church History, The Southern Baptist Theological Seminary

"There is no doubting the significance of Bishop J. C. Ryle in both his own lifetime and the present day. In *Ryle on the Christian Life*, he speaks to us in his own words, a fiery preacher addressing his apathetic culture and constantly evangelizing. He was shaped by Reformation Anglicanism and appealed always to the full teaching of Scripture as the sole word of God. I was frequently challenged by this book and warmly commend it."
    Peter Jensen, former Archbishop of Sydney, Australia

"Although he was very much a man of the nineteenth century, J. C. Ryle's voice still speaks with forceful clarity today. He was an evangelist, both in his ministry to non-Christians, chiefly through numerous tracts, and in his appeal to Christians to hold firmly to the 'old paths' of the gospel and apply them deeply to the heart. There remains a contemporary power to his writing, with his lively exposition of Scripture, vivid illustrations, and down-to-earth applications. Andrew Atherstone has done a wonderful job in introducing Ryle's life and teaching, both for those new to his ministry and for old hands, who will discover much fresh material in this book."
    Vaughan Roberts, Rector, St Ebbe's Church, Oxford, United Kingdom

"In *Ryle on the Christian Life*, Andrew Atherstone offers a fresh and engaging introduction to J. C. Ryle's theology of the Christian life. With clarity and conviction, he shows how Ryle's gospel-centered emphasis on grace, holiness, and Scripture speaks powerfully to believers today. This book is both a tribute to a faithful evangelical voice and a timely guide for anyone seeking to grow in godliness. I warmly commend it to all who desire to follow Christ more closely."
    Samuel Morrison, former Bishop of Valparaíso, Chile

"Andrew Atherstone introduces modern readers to Ryle's essential tracts on the Christian life, rooted in foundational themes like faith and grace. Ryle championed the Bible as the infallible word of God, the ultimate authority by which all teaching must be tested. For modern readers seeking grounded, practical wisdom for the journey of faith, Ryle's classic evangelical teaching remains profoundly relevant today."

Samy Fawzy Shehata, Bishop of Egypt; Archbishop of the Anglican Province of Alexandria

"Andrew Atherstone brings J. C. Ryle and his Victorian world vividly to life. With deep historical insight into an age of novelty and restlessness, Atherstone shows how Ryle responded to the spiritual needs of his time as a passionate preacher and courageous evangelist. Just as Ryle drew timeless wisdom from Reformation history and Puritan classics to serve his own generation, this book helps us hear afresh a faithful voice from the past—with clarity, conviction, and relevance for today. I warmly commend it!"

Christy Wang, JSPS Fellow, The University of Tokyo, Japan

"Andrew Atherstone has done the hard work of distilling J. C. Ryle's thoughts on the Christian life—no small feat, given the numerous tracts Ryle wrote. This book orients us to Ryle's evangelical convictions on the reality of sin, the need for conversion, the role of the Holy Spirit, the supremacy of Scripture, and so on. I highly recommend it to those seeking inspiration on evangelical truths."

Titus Chung, Bishop of Singapore; Archbishop of the Anglican Province of South-East Asia

RYLE
on the Christian Life

THEOLOGIANS ON THE CHRISTIAN LIFE

EDITED BY JUSTIN TAYLOR AND THOMAS KIDD

Grimké on the Christian Life:
Christian Vitality for the Church and World,
Drew Martin

Ryle on the Christian Life:
Growing in Grace,
Andrew Atherstone

Whitefield on the Christian Life:
New Birth to Enjoy God,
Tom Schwanda and Ian Maddock

EDITED BY STEPHEN J. NICHOLS AND JUSTIN TAYLOR

Augustine on the Christian Life:
Transformed by the Power of God,
Gerald Bray

Bavinck on the Christian Life:
Following Jesus in Faithful Service,
John Bolt

Bonhoeffer on the Christian Life:
From the Cross, for the World,
Stephen J. Nichols

Calvin on the Christian Life:
Glorifying and Enjoying God Forever,
Michael Horton

Edwards on the Christian Life:
Alive to the Beauty of God,
Dane C. Ortlund

Lewis on the Christian Life:
Becoming Truly Human in
the Presence of God,
Joe Rigney

Lloyd-Jones on the Christian Life:
Doctrine and Life as Fuel and Fire,
Jason Meyer

Luther on the Christian Life:
Cross and Freedom,
Carl R. Trueman

Newton on the Christian Life:
To Live Is Christ,
Tony Reinke

Owen on the Christian Life:
Living for the Glory of God in Christ,
Matthew Barrett and
Michael A. G. Haykin

Packer on the Christian Life:
Knowing God in Christ,
Walking by the Spirit,
Sam Storms

Schaeffer on the Christian Life:
Countercultural Spirituality,
William Edgar

Spurgeon on the Christian Life:
Alive in Christ,
Michael Reeves

Stott on the Christian Life:
Between Two Worlds,
Tim Chester

Warfield on the Christian Life:
Living in Light of the Gospel,
Fred G. Zaspel

Wesley on the Christian Life:
The Heart Renewed in Love,
Fred Sanders

RYLE
on the Christian Life

GROWING IN GRACE

ANDREW ATHERSTONE

❖ CROSSWAY®
WHEATON, ILLINOIS

Ryle on the Christian Life: Growing in Grace

© 2025 by Andrew Atherstone

Published by Crossway
        1300 Crescent Street
        Wheaton, Illinois 60187

All rights reserved. No part of this publication may be reproduced, stored in a retrieval system, or transmitted in any form by any means, electronic, mechanical, photocopy, recording, or otherwise, without the prior permission of the publisher, except as provided for by USA copyright law. Crossway® is a registered trademark in the United States of America.

Cover design: Josh Dennis

Cover image: Richard Solomon Artists, Mark Summers

First printing 2025

Printed in the United States of America

Scripture quotations are from the King James Version of the Bible, the translation with which Ryle and his Victorian hearers and readers were most familiar. Public domain.

Trade paperback ISBN: 978-1-4335-6734-6
ePub ISBN: 978-1-4335-6737-7
PDF ISBN: 978-1-4335-6735-3

Library of Congress Cataloging-in-Publication Data

Names: Atherstone, Andrew, author
Title: Ryle on the Christian life : growing in grace / Andrew Atherstone.
Description: Wheaton, Illinois : Crossway, [2025] | Series: Theologians on the Christian life | Includes bibliographical references and index.
Identifiers: LCCN 2024059353 (print) | LCCN 2024059354 (ebook) | ISBN 9781433567346 trade paperback | ISBN 9781433567353 pdf | ISBN 9781433567377 epub
Subjects: LCSH: Ryle, J. C. (John Charles), 1816-1900 | Christian life
Classification: LCC BX5199.R9 A84 2025 (print) | LCC BX5199.R9 (ebook) | DDC 248.4—dc23/eng/20250624
LC record available at https://lccn.loc.gov/2024059353
LC ebook record available at https://lccn.loc.gov/2024059354

Crossway is a publishing ministry of Good News Publishers.

VP		34	33	32	31	30	29	28	27	26	25			
15	14	13	12	11	10	9	8	7	6	5	4	3	2	1

*For the students and friends of
Wycliffe Hall, Oxford,
the evangelical seminary
which J. C. Ryle helped to establish
in his old university city*

CONTENTS

Series Preface ... ix
Introduction: Prince of Tract Writers ... 1

1. Scripture's Supremacy ... 9
2. Sin and Salvation ... 21
3. Conversion ... 39
4. Sovereign Grace ... 57
5. Heart Religion ... 71
6. Fruits of Faith ... 85
7. Fighting for Holiness ... 101
8. Means of Grace ... 115
9. Preaching ... 133
10. Sorrow and Affliction ... 147
11. Facing Eternity ... 161

Further Reading ... 177
General Index ... 179
Scripture Index ... 187

SERIES PREFACE

Some might call us spoiled. We live in an era of significant and substantial resources for Christians on living the Christian life. We have ready access to books, videos, online material, seminars—all in the interest of encouraging us in our daily walk with Christ. The laity, the people in the pew, have access to more information than scholars dreamed of having in previous centuries.

Yet, for all our abundance of resources, we also lack something. We tend to lack the perspectives from the past, perspectives from a different time and place than our own. To put the matter differently, we have so many riches in our current horizon that we tend not to look to the horizons of the past.

That is unfortunate, especially when it comes to learning about and practicing discipleship. It's like owning a mansion and choosing to live in only one room. This series invites you to explore the other rooms.

As we go exploring, we will visit places and times different from our own. We will see different models, approaches, and emphases. This series does not intend for these models to be copied uncritically, and it certainly does not intend to put these figures from the past high upon a pedestal like some race of super-Christians. This series intends, however, to help us in the present listen to the past. We believe there is wisdom in the past twenty centuries of the church, wisdom for living the Christian life.

Justin Taylor and Thomas Kidd

INTRODUCTION

PRINCE OF TRACT WRITERS

John Charles Ryle (1816–1900) was one of the most popular theological writers of the Victorian period, and the most prominent evangelical clergyman in the Church of England. His ministry almost exactly spanned the reign of Queen Victoria—he was converted to Christ in 1837, just a few months after the young Queen's accession to the British throne, and died at the dawn of the new century in 1900, just a few months before the monarch's own death.

An Era of Change

The Victorian age was an era of remarkable social, political, and technological upheaval. Industrial powerhouses like London, Manchester, and Birmingham drove Britain's economic boom. Railways crisscrossed the nation, superseding the old canal network, while steamships traversed the Atlantic, and the revolutionary "penny post" enabled affordable communications throughout the United Kingdom. The 1851 Great Exhibition in the Crystal Palace promoted Victorian ingenuity in science and manufacturing, while artistic creativity attracted royal patronage from Prince Albert, the prince consort. The Palace of Westminster, home to the British Parliament, was rebuilt in the 1840s and 1850s as a showcase for artistic talent and national mythologizing. Engineering wonders like the Clifton Suspension Bridge and the London Underground, both opened in the 1860s, enthralled the public. The frontiers of knowledge were pushed back in every area, from archaeology and astronomy to linguistics and medicine, while popular authors like Charles Dickens (1812–1870), George Eliot (1819–1880), and Lewis Carroll (1832–1898) added classics to the English literary canon. Meanwhile, Victoria's global empire demonstrated an avaricious appetite for land and riches, colonizing swaths of new territory across India, Africa, and Australasia, defended by the British military from the Punjab to the Transvaal.

During this age of exploration and conquest, many of Britain's historic Christian institutions were progressively secularized. The Houses of Parliament, an exclusively Anglican preserve until the late 1820s, formally admitted atheists for the first time in the 1880s. The two ancient universities at Oxford and Cambridge, also bastions of the Church of England, were secularized by acts of Parliament, removing all religious prerequisites. The Church of Ireland was disestablished and disendowed by William Gladstone's Liberal government, and the Liberation Society (founded 1844) campaigned for the disestablishment of the Church of England also. Yet national religion was on the rise as the churches embraced the mood of Victorian optimism and expansionism, with thousands of ambitious church building projects and the growth of powerful mission agencies. Denominations sought to outdo one another in the rush for cultural capital, but some of them joined forces in political and moral crusades for elementary education, sanitation, workers' rights, temperance, and sexual purity, or for evangelistic enterprise. Christian leaders became national celebrities, like Cardinal John Henry Newman (1801–1890), a Roman Catholic convert from Anglicanism, and Charles Haddon Spurgeon (1834–1892), Baptist preacher at London's Metropolitan Tabernacle who enjoyed a global following.

Competitiveness was also evident within the Church of England, which held a privileged position in national life and covered every square mile of the country with its network of over twelve thousand parishes and over twenty thousand clergymen. Tractarianism, born in Oxford in the 1830s, helped to foster the revival of Catholic theology and later morphed into Anglican ritualism, provoking expensive court cases over the legitimate boundaries of Anglican doctrine and liturgy. The "broad church" movement, forerunners of theological liberalism, also experimented with new interpretations, seeking to integrate modern discoveries with ancient orthodoxies, while Charles Darwin's *On the Origin of Species* (1859) stimulated new paradigms in Christian anthropology. Evangelicals within the establishment were likewise a vibrant and diverse array, engaged in a plethora of missional and reformist activities, and they contributed to the theological ferment. They had grown in influence from their Georgian roots as a beleaguered minority, associated with personalities like the former slave trader John Newton (1725–1807), literary "blue-stocking" Hannah More (1745–1833), parliamentary campaigner William Wilberforce (1759–1833), and Cambridge preacher Charles Simeon (1759–1836), to achieve a new position of dominance by the mid-Victorian period. A succession of evangelicals were promoted as bishops and cathedral deans, including John Bird Sumner (1780–1862), who in 1848 was the first evangelical to be elevated as archbishop of Canterbury. The philanthropist Lord Shaftesbury (1801–1885), best known for his parliamentary agitations on behalf of the poor, had the ear of Prime Minister Palmerston, which ensured a steady stream of evangelical appointments to high office. Anglican evangelical societies and conferences permeated the country, often drawing large audiences and sizeable donations, while their publications were multitudinous, including monthly journals like *The Christian Observer* and *The Churchman*, and newspapers like *The Record* and *The Rock*. Evangelical parishes also multiplied. It was said that in 1800 the number of Anglican evangelical churches in London and its environs could be counted on a child's fingers, but two generations later, "You could hardly count them now on the fingers of the hundred-handed Briareus," a mythological giant.[1]

Enter Ryle

Ryle was a figurehead within this burgeoning Anglican evangelical movement. He was a natural orator and platform speaker who had honed his skills as a teenager in the debating society at Eton College, and had ambitions to follow his father as a member of Parliament. But Ryle's Christian conversion in 1837, in his final months as an undergraduate at the University of Oxford, combined with the collapse of the family bank in Macclesfield in 1841, drove him instead into Christian ministry. After a curacy in the New Forest in Hampshire, he spent the bulk of his ministry in two villages in rural Suffolk, as rector of Helmingham (1844–1861) and vicar of Stradbroke (1861–1880), in the diocese of Norwich. On the nomination of Prime Minister Benjamin Disraeli, Ryle was transferred to a very

---

[1] Quoted in Andrew Atherstone, "Anglican Evangelicalism," in *The Oxford History of Anglicanism*, vol. 3, *Partisan Anglicanism and Its Global Expansion, 1829–c. 1914*, ed. Rowan Strong (Oxford University Press, 2017), 166.

different scene of ministry in 1880, as the first bishop of Liverpool, a new urban diocese with 1.1 million inhabitants, where he labored for the last two decades of his life.

It was in Suffolk that Ryle established his fame as a conference speaker and prolific tract writer. He recalled in his autobiography—dictated in 1873 and rediscovered in 2015—that in Helmingham, with only three hundred parishioners, the ministerial load was light, and he had "plenty of spare time" for reading and writing.[2] From the mid-1840s, he began to publish short tracts, initially as exhortations to his own congregation, which soon won an eager readership across the country. As an author, Ryle was at the height of his powers between the 1850s and the 1870s, his most fruitful and creative period. Although he published some longer books, such as *Expository Thoughts on the Gospels* in seven volumes between 1856 and 1873, the tract was his vehicle of choice. After his consecration as a bishop, his energies were absorbed by diocesan administration, which allowed much less facility to write, though he continued to publish occasional sermons and addresses. Ryle was also an inveterate correspondent to the evangelical newspapers, under pseudonyms such as "A Suffolk Incumbent," "A Northern Churchman," and "An Old Soldier," a significant dimension of his literary legacy that has been overlooked until recently.[3]

Many of Ryle's tracts began as sermons, and he knew how to grab his readers' attention. His appeals were direct and vigorous, with pithy titles designed to startle and awaken: *Are You Forgiven?*, *Are You Happy?*, *Are You Holy?*, *Do You Believe?*, *Are You Free?*, *Do You Love Christ?*, *Repent or Perish!* He often made use of national events and crises, or of moments for sober reflection, like Christmas and the New Year, to claim a hearing.[4] For example, in his tract for New Year 1851, Ryle urged:

> Oh! reader, if you never came to Christ for life before, come to Him this very year. Come to Him with the penitent's prayer for mercy and grace. Come to Him without delay. Come to Him while the name of 1851 is still strange to you. Come to Him before the winter is past, and let the spring find you a new creature.[5]

Likewise, his tract for New Year 1854 exhorted:

---

[2] *Bishop J. C. Ryle's Autobiography: The Early Years*, ed. Andrew Atherstone (Banner of Truth, 2016), 117.
[3] *Bishop J. C. Ryle's Letters: The Later Years*, ed. Andrew Atherstone (Banner of Truth, forthcoming).
[4] J. C. Ryle, *Christmas Thoughts*, ed. Andrew Atherstone (Banner of Truth, 2022).
[5] J. C. Ryle, *Wheat or Chaff? A Question for 1851* (Ipswich, 1851), 30.

Reader, I charge you not to lie down on your bed tonight without trying to answer my question. I summon you before you sleep to bring the matter to an issue. We stand at the end of an old year. We live in an old worn-out, sin-laden world. Who can tell what a year may bring forth? Who shall live to see 1855?[6]

Ryle's tracts were also intensely practical. "I hold it to be of cardinal importance," he declared, "not to be content with generalities in delivering God's message to souls." He did not want anyone to finish one of his tracts unable to answer the question "What practical lesson have I learned?"[7] With evangelistic urgency, Ryle therefore always demanded a response. In his tract on prayer, for example, he called his readers to take action: "Wait for nothing. Wait for nobody. Waiting comes from the devil. Just as you are, go to Christ."[8]

The tract, second only to the sermon, was widely utilized by Victorian Christians of all stripes to campaign and communicate. For Ryle it was principally a spiritual tool, which he harnessed energetically. "May it be recorded in heaven," he wrote in 1857, "that by reading this tract some souls were saved!"[9] He prayed that the Holy Spirit would turn his New Year tract for 1860 into "an arrow to pierce many hearts!"[10] It was a popular and powerful but inherently transient form of literature. Some of Ryle's original tracts are now extremely rare, even from print runs of tens of thousands, and others have disappeared altogether. They were usually short (sometimes only a few pages), cheaply manufactured, and sold in bulk for mass circulation. Most were given away for free by evangelical ministers, or local tract distributors, as a missional strategy. The response was therefore inevitably mixed. Some were immediately thrown away, burned, or otherwise destroyed by hostile recipients, perhaps in large numbers. Others lay unwanted and unread. In one of his 1858 tracts, Ryle pleaded:

My heart's desire and prayer to God is this, that this tract may be greatly useful to your soul. I entreat you to give it a fair reading. Do not put it in the fire. Do not tear it in pieces. Read it! Read it! Read it to the end! Who can tell but the Holy Ghost may employ this tract for the saving of your soul?[11]

---
[6] J. C. Ryle, *Have You the Spirit? A Question for 1854* (Ipswich, 1854), 26.
[7] J. C. Ryle, *"He Whom Thou Lovest Is Sick": A Tract on Sickness, Being Thoughts on John xi. 3* (Ipswich, 1859), 14.
[8] J. C. Ryle, *Do You Pray? A Question for 1852* (Ipswich, 1852), 23.
[9] J. C. Ryle, *Your Soul! Being Thoughts on Mark viii. 36, 37* (Ipswich, 1857), 3.
[10] J. C. Ryle, *Is Thy Heart Right? A Question for Everybody* (Ipswich, 1860), 4.
[11] J. C. Ryle, *Where Are Your Sins? A Question for Everybody* (Ipswich, 1858), 3–4.

Likewise, at New Year 1861, Ryle warned that salvation was at stake, so the reader should not "throw down this tract in anger or impatience" but read it through.[12] At Christmas the following year, he opened with a promise that his tract would not take long to read: "Do not throw it aside. Do not turn it into food for jesting and ridicule. It is written with a sincere desire to do good. May God the Holy Ghost apply it with power to your conscience, head, heart, and soul!"[13] Although Ryle's tracts made him globally famous and won him an eager Christian readership, many of them were originally designed for a more hostile environment, to awaken the unconverted.

Ryle became known as "the prince of tract writers."[14] According to contemporary estimates, twelve million copies of his tracts were in circulation during his lifetime.[15] They also appeared in translation, beginning with *Living or Dead?* (1849), which was circulated in French as *Mort ou Vivant?* (1851) and in German as *Lebendig oder Todt?* (1851).[16] Other tracts were translated into Welsh, Gaelic, Dutch, Portuguese, Spanish, Italian, Norwegian, Swedish, Danish, Russian, Chinese, and Hindustani.[17]

Ryle established a long and fruitful partnership with Edward Hunt (1792–1862) and his son William Hunt (1823–1901), booksellers and publishers from Ipswich with a genius for marketing. They sold Ryle's tracts in many different formats, frequently revised, abridged, or cut down into shorter sections, sometimes only four or eight pages long. They also identified an audience who preferred longer and more durable books, so Ryle's tracts were edited and repackaged as compilation volumes. During the 1850s Ryle published seven compilations, entitled *Home Truths*, with about nine or ten tracts per volume. Later he marketed larger compilations, with about nineteen or twenty tracts per volume, which helped to establish his reputation as a serious theological author. The best known were *Knots Untied* (1874), *Old Paths* (1877), *Practical Religion* (1878), *Holiness* (1879), *Principles for Churchmen* (1884), *The Upper Room* (1888), and *Light from Old Times* (1890). There was also a volume of his preaching, *The Christian Race and Other Sermons* (1900), taken from his manuscripts. After his death, Ryle's

---

[12] J. C. Ryle, *Do You Believe? A Question for 1861* (Ipswich, 1860), 5.
[13] J. C. Ryle, *Do You Love Christ? A Question for All!* (London, 1862), 4.
[14] G. R. Balleine, *A History of the Evangelical Party in the Church of England* (Longmans, Green, 1908), 272. See also Alan Munden, "J. C. Ryle: Prince of Tract-Writers," in *Stand Firm and Fight On: J. C. Ryle and the Future for Anglican Evangelicals*, ed. Lee Gatiss (Lost Coin, 2016), 93–101.
[15] W. F. Machray, *The First Bishop of Liverpool: John Charles Ryle* (Thynne, 1900), 43.
[16] J. C. Ryle, *Mort ou Vivant? Question Adressée à Chacun* (Ipswich, 1851); Ryle, *Lebendig oder Todt? Eine Frage für Jedermann* (Ipswich, 1851).
[17] Machray, *The First Bishop of Liverpool*, 44.

episcopal speeches were gathered together by another enterprising publisher and marketed as *Charges and Addresses* (1903).

Although Ryle was largely forgotten in the first half of the twentieth century, dismissed as a backward-looking Victorian from a bygone age, there was an unexpected resurgence of interest in his theology after the Second World War. When *Holiness* was republished in 1956, Martyn Lloyd-Jones celebrated the rediscovery of Ryle as "one of the most encouraging and hopeful signs I have observed for many a long day."[18] Many of Ryle's compilation volumes are now back in print for a global Christian audience hungry for classic evangelical teaching. He is more widely read today than at any period since his own lifetime.

Ryle on the Christian Life

This book, *Ryle on the Christian Life*, is not a biography. It does not analyze Ryle's education or his parochial ministry or his evangelical networks across the United Kingdom or his diocesan administration. It neglects many important themes, such as Ryle's deep participation in Church of England affairs, his campaigns for church reform, his controversial involvement in the annual Church Congress movement, his connection with the antiritualist Church Association, his nationwide travels on deputation for evangelical mission agencies, and his didactic use of Reformation history.[19] Likewise, it leaves aside his addresses to children and his views on contested subjects such as disestablishment, Roman Catholicism, relations with Nonconformity, and the place of Israel in prophetic fulfillment. Instead, this book aims to introduce modern readers to Ryle's many tracts on the Christian life, especially his publications designed for a mass market from the late 1840s to the early 1880s. Ryle is most often encountered today via his compilation volumes, but, importantly, *Ryle on the Christian Life* examines his tracts in their earliest published forms, where the original context and setting generate richer interpretations.

---

[18] D. M. Lloyd-Jones, foreword to J. C. Ryle, *Holiness: Its Nature, Hindrances, Difficulties, and Roots* (James Clarke, 1956), iii.
[19] For Ryle's approach to history, see Andrew Atherstone, "J. C. Ryle and Evangelical Churchmanship," in *Making Evangelical History: Faith, Scholarship and the Evangelical Past*, ed. Andrew Atherstone and David Ceri Jones (Routledge, 2019), 81–101.

CHAPTER 1

SCRIPTURE'S SUPREMACY

The Bible was the foundational text for Ryle's Christian life and public ministry. It played a prominent role in his ordination by the bishop of Winchester, in the chapel at Farnham Castle in Surrey, when Ryle was twenty-five years old. One of the first questions he was asked by the bishop on his admission to the diaconate in December 1841 was "Do you unfeignedly believe all the Canonical Scriptures of the Old and New Testament?" To this Ryle affirmed, "I do believe them."[1] The following December, 1842, on Ryle's ordination to the presbyterate, the bishop asked whether he was persuaded of the Bible's sufficiency "for eternal salvation through faith in Jesus Christ" and was determined to teach that scriptural gospel to "the people committed to your charge"? Again the young clergyman replied, "I am so persuaded, and have so determined by God's grace."[2] Throughout the next six decades of his ministry, he viewed these ordination promises with great seriousness. He aimed to promote a model of the Christian life deeply shaped by the Bible in every way.

Ryle urged his congregations always to hold him to account by testing his doctrine at the bar of Scripture. He deemed it the obligation of every Christian, not only ordained ministers, to judge every religious teaching by the word of God. Ryle expounded this Reformation principle—"the right of private judgment"—when preaching before the British Reformation Society

---

[1] Ordinal (1662) in *The Book of Common Prayer: The Texts of 1549, 1559, and 1662*, ed. Brian Cummings (Oxford University Press, 2011), 630.
[2] Ordinal (1662), 637.

at London's Portman Chapel in May 1851.[3] The sermon was published as *Prove All Things*, echoing Paul's injunction to the early Christians (1 Thess. 5:21). No doctrine was to be believed simply because it was taught by a bishop, evangelist, preacher, or synod. Whether the teaching authority was an early church father or sixteenth-century Reformer, pope or Puritan, or even the universal church itself, all must be tested. Ryle exclaimed:

> Prove all things by the Word of God—all ministers, all teaching, all preaching, all doctrines, all sermons, all writings, all opinions, all practices—prove all by the Word of God. Measure all by the measure of the Bible. Compare all with the standard of the Bible. Weigh all in the balances of the Bible. Examine all by the light of the Bible. Test all in the crucible of the Bible. That which can abide the fire of the Bible, receive, hold, believe, and obey. That which cannot abide the fire of the Bible, reject, refuse, repudiate, and cast away.[4]

It is wrong to believe a doctrine simply because it is the majority view in the church, Ryle insisted. Even great ecumenical councils "sometimes have erred," stated the Church of England's Thirty-Nine Articles of Religion. "Wherefore things ordained by them as necessary to salvation, have neither strength nor authority, unless it may be declared that they be taken out of holy Scripture."[5] Ryle emphasized: "Oh! Reader, it were surely a thousand times better for a man to stand alone, and be saved, than to err in company with the Church, and be lost! It were better to prove all things, and go to heaven, than to say, 'I dare not think for myself,' and go to hell." He praised the determination of the English Reformers, who "broke the fetters of tradition, and dared to think for themselves."[6]

No church is infallible, and even the best ministers make terrible mistakes, Ryle observed. Therefore, acknowledging his own frailty, he pleaded with his hearers: "Follow us so far as we follow Christ, but not a hair's breadth farther. Believe whatever we can show you out of the Bible, but do not believe a single word more."[7] He derided the "blindfold system" of mindlessly believing ordained leaders, and proclaimed, "Let the Bible and not any Church upon earth, or any minister upon earth, be your rule of

---

[3] J. C. Ryle, "British Reformation Society Annual Sermon, Preached at Portman Chapel, Baker Street, on Wednesday, May 14th, 1851," *British Protestant*, June 1851, 117–34.
[4] J. C. Ryle, *Prove All Things: A Tract on Private Judgment, Being Thoughts on 1 Thess. v. 21* (Ipswich, 1851), 5.
[5] Article 21 ("Of the Authority of General Councils"), in Cummings, *The Book of Common Prayer*, 679.
[6] Ryle, *Prove All Things*, 8–9, 11.
[7] Ryle, *Prove All Things*, 9.

faith."[8] In another tract, Ryle spoke of the Bible as "this infallible umpire."[9] "It is here alone that infallibility resides," he reiterated. "It is not in the church. It is not in the councils. It is not in ministers. It is only in the written Word."[10]

Bible Education

Ryle's doctrine of Scripture was laid out most fully in *How Readest Thou?*, his New Year tract for 1853, an exposition of Jesus's probing question "What is written in the law? how readest thou?" (Luke 10:26). Two decades later, he reworked this material as *Whose Word Is This?* (1877), republished as *Bible Inspiration: Its Reality and Nature* (1877).

Ryle rejoiced in the 1850s that educational standards were rapidly rising across Britain, with the founding of many new schools and colleges, the reform of the ancient universities of Oxford and Cambridge, and the burgeoning of the book publishing industry. "More is being taught—more is being learned—more is being read, than there ever was since the world began." Nevertheless, he insisted, general knowledge is insufficient because "all the education a man's head can receive, will not save his soul from hell, unless he knows the truths of the Bible." In a lively series of contrasts, Ryle drew a distinction between formal education and biblical faith. Some might possess "prodigious learning," be accomplished in many languages, and have read enough books to be "a walking cyclopaedia" yet remain ignorant of the gospel. "Chemistry never silenced a guilty conscience. Mathematics never healed a broken heart. All the sciences in the world never smoothed down a dying pillow." Conversely, another person might be entirely illiterate, with no grasp of the most basic elements of geography, arithmetic, history, politics, or science, and yet be saved. This motivated Ryle's ministry in rural Suffolk and urban Liverpool, where many of his hearers were farm and factory laborers with little formal education and no concept of university life. "A man may get to heaven without money, learning, health, or friends," he observed, "but without Bible knowledge, he will never get there at all. A man may have the mightiest of minds, and a memory stored with all that mighty mind can grasp—and yet, if he does not know the things of the Bible, he will make shipwreck of his soul for ever."[11]

---
[8] Ryle, *Prove All Things*, 14–15.
[9] J. C. Ryle, *Is Thy Heart Right? A Question for Everybody* (Ipswich, 1860), 5.
[10] J. C. Ryle, *How Readest Thou? A Question for 1853* (Ipswich, 1852), 20.
[11] Ryle, *How Readest Thou?*, 3–5.

In his own education at Eton and Oxford, Ryle was deeply schooled in classics. Allusions to Greek and Roman history and literature frequently populate his sermons and writings. He often lamented that he wished he knew his Bible as well as he knew the Roman poet Horace, who was drummed into him by heart as a teenager.[12] For all their brilliance as philosophers, when these ancient authors attempted to write on religious subjects like the soul and eternity, they merely displayed their ignorance, because they lacked biblical revelation.

> They grope like the blind. They speculate. They conjecture. They generally make the darkness more visible, and land us in a region of uncertainty and doubt. How little did the wisest of the heathen know! How dim were the views of Solon, Socrates, Aristotle, Plato, Cicero, and Seneca! A well-taught Sunday-school child, in the present day, knows more eternal truth than all these sages put together.[13]

The purpose of the Bible, of course, is not to train someone to be a mathematician, doctor, or engineer. Ryle explained that anyone wanting to be a lawyer should read the famous English jurists Sir William Blackstone (1723–1780), or Sir Edward Sugden (1781–1875), lord high chancellor in 1852. The person hoping to be an astronomer should study the groundbreaking discoveries of Sir William Herschel (1738–1822) and his son Sir John Herschel (1792–1871), presidents of the Royal Astronomical Society. Any budding geologist should follow William Buckland (1784–1856), the famous paleontologist and fossil hunter. But for knowledge of salvation, the only place to turn, Ryle insisted, is to the pages of Scripture.[14]

Ryle celebrated that the Bible was designed by God to meet the spiritual needs of every human being in every class, culture, and climate across the globe. It "feeds the mind of the labourer in his cottage" but also "satisfies the gigantic intellects" of scientists and scholars such as Isaac Newton, Thomas Chalmers, David Brewster, and Michael Faraday. It was valued not only by British statesmen and orators like Baron Macaulay (1800–1859) and John Bright (1811–1889), and brilliant editorial writers in *The Times*, but also by "the converted New Zealander in the southern hemisphere, and the Red River Indian in the cold north of America, and the Hindoo under

---

[12] "Herbert Ryle on His Father's Schooldays," in *Bishop J. C. Ryle's Autobiography: The Early Years*, ed. Andrew Atherstone (Banner of Truth, 2016), 193.
[13] Ryle, *How Readest Thou?*, 8–9.
[14] Ryle, *How Readest Thou?*, 18–19.

the tropical sun." Furthermore, the Bible is "always fresh and evergreen and new," no matter how much it is studied and expounded. Theologians for centuries have "incessantly dug down into the mine of Scripture, and yet never exhausted it. It is a well never dry, and a field which is never barren." It meets the deepest longings of every person in every generation, from early Christian women in Rome like Tryphaena and Tryphosa (Rom. 16:12), to Elizabeth Wallbridge (1770–1801) from the parish of Arreton on the Isle of Wight, whose conversion story was immortalized in Legh Richmond's classic *The Dairyman's Daughter* (1814). The Bible, Ryle exclaimed, was equally suited to English aristocrats as to converted Africans in the British colony of Sierra Leone.[15]

Ryle rejoiced that the Bible is "utterly unrivalled" when compared to all other books in wisdom and purity. "There are no weak points, and motes, and flaws, and blemishes. There is no mixture of infirmity and feebleness, such as you will find in the works of even the best Christians." It is therefore "blasphemous folly" to compare the Bible with great literature by William Shakespeare or John Milton. To move from Scripture to these human authors is like exchanging "gold for base metal, and heaven for earth."[16] Every other book, however good or useful, is defective. "The Bible alone is absolutely perfect."[17] For similar reasons, it is "positively absurd" to compare the Bible with other religious texts like the Muslim Qur'an and the Hindu Shastras, or the Book of Mormon, a modern American product that was rapidly gaining adherents in mid-nineteenth-century Britain. Ryle offered several dramatic images to highlight the sharp contrast between the Bible and these rival religious texts. It was like comparing the blazing sun with "a rushlight," a cheap substitute for a candle, popular among the Victorian rural poor. Or like comparing Mont Blanc in the French Alps and Skiddaw in the English Lake District with a mole hill; or the grandeur of St Paul's Cathedral with a hut. Or like comparing the precious Portland Vase—a decorated first-century Roman glass vase, owned by the Duke of Portland and displayed at the British Museum since 1810—with "a garden pot." Or like comparing the Koh-i-Noor diamond—acquired by Queen Victoria in 1849 after the annexation of the Punjab, and displayed at the Great Exhibition in 1851—with a piece of glass. "God seems to have allowed the existence of

---
[15] J. C. Ryle, *Whose Word Is This? Being Thoughts About 2 Tim iii. 16: A Question for 1877* (London, 1877), 15.
[16] Ryle, *Whose Word Is This?*, 12–13.
[17] J. C. Ryle, "Bible-Reading," in *Practical Religion: Being Plain Papers on the Daily Duties, Experience, Dangers, and Privileges of Professing Christians* (London, 1878), 99.

these pretended revelations, in order to prove the immeasurable superiority of His own Word," Ryle concluded.[18]

When describing the Bible's global impact, Ryle turned to contemporary examples of "mighty power" that were attracting national attention in the early 1850s. Thousands of visitors flocked to Portsmouth Harbour every year for tours of *HMS Victory*, the flagship in which Admiral Nelson led the British to triumph over the French and Spanish fleets at the Battle of Trafalgar in 1805. Visits by Queen Victoria boosted public interest.[19] In North Wales, attention was fixed on the construction of the impressive Britannia Bridge over the Menai Strait, linking Anglesey by railway to the rest of the country. Its heavy sections were slowly raised into place during 1849–1850 by hydraulic cylinders, an innovative process overseen by engineer Robert Stephenson. These mighty symbols of Britain's naval and engineering prowess were spectacular, Ryle agreed, but the Bible was "an instrument a thousand-fold mightier still."[20] The Bible had shaken the world more completely than any revolution witnessed in the annals of England or France, or narrated by Roman Catholic clergyman René Aubert de Vertot (1655–1735) in his histories of revolutions in Portugal, Sweden, and ancient Rome. "This is the book on which the well-being of nations has always hinged," Ryle declared, "and with which the best interests of every nation in Christendom at this moment are inseparably bound up."[21]

Bible Inspiration

The Bible was "given by inspiration of God" (2 Tim. 3:16), and its authors "spake as they were moved by the Holy Ghost" (2 Pet. 1:21). Therefore, Ryle argued, the Bible is "utterly unlike" any other writing. "When you read it, you are not reading the self-taught compositions of poor imperfect men like yourself, but the words of the eternal God. When you hear it, you are not listening to the erring opinions of short-lived mortals, but to the unchanging mind of the King of kings." He believed this to be "the very keel and foundation of Christianity," because without a "divine book" as the warrant for their teaching, Christians are "building on a quicksand, and their faith is vain."

---

[18] Ryle, *How Readest Thou?*, 7; Ryle, *Whose Word Is This?*, 12–13. See also Danielle C. Kinsey, "Koh-i-Noor: Empire, Diamonds, and the Performance of British Material Culture," *Journal of British Studies* 48, no. 2 (2009): 391–419.
[19] Alan Aberg, "Saving the Victory," *Mariner's Mirror* 91, no. 2 (2005), 359.
[20] Ryle, *How Readest Thou?*, 18.
[21] Ryle, *How Readest Thou?*, 16.

The nature of Scripture therefore has "tremendously grave consequences" for all readers. If the Bible is not the word of God, then Christians are living under "an immense delusion," and their churches are "monuments of folly." But if the Bible is the word of God, then "all who refuse to believe it are in fearful danger—they are living on the brink of eternal misery."[22]

Ryle believed in the plenary verbal inspiration of Scripture (that every word is divinely inspired). Yet, when it came to explaining the process of inspiration, his emphasis shifted between the early 1850s and the late 1870s. In his 1853 tract *How Readest Thou?*, Ryle announced that God "taught the writers" what to say and "guided their pens." "They all write as if they were under one dictation," he observed. "The handwriting may vary, but the mind that runs through their work, is always one and the same." The style of the different biblical authors showed that "each had a distinct individual being; but the Divine Guide who dictates and directs the whole is always one. All is alike inspired. Every chapter, and verse, and word, is from God."[23] However, in his 1877 tract *Whose Word Is This?*, Ryle cautiously distanced himself from the more radical theories of divine "dictation," which removed human personality from the writing process:

> I do not admit for a moment that they were mere machines holding pens, and, like type-setters in a printing-office, did not understand what they were doing. I abhor the "mechanical" theory of inspiration. I dislike the idea that men like Moses and St Paul were no better than organ-pipes, employed by the Holy Ghost, or ignorant secretaries or amanuenses who wrote by dictation what they did not understand.

Inspiration was miraculous, Ryle insisted, and therefore, like all miracles, is difficult to comprehend or to explain fully. He held that "in some marvellous manner" the Holy Spirit used the natural memory, reason, intellect, and style of the authors, while putting ideas into their minds and guiding their pens, but Ryle was content to remain agnostic about the precise details of the process.[24]

Concerning the extent of the Holy Spirit's involvement, Ryle rejected the notion that biblical inspiration was merely partial or related only to matters of salvation or covered only the ideas and not the words, or that

---

[22] Ryle, *Whose Word Is This?*, 3, 5.
[23] Ryle, *How Readest Thou?*, 5–6, 8.
[24] Ryle, *Whose Word Is This?*, 21.

occasional mistakes had been permitted. He believed that "every book, and chapter, and verse, and syllable of the Bible was given by inspiration of God. . . . I hold that Scripture not only *contains* the Word of God, but *is* the Word of God." One significant implication was that the stories in Genesis and the family trees in Chronicles were as much written by inspiration as the Acts of the Apostles. Apparently unimportant details like the twenty-nine knives returned to Jerusalem by Emperor Cyrus (Ezra 1:9) or the cloak left by Paul at Troas (2 Tim. 4:13) were as much written by divine direction as superlative passages like Exodus 20, John 17, and Romans 8. Ryle clarified: "I do not say, be it remembered, that all these parts of the Bible are of equal importance to our souls. Nothing of the kind! But I do say they were all equally given by inspiration."[25]

In maintaining this view of Scripture's origins and authority, Ryle affirmed that he was standing in a long line of Christian thinkers, from the early church fathers to the Reformers and Puritans. For example, he quoted, with approval, from the posthumous treatise on Holy Scripture by Bishop John Jewel (1522–1571): "There is no sentence, no clause, no word, no syllable, no letter, but it is written for thy instruction. There is not one jot, but it is signed and sealed with the blood of the Lamb."[26] Ryle also claimed a catena of Victorian theologians in his favor, all of whom had published on the inspiration of Scripture, such as Robert Haldane and Thomas Chalmers from Scotland, Louis Gaussen from Switzerland, Alexander McCaul and William Lee from Ireland, and Bishop Christopher Wordsworth and John Burgon from England.[27] Preaching before the University of Oxford in 1860, Burgon declared that the Bible is "none other than *the voice of Him that sitteth upon the Throne!* Every Book of it—every Chapter of it—every Verse of it—every word of it—every syllable of it—(where are we to stop?)—every letter of it—is the direct utterance of the Most High!"[28] Ryle concurred. In *Expository Thoughts*, he urged Christians to defend the doctrine of plenary verbal inspiration "as we would the apple of our eye," and to insist, "I cannot give up a single word of my Bible."[29] He acknowledged that there are difficulties with this doctrine, because of apparent inaccura-

---
[25] Ryle, *Whose Word Is This?*, 23.
[26] Ryle, *How Readest Thou?*, 13.
[27] Ryle, *Whose Word Is This?*, 24.
[28] John William Burgon, *Inspiration and Interpretation: Seven Sermons Preached Before the University of Oxford* (Oxford, 1861), 89.
[29] J. C. Ryle, *Expository Thoughts on the Gospels, for Family and Private Use: St John*, vol. 2 (London, 1869), 244–45.

cies and inconsistencies in Scripture, but suggested that future discoveries might resolve them. As a parallel, he pointed to the recent discovery of the planet Neptune in 1846. Previously, astronomers had been troubled by the orbit of Uranus, but the existence of Neptune explained the difficulties.[30]

One significant implication of the Bible's inspiration is its faultlessness, Ryle explained. Unlike human innovations, the Bible can never be improved and is never obsolete or in need of reform or amendment. "The wisdom of wise men never gets beyond it. The science of philosophers never proves it wrong. The discoveries of travellers never convict it of mistakes."[31] In *Expository Thoughts*, Ryle addressed apparent mistakes that had puzzled generations of interpreters. For example, Matthew's Gospel quotes a passage from Zechariah but attributes it to Jeremiah (Matt. 27:9). Ryle laid out various possible solutions to this conundrum but dismissed out of court the idea that the apostle might have "made a blunder."[32] Likewise, according to Mark's Gospel, Abiathar was high priest when David ate the showbread (Mark 2:26), but in 1 Samuel the priest's name was Ahimelech (1 Sam. 21:1). Ryle acknowledged that this may have been a copyist's error, but the original authors were "inspired in the writing of every word, and therefore could not err."[33] According to Luke's Gospel, at the time of Jesus's birth Cyrenius (or Quirinius) was governor of Syria (Luke 2:2), but nonbiblical texts dated him eight or ten years later. Ryle simply replied that "St Luke was infinitely more likely to be correct about a matter of fact, than any uninspired historians."[34]

Concerning wider aspects of ancient history, Ryle observed that "it is generally safer and wiser to believe that Bible history is right and other history wrong." New historical evidence was continually being dug up, and he claimed that all recent archaeological research in Assyria, Babylon, Palestine, and Egypt tended to confirm "the perfect accuracy of the Word of God."[35] For example, the famous excavations in the 1840s of the ruins of ancient Nineveh by the English Assyriologist Austen Henry Layard (1817–1894) had not overturned "one jot or tittle" of the historical statements in the Bible.[36] There was similar national excitement twenty-five years

---
[30] Ryle, *Whose Word Is This?*, 34–35.
[31] Ryle, *How Readest Thou?*, 6.
[32] J. C. Ryle, *Expository Thoughts on the Gospels, for Family and Private Use: St Matthew* (Ipswich, 1856), 382.
[33] J. C. Ryle, *Expository Thoughts on the Gospels, for Family and Private Use: St Mark* (Ipswich, 1857), 39.
[34] J. C. Ryle, *Expository Thoughts on the Gospels, for Family and Private Use: St Luke*, vol. 1 (Ipswich, 1858), 54.
[35] Ryle, *Whose Word Is This?*, 29.
[36] Ryle, *How Readest Thou?*, 6.

later at the remarkable discoveries of another pioneer Assyriologist and cuneiformist, George Smith (1840–1876), who won global fame in 1872 by translating the flood epic of Gilgamesh. Ryle commented: "There are buried evidences which God seems to keep in reserve for these last days. If Bible history and other histories cannot be made to agree at present, it is safest to wait."[37]

Additions and Subtractions

Ryle discerned two chief threats to biblical authority: traditionalism and skepticism. In *Expository Thoughts*, he warned, "It is just as easy to destroy the authority of God's word by addition as by subtraction, by burying it under man's inventions as by denying its truth."[38] He saw these two tendencies as represented by Pharisees and Sadducees in the first century, and by Roman Catholics and "Neologians" in the nineteenth century. The Pharisees, for example, were rebuked by Jesus for "making the word of God of none effect through your tradition" (Mark 7:13). Yet Ryle mourned that there was abundant proof of the Christian church frequently following the same degenerative pattern. He urged Christians to draw a clear distinction between injunctions plainly taught by God in the Bible and those devised by the church. "What God commands is necessary to salvation. What man commands is not."[39] Ryle cautioned, "The moment a Christian departs from God's Word written, and allows 'Catholic tradition' any authority, he plunges into a jungle of uncertainty, and will be happy if he does not make shipwreck of his faith altogether."[40]

Later in his ministry, Ryle's attention was drawn increasingly to the parallel dangers of skepticism and agnosticism. As a bishop, he often found himself addressing university audiences and other groups of public intellectuals. For example, the British Association for the Advancement of Science (founded in 1831) held its annual meeting at Southport, near Liverpool, in September 1883. Ryle welcomed attendees to his diocese and preached for them at Christ Church, Southport—a sermon later republished as "Thoughts for Sceptics." He suggested that "a wave of unbelief" was flowing through late Victorian society, "like a wave of fever, cholera, diphtheria, or plague." This "sceptical" and "doubting spirit" was spreading even

---
[37] Ryle, *Whose Word Is This?*, 29.
[38] Ryle, *St Mark*, 139.
[39] Ryle, *St Mark*, 139.
[40] J. C. Ryle, *Expository Thoughts on the Gospels, for Family and Private Use: St John*, vol. 3 (London, 1873), 526.

within the church, where growing numbers of Christians were questioning the veracity of Scripture and abandoning the "old creed."[41] Ryle celebrated that science was adding every year to the fund of human knowledge, but he was convinced that scientific exploration ("the Book of Nature") and biblical revelation ("the Book of God") were entirely compatible. He therefore challenged the "scientific infidel," who claimed to believe only what he could fully understand, to investigate the Bible "with the same careful pains which he exercises when he uses his microscope, his telescope, his spectroscope, his dissecting knife, or his chemical apparatus."[42] Ryle observed that, as with Christianity, there were many scientific fields not yet understood, but it would be foolish to reject science on that basis. He listed astronomy, geology, viruses, snakebites, and "recent awful catastrophes" like the Casamicciola earthquake in July 1883, which killed over twenty-three hundred people on the island of Ischia, in the Bay of Naples, and the enormous volcanic eruption in August 1883 on the island of Krakatoa, in Indonesia, which left over thirty-six thousand dead.[43] The bishop rebuked "those weak-kneed Christians, who seem to think that science and religion can never harmonize, and that they must always scowl and look askance at one another, like two quarrelsome dogs." On the contrary, he believed that scientific advance would prove the compatibility between the "words of God's mouth" and the "works of God's hands."[44]

Ryle lamented the prevalence of "unbelief" in nineteenth-century Britain. A growing proportion of the population did not attend church or profess religious faith of any sort. He described skepticism, or agnosticism, as "one of the commonest spiritual diseases in this generation." Many reckoned it was "clever and intellectual" to throw doubt on biblical revelation, while a Christian who avowed belief in everything in the Bible was "smiled at contemptuously, and thought an ignorant and weak man."[45] Nevertheless, Ryle told the British Association, much professed skepticism was not a matter of genuine conviction but "mere show and pretence" in order to "seem clever, and to win the temporary applause of clever men." He had learned from years of pastoral experience that, when

---
[41] J. C. Ryle, "What Canst Thou Know?" (Job xi. 7, 8): A Question for the Times (London, 1884), 4–5; republished as Ryle, "Thoughts for Sceptics," in Principles for Churchmen: A Manual of Positive Statements on Doubtful or Disputed Points (London, 1884).
[42] Ryle, What Canst Thou Know?, 7–8.
[43] Ryle, What Canst Thou Know?, 9–10.
[44] Ryle, What Canst Thou Know?, 11–12.
[45] Ryle, What Canst Thou Know?, 18–19.

faced by sickness and death, many "so-called sceptics are no sceptics at all."[46] Therefore, Christians should not take fright at encroaching unbelief. He noticed that every time a new lecture or book was published by authors like Charles Darwin (1809–1882) or John Colenso (1814–1883), Christians were "scared and panic-stricken, and run from clergyman to clergyman to pour out their anxieties and fears, as if the very ark of God was in danger." Yet Ryle insisted that these attacks could no more shake Christianity "than the scratch of a pin shakes the great Pyramid of Egypt." The problem, he discerned, was that so few were properly schooled in the "defensive armour" of Christian "evidences." They had probably never read a page of famous apologists like William Paley (1743–1805), author of *Evidences of Christianity* (1794). Christians must be better educated, Ryle declared, not just to love the Bible but to be able to explain why they believe the Bible to be true.[47]

In Ryle's understanding of the Christian life, the Bible remained always the fundamental anchor and authority. From the first day of his ordination to the final years of his episcopate, he wanted Scripture to be shaping the perspective of every Christian at the most profound level. Here was the message of "eternal salvation through faith in Jesus Christ." Here was the infallible, inspired word of God to humanity. Here were the authoritative, never-changing, God-given instructions for Christian life and growth. Everything Ryle taught about the Christian life flowed from his engagement with the biblical text.

---

[46] Ryle, *What Canst Thou Know?*, 21.
[47] Ryle, *What Canst Thou Know?*, 23–25.

CHAPTER 2

SIN AND SALVATION

Lecturing to the Church Association in London in 1867, Ryle attempted to distill the leading features of "Evangelical Religion." He identified the supremacy of Scripture, the depth of human sinfulness and corruption, the saving work of Jesus Christ, and the regenerating and sanctifying work of the Holy Spirit as evangelicalism's distinctive doctrines, which seemed "to stand out in the theological horizon like Tabor and Hermon among the mountains, and to tower upward like cathedral spires in our English plains." Other theological schools also accepted these tenets to a certain extent, Ryle acknowledged, but not with the same prominence and priority. Put epigrammatically, he affirmed, "Man is radically diseased, and man needs a radical cure."[1] Foundational to Ryle's understanding of the Christian life was not just the existence of sin but its enormous depth and awful consequences, from which humanity could be rescued only by a great Savior.

The Sinfulness of Sin

Ryle frequently expounded the "sinfulness of sin" in his tracts, with titles such as *Are You Forgiven?* (1850), *Where Are Your Sins?* (1858), and *About Sin!* (1876). For much fuller treatment, he recommended the works of seventeenth-century Puritans like John Owen, Anthony Burgess, Thomas Manton, and Thomas Watson, all of them "masters of experimental

---
[1] J. C. Ryle, *Evangelical Religion: What It Is, and What It Is Not* (London, 1868), 8, 10.

theology"—that is, theology connected with deep personal experience.[2] Ryle was primarily a popularizer who aimed to distill biblical wisdom from the Puritans and repackage it in pithy form to attract busy Victorians. His gift was for succinct summary and memorable illustration. He was also at pains to show that these were not novel ideas but mainstream Church of England teaching as expressed in the Book of Common Prayer and the Thirty-Nine Articles of Religion.

Ryle's tract *About Sin!* began as an address to a conference for the "Promotion of Spiritual Life," held at St James's Hall, London, in February 1876. The following year, he republished it as the opening chapter in *Holiness*, arguing that mistakes about holiness could usually be traced to mistakes about sin.[3] He told the conference that a correct understanding of sin is the foundation of Christian teaching. Conversely, a wrong view of sin "is the origin of most of the errors, heresies, and false doctrines of the present day. If a man does not realize the dangerous nature of his soul's disease you cannot wonder if he is content with false or imperfect remedies."[4]

Ryle described sin as a "vast moral disease" affecting the whole human race. "The slightest outward or inward departure from absolute mathematical parallelism with God's revealed will and character constitutes a sin, and at once makes us guilty in God's sight." Ryle was concerned that many Christians seemed unaware of the depths of their own sinfulness, and he recommended they study the book of Leviticus. Sin is not the result of poor upbringing or unhealthy role models but a "family disease" inherited from Adam and Eve, he argued:

> The fairest babe that has entered life this year, and become the sunbeam of a family, is not, as its mother perhaps fondly calls it, a little "angel," or a little "innocent," but a little sinner. Alas, as it lies smiling and crowing in its cradle, that little creature carries in its heart the seeds of every kind of wickedness!

This is increasingly apparent, Ryle continued, as a child grows older. The child displays deceit, temper, obstinacy, greed, and jealousy, all without being taught to do wrong. One of the most foolish things parents could say

---
[2] J. C. Ryle, *About Sin!* (London, 1876), 16.
[3] J. C. Ryle, "Sin," in *Holiness and Other Kindred Subjects* (London, 1877), 31.
[4] Ryle, *About Sin!*, 3.

Sin and Salvation 23

about their wayward son, Ryle suggested, was that he had been led astray at school and fallen into bad company, but fundamentally he had "a good heart." Ryle retorted: "The truth, unhappily, is diametrically the other way. The first cause of all sin lies in the natural corruption of the boy's own heart."[5]

This is true of every human being, from every corner of the globe, without exception, Ryle insisted. He encouraged his congregation to sit down with pen and paper to calculate the number of their sins. Reckoning two sins per hour and fifteen waking hours per day, made thirty sins per day and 210 sins per week. These accumulated to over a hundred thousand sins per decade. Yet Ryle suggested that this was a gross underestimate, and the true number is nearer a million. "Oh! cease from your self-righteousness," he urged. "Lay aside this proud affectation of 'not being so very bad,' in which you are trying to wrap yourself up. Be bold enough to confess the truth."[6] The many impressive advances in British industry and technology in the mid-nineteenth century, and the global dominance of its empire, had not changed this fundamental fact: Britain was still, in God's sight, "an island full of sinners."[7]

Turning to the rest of the world, Ryle offered the same diagnosis. Despite all the differences between nations, they had this one factor in common. From Iceland to India, and Paris to Peking (Beijing), "all alike have the mark of sin."[8] There was no distant paradise, uncontaminated by modernity, where sin had not reached. "Is there no happy valley—no secluded island, where innocence is to be found? Is there no tribe on earth, where far away from civilization, and commerce, and money, and gunpowder, and luxury, and books, morality and purity flourish? No! reader, there is none." Ryle observed that all the navigations of the globe, from Christopher Columbus (1451–1506) to Captain James Cook (1728–1779), proved this assertion. Even the idyllic Pacific islands, cut off from the iniquities of major European cities like Paris and London, were found to be "full of impurity, cruelty, and idolatry. The footprints of the devil have been traced on every shore."[9] This was historical evidence, Ryle suggested, for the doctrine of the fall. When he reprinted these observations in his compilation volume *Knots Untied* (1874), he added as further proof the explorations in

---
[5] Ryle, *About Sin!*, 4, 6–7.
[6] J. C. Ryle, *Where Are Your Sins? A Question for Everybody* (Ipswich, 1858), 7.
[7] J. C. Ryle, *Are You Forgiven? A Question for 1850* (Ipswich, 1849), 5.
[8] Ryle, *Are You Forgiven?*, 5.
[9] J. C. Ryle, *Only One Way: A Tract for the Times, Being Thoughts on Acts iv. 12* (Ipswich, 1850), 7.

central Africa by the recently deceased missionary hero David Livingstone (1813–1873).[10]

The global pervasiveness and misery of sin was also a theme in Ryle's 1882 sermon on the parable of the good Samaritan. He noted how violence on the Jericho road in the first century and many similar outrages in every part of the world in the nineteenth century showed human nature to still be the same. For example, he pointed to the African slave trade, abolished in British dominions in 1807 but still prevalent in the 1880s on the east coast of Africa and in the Sudan. The shocking massacres of women and children during the so-called Indian Mutiny in 1857 were seismic in their consequences for British rule in India, but they were part of a repeated pattern of violence, Ryle suggested. He drew attention to similar recent outrages in Egypt, where Christians had been massacred in mob violence at Alexandria and Tantah during the Anglo-Egyptian War of 1882. Closer to home, British newspapers were filled every week with accounts of murder, "not least in Ireland," where Lord Frederick Cavendish (chief secretary for Ireland) and Thomas Burke (permanent undersecretary) had been assassinated in May 1882 in Dublin's Phoenix Park by Irish republicans. The victims of violence and oppression were to be found everywhere: "They dwell by the banks of the Seine as well as the banks of the Thames—by the banks of the Mississippi and Amazon as well as the banks of the Niger or Ganges. They abound under republics as well as under monarchies—under liberal governments as well as under despotism."[11]

Sin pervades not only every part of human society but also every part of the human person, Ryle observed. Although he avoided the technical Calvinist phrase *total depravity*, he expressed the same idea in popular form. He described sin as a disease running through "every part of our moral constitution and every faculty of our minds," including human reason and conscience. "In short, from the crown of the head to the sole of the foot there is no soundness about us." Sin might have been thinly veiled by Victorian politeness and good manners, but it is rooted deeply within human nature. Ryle agreed that human beings still possess many noble characteristics and immense capacity for creativity, but even their best efforts are "intermingled with corruption." As historical proof of this doctrine,

---

[10] J. C. Ryle, "Only One Way of Salvation," in *Knots Untied: Being Plain Statements on Disputed Points in Religion, from the Standpoint of an Evangelical Churchman* (London, 1874), 35.
[11] J. C. Ryle, *"Go, and Do Thou Likewise" (Luke x. 37): Thoughts on a Much-Neglected Duty* (London, 1883), 5–6. For reference to the Sudan slave trade, see his compilation version, Ryle, "Real Church Work," in *Principles for Churchmen: A Manual of Positive Statements on Doubtful or Disputed Points* (London, 1884), 286.

he observed that ancient communities were capable of erecting impressive structures like the Carnac standing stones in Brittany, the Egyptian temples and tombs near Luxor, and the Parthenon in Athens, and yet they worshiped "vile gods and goddesses" in the form of birds and reptiles. They produced majestic literature like the tragedies of Aeschylus and Sophocles, and the histories of Thucydides, and yet they were enslaved to "abominable vices" like those described in Romans 1. Ryle argued that only the Bible's doctrine of the fall can satisfactorily explain these dichotomies.

> We can acknowledge that man has all the marks of a majestic temple about him—a temple in which God once dwelt, but a temple which is now in utter ruins—a temple in which a shattered window here, and a doorway there, and a column there, still give some faint idea of the magnificence of the original design, but a temple which from end to end has lost its glory and fallen from its high estate.[12]

Elsewhere Ryle likened sin to "birdlime"—a very sticky substance, familiar in nineteenth-century agricultural contexts, used to trap birds. "Oh! what unutterable corruption sticks, like birdlime, to all our motives, all our thoughts, all our words, all our actions!"[13] Varying the image, in startling language he described sin as "a serpent that will bite you to death."[14] Humanity is therefore helpless and hopeless without the intervention of "a mighty Saviour."[15]

Peace with God

In September 1854, British troops, in alliance with France, landed on the Crimea peninsula off the coast of the Black Sea to wage war against the Russian Empire for influence in Eastern Europe. It was Britain's first involvement in a major European conflict for a generation, since the Battle of Waterloo in 1815 brought an end to the Napoleonic Wars. After Napoleon's defeat, some had prophesied that war in Europe would never occur again, but the shocking accounts of bloodshed at the Battle of Balaclava in October 1854, including the ill-fated Charge of the Light Brigade, destroyed those naive hopes. The British newspapers were filled day after day with

---
[12] Ryle, *About Sin!*, 7–8.
[13] J. C. Ryle, *Are You an Heir? A Question for Everybody* (Ipswich, 1852), 26.
[14] J. C. Ryle, "Repentance: Its Nature and Necessity," in *Twelve Sermons Preached at the Special Services for the Working Classes, in Exeter Hall, July, August, September, 1858* (London, 1858), 126.
[15] Ryle, *Only One Way*, 8.

reports from the battlefield and the Siege of Sevastopol. "The whole attention of the country is fixed on the war," Ryle observed, "and nothing but the war." In the early months of the conflict, in December 1854, he saw the opportunity for an evangelistic tract on peace. Formulated, as usual, as a direct question—*Have You Peace?*—it expounded the New Testament affirmation "Being justified by faith, we have peace with God through our Lord Jesus Christ" (Rom. 5:1). The disaster unfolding in Crimea framed Ryle's treatment:

> Battle and disease are doing their deadly work among our gallant soldiers and sailors. Gentle and simple blood is being shed like water in far distant lands. Many of the best and bravest of our countrymen are lying cold in untimely graves. Hearts in England are being broken by sudden, stunning, crushing bereavements.

He hoped that, in God's providence, the war years would prove "a time of blessing to many souls" because affliction and bereavement would draw them to Christ in a way that prosperity did not. "I suspect that many an aching heart will discover at length that the world is a miserable comforter, and that nothing can fill up the void in their affections, and cure their sorrow, but the truth as it is in Jesus."[16]

Yet the focus of Ryle's tract was a peace that did not depend on human armies or governments—peace with God. Ryle defined it as "friendship with the Lord of heaven and earth," no longer facing God's anger at sin. When life is over, this is the only question that matters. "Your body may be carried to the grave with pomp and ceremony. A solemn service may be read over your coffin. A marble monument may be put up in your honour. But after all it will be but a pauper's funeral, if you die without peace with God."[17] Therefore, Ryle urged everyone worried about friends and relations on the Crimean battlefield to seek Christ. Writing, in particular, to anxious wives who had sent their husbands off to war knowing they might never return, he invited them to become acquainted with Jesus Christ, "a husband that never dies."[18]

False peace is deceptive, "a perilous dream." Ryle encouraged his readers to imagine they were standing in one of the large London hospitals at

---
[16] J. C. Ryle, *Have You Peace? A Question for 1855* (Ipswich, 1854), 3–5.
[17] Ryle, *Have You Peace?*, 6, 8.
[18] Ryle, *Have You Peace?*, 27.

Sin and Salvation

the bedside of a patient dying from an incurable disease. The patient might lie comfortably on his pillow, "dreaming of home, and his mother, and his youth," without complaining of pain. But was he healthy? "Oh! no! no! It is only the effect of opiates. Nothing can be done for him. He is dying daily." Next, Ryle encouraged his readers to imagine they were visiting a lunatic asylum where one of the inmates believed himself to be a king, twisting straw into a crown and thinking that stones and gravel were diamonds and pearls. The mentally ill man might appear happy but would be living a delusion.[19] By contrast, authentic peace with God is not merely a perception but an objective reality.

Have You Peace? was republished in Ryle's compilation volume *Old Paths* (1877) under the more technical title "Justification." He pictured a scene familiar to Victorian readers, the arrival of the court of assize in the local county town to judge the most serious crimes, which often resulted in capital punishment. This was part of the English circuit justice system, stretching back to the Middle Ages, and was a major local event involving proclamations, sermons, bell ringing, and lavish dinners; and the visiting judges were ceremonially heralded by a fanfare of trumpeters. To innocent people, the assize fanfare was no cause for concern. But to the criminal waiting in his cell, Ryle noted, "Those trumpets are a knell of despair." They announced that he would soon be required to "stand at the bar of justice," to face trial and punishment.[20] A similar day is coming at God's grand assize, Ryle warned, for every unjustified sinner who has broken God's law. But those who are "justified by faith" will escape the punishment they deserve, because Christ suffered in their place as their substitute. Varying the image from the assize court to the debtors' court, Ryle declared that Christ, by shedding his blood, had discharged the debt owed by the Christian "to the uttermost farthing."[21]

The Cross of Christ

Ryle's preoccupation with the atonement permeated his tracts and was expounded most fully in *The Cross* (1852), a celebration of Saint Paul's exclamation "God forbid that I should glory, save in the cross of our Lord Jesus Christ" (Gal. 6:14). The apostle, Ryle noted, "loved to think of what Christ

---
[19] Ryle, *Have You Peace?*, 10–11.
[20] Ryle, *Have You Peace?*, 11–12.
[21] Ryle, *Have You Peace?*, 14–15.

had done, and Christ had suffered—of the death of Christ, the righteousness of Christ, the atonement of Christ, the blood of Christ, the finished work of Christ."[22] In the same way, Ryle wanted his own preaching and tracts to be saturated with Christ.

Ryle described the atonement as "the centre truth in the whole Bible." Building on the Victorian fascination with Egypt, he alluded to recent advances in deciphering hieroglyphs. The famous Rosetta Stone had been displayed in the British Museum since 1802, after being transferred the previous year from French to British possession with other Egyptian antiquities under the terms of the Capitulation of Alexandria. The stele's parallel texts in hieroglyphic, Demotic, and Greek enabled a major breakthrough in decipherment in the 1820s by Jean-François Champollion (1790–1832) and Thomas Young (1773–1829), which was extended in subsequent decades by pioneer Egyptologists like Karl Richard Lepsius (1810–1884) and Emmanuel de Rougé (1811–1872). Ryle argued that, in a similar way, the atonement is the interpretative key to the whole of Scripture, from Genesis to Revelation. "Take away the cross of Christ, and the Bible is a dark book. It is like the Egyptian hieroglyphics, without the key that interprets their meaning—curious and wonderful, but of no real use." Ryle exhorted his readers that however much they knew about the Bible, if they had not yet discovered that Christ crucified is "the foundation of the whole volume," then they missed its true purpose. "Your religion is a heaven without a sun, an arch without a keystone, a compass without a needle, a clock without spring or weights, a lamp without oil. It will not comfort you. It will not deliver your soul from hell."[23]

Ryle argued that the crucifixion was part of God's eternal salvation plan. "Not one throb of pain did Jesus feel, not one precious drop of blood did Jesus shed, which had not been appointed long ago. Infinite wisdom planned that redemption should be by the cross." The atoning sacrifice of Christ bridged the "mighty gulf" between humanity and God, which otherwise was impassable. The crucifixion proved God's deep love for sinners and opened a way to heaven for "the very vilest of men." "The longer I dwell on the cross in my thoughts," Ryle wrote, "the more I am satisfied that there is more to be learned at the foot of the cross than anywhere else in the world."[24] He described it as "the crown and glory of the Gospel," and it riveted his attention. As an ordained minister, Ryle remarked that without the

---

[22] J. C. Ryle, *The Cross: A Tract for the Times* (Ipswich, 1852), 11.
[23] Ryle, *The Cross*, 12–14.
[24] Ryle, *The Cross*, 17–18, 20.

Sin and Salvation

message of the cross, he would feel "like a soldier without arms—like an artist without his pencil—like a pilot without his compass—like a labourer without his tools." Furthermore, he celebrated the cross as the heartbeat of Christian missions and as "the weapon that has won victories over hearts of every kind, in every quarter of the globe. Greenlanders, Africans, South-Sea Islanders, Hindoos, Chinese, all have alike felt its power."[25] Here is the foundation of the church's prosperity and its first priority, Ryle proclaimed. Any congregation that fails to put Christ crucified at the center of its ministry is useless, he announced. It is little better than

> a dead carcase, a well without water, a barren fig tree, a sleeping watchman, a silent trumpet, a dumb witness, an ambassador without terms of peace, a messenger without tidings, a lighthouse without a fire, a stumbling-block to weak believers, a comfort to infidels, a hot-bed for formalism, a joy to the devil, and an offence to God.[26]

This emphasis on the atonement was central to Ryle's concerns. For example, preaching at London's Exeter Hall in 1857, he proclaimed that "Christ by His death has made satisfaction to the holy law of God, which we have broken." The crucifixion was not merely an example of self-denial, nor an act of martyrdom, but "a sacrifice and propitiation for the sin of the whole world." It was "the vicarious death of an almighty substitute, surety, and representative of the sons of men. It paid our enormous debt to God. . . . It purchased reconciliation with Him. . . . The prison-doors were set open, when Jesus died."[27] Likewise, the following year, in *Where Are Your Sins?*, Ryle urged his readers to think highly of Christ's incarnation, miracles, teaching, resurrection, intercession, and second coming. "But think highest of all of Christ's sacrifice and the propitiation made by His death. . . . Never, never be ashamed to let men know that you derive all your comfort from the atoning blood of Christ, and from His substitution for you on the cross."[28]

Only One Way

On New Year's Day 1850, Ryle lectured at St Clement's Church in Ipswich—the county town of Suffolk, nine miles from his Helmingham parish—

---
[25] Ryle, *The Cross*, 23–24.
[26] Ryle, *The Cross*, 26.
[27] Ryle, *Your Soul!*, 14–15.
[28] Ryle, *Where Are Your Sins?*, 29.

on Acts 4:12, "Neither is there salvation in any other: for there is none other name under heaven given among men, whereby we must be saved." This Bible text was directly quoted in the formularies of the Church of England in Article 18 of the Thirty-Nine Articles, entitled "Of obtaining eternal salvation only by the name of Christ." Ryle therefore insisted that it was the obligation of every Church of England minister to teach this doctrine. His lecture was soon published for a wider readership as *Only One Way* (1850). In it he proclaimed: "Christ's blood alone can cleanse us. Christ's righteousness alone can clothe us. Christ's merit alone can give us a title to heaven. Jews and Gentiles—learned and unlearned—kings and poor men—all alike must either be saved by Jesus, or lost for ever."[29] Later he summarized, aphoristically, "salvation in Christ to the very uttermost—but out of Christ no salvation at all."[30]

Ryle argued that this teaching runs like a "golden chain" through the whole of Scripture from beginning to end.[31] The claims of Christ are total:

> Remember that heaven is before you, and Christ the only door into it—hell beneath you, and Christ alone able to deliver you from it—the devil behind you, and Christ the only refuge from his wrath and accusations—the law against you, and Christ alone able to redeem you—sin weighing you down, and Christ alone able to put it away.[32]

Some of Ryle's theological critics warned that such exclusive teaching was uncharitable to other viewpoints. But he retorted that "the greatest charity is to tell the greatest quantity of truth." It would not be charitable to watch a neighbor drinking poison or an emigrant embarking on an ocean voyage in a leaking ship or a blind man walking near a precipice and not intervene to warn of the danger. In the same way, Ryle suggested, it was his duty to cry alarm whenever he encountered people who believed they could be saved outside of Christ, because they were heading for eternal ruin.[33]

Ryle's faith was thoroughly Christocentric. He denounced the deists, who spoke not of Jesus Christ but only in general terms of "God" or "Providence." Ryle rejected their teaching as "an utter delusion. The god of such people is an idol of their own invention, and not the glorious God of the

---

[29] Ryle, *Only One Way*, 4.
[30] Ryle, *Only One Way*, 18.
[31] Ryle, *Only One Way*, 11.
[32] Ryle, *Only One Way*, 6.
[33] Ryle, *Only One Way*, 13.

Scriptures." Likewise, he derided the unitarian doctrines of the Socinians as "ruinous to men's souls" and as striking at "the root of the whole plan of salvation which God has revealed in the Bible. . . . The name whereby alone you and I can be saved, is a name above every name, and the slightest contempt poured upon it is an insult to the King of kings." Next, Ryle criticized Roman Catholics for adding to "the simple way of the Gospel" with "inventions" like penances and masses. But some of his sternest rebukes were reserved for sectarian Protestants who seemed to lay as much weight upon denominational distinctives as upon salvation. In reply to the question "What shall I do to be saved?," they answered not only "Believe on the Lord Jesus Christ" but also "Come and join us." "In the things of God's word," Ryle proclaimed, "be it remembered, addition, as well as subtraction, is a great sin."[34]

Ryle also rejected a "very common heresy" that was growing in popularity in liberal circles in the mid-nineteenth century, that what mattered most about religious faith was not doctrinal truth but personal sincerity. On that basis, he observed, it would be possible to defend druidical sacrifices in early Britain before the arrival of Christianity; the burning of Protestants in the fires of Smithfield in the 1550s during the Marian persecutions; and religious traditions in the recent history of India like *sati* (the burning of a Hindu widow on her husband's funeral pyre), *thuggee* (the ritual strangulation of travelers by gangs of Hindu assassins), and the crushing of Hindu pilgrims under the chariot of the god Jagannath, all of which the British Raj had attempted to eradicate. Ryle insisted, "Sincerity is not Christ, and therefore sincerity cannot put away sin." He warned that a rising challenge to Christianity came not from atheism but from pluralism—not from the philosophy that said there is no God and no Savior but from the philosophy that said there are "many Saviours, and many ways to peace." Pluralism gave equal honor to all creeds and to all religious texts and teachers—the Bible and the Qur'an, the Hindu Vedas and the Zoroastrian Avesta, the antitrinitarian Racovian Catechism (1605) of the Polish Brethren and the Thirty-Nine Articles of the Church of England, and "revelations" from heaven claimed by the Scandinavian mystic Emanuel Swedenborg (1688–1772) and the American founder of Mormonism, Joseph Smith (1805–1844). This liberal philosophy of religion was "so scrupulous about the feelings of others, that we are never to say they are wrong," Ryle protested, whereas anyone who claimed to be right was denounced as

---
[34] Ryle, *Only One Way*, 14–17.

"a bigot." Yet he dismissed this modern "liberality" as a form of idolatry, "a sacrificing of truth upon the altar of a caricature of charity." Alexander Pope's philosophical poem *An Essay on Man* (1732–1734), included the famous line "He can't be wrong whose life is in the right." Pope might have been a great poet, Ryle admitted, but nonetheless he was "a wretched divine." The only path to salvation, Ryle insisted, was faith in Christ.[35]

Emancipation

Throughout Ryle's ministry, he hammered home these Christocentric themes from multiple angles. He often looked for a question in the media, or in public discourse, as the springboard for his gospel proclamations. For example, in the mid-1860s, England was gripped by feverish excitement about the growth of democracy and the extension of the franchise, which culminated in 1867 in the Second Reform Act, championed by Benjamin Disraeli. Although still a long way from universal suffrage, it almost doubled the number of men who were eligible to vote in parliamentary elections, from 1.3 million to 2.5 million, out of a total adult male population of 7 million. The cause of political freedom dominated public discussions, and many British citizens viewed themselves as pioneering a democratic standard for the rest of the world to follow.[36] Ryle saw the opportunity for a tract entitled *Are You Free?*, published at New Year 1867, an exposition of John 8:36, "If the Son therefore shall make you free, ye shall be free indeed." It opened with a pertinent question: "You live in a land which is the very cradle of freedom. But are you yourself free?" Many were pushing for parliamentary reform, and it was "the grand aim and ambition of myriads" to secure the vote. Yet Ryle announced a freedom that was "independent of all political changes—a freedom which neither Queen, Lords and Commons, nor the cleverest popular leaders can bestow." This "true liberty" was within reach of everyone, he promised, and was found in Jesus Christ. "Think not for a moment that this is going to be a political tract," Ryle apologized. "I am no politician. I have no politics but those of the Bible. The only party I care for is the Lord's side. . . . The Government I want to support is the government which is on the shoulder of my Lord and Saviour Jesus Christ."[37]

---

[35] Ryle, *Only One Way*, 17–20.
[36] Robert Saunders, *Democracy and the Vote in British Politics, 1848–1867: The Making of the Second Reform Act* (Ashgate, 2011).
[37] J. C. Ryle, *Are You Free? A Question for 1867* (London, 1867), 3–4.

Sin and Salvation 33

Ryle rejoiced in the blessings of living in England, a land of civil, religious, and personal freedoms. "We have free bodies, free consciences, free speech, free thought, free action, free Bibles, a free press, and free homes. How vast is this list of privileges!" He praised the champions of freedom down the centuries, from Alfred the Great (ca. 848–899) in Wessex and Robert the Bruce (1274–1329) in Scotland to the legendary William Tell in fourteenth-century Switzerland and George Washington (1732–1799) in the United States of America. Yet Ryle proclaimed that there was no country on earth with as much liberty as England. In particular, he compared England favorably with the United States, where the Civil War had only recently drawn to a close, and he denounced the American enslavement of Africans as "that enormous fountain of wretchedness."[38] The focus of his tract, however, was upon liberation from the tyranny of sin and bondage to Satan. "What is the use of living in a free land like England, with free thought, free speech, free action, free conscience, so long as you are a slave to sin, and a captive to the devil?" Ryle suggested that many English people did not realize that they themselves were slaves, in spiritual chains "as true and heavy and soul-withering as ever crushed the limbs of an African."[39] Spiritual freedom, true liberty, had been won for them by Christ's death on the cross.

The way to be set free by Christ is not baptism or church membership but "by faith, simple faith in Him as our Saviour and Redeemer.... It is by receiving Christ, trusting Christ, committing ourselves to Christ, reposing our whole weight on Christ—it is by this, and by no other plan, that spiritual liberty is made our own."[40] Ryle therefore exhorted his readers:

> Let not political struggles and party strife make you forget your precious soul. Take any side in politics you please, and follow honestly your conscientious convictions. But never, never forget that there is a liberty far higher and more lasting than any that politics can give you. Rest not till that liberty is your own. Rest not till YOUR SOUL IS FREE.

No extension of the franchise could ever raise the status of the Christian in God's sight, Ryle insisted. "Grace now, and the hope of glory hereafter, are more lasting privileges than the power of voting for twenty boroughs or

---
[38] Ryle, *Are You Free?*, 5–6.
[39] Ryle, *Are You Free?*, 9.
[40] Ryle, *Are You Free?*, 16.

counties." He therefore urged them to make every effort to promote "spiritual emancipation" through Christ, as an evangelistic duty. "If we have tasted the blessings of freedom, let us spare no pains to make others free."[41]

Faith and Repentance

Ryle repeatedly argued that peace with God, made possible by the death of Christ, is accessed freely by "simple faith," not by human merit, morality, or religious observance. Good works and personal holiness are essential evidence of Christian faith, he agreed, but they are themselves defective and play no part in justification. For example, in *Where Are Your Sins?*, Ryle described faith as "the one thing needful" to enjoy the benefits of salvation. This faith is not intellectual assent to doctrines and articles, or mere subscription to orthodox statements like John Pearson's *Exposition of the Creed* (1659) and William Paley's *Evidences of Christianity* (1794), both standard textbooks in the training curriculum for Victorian clergy.

> It is simply the grasp of a contrite heart on the outstretched hand of an Almighty Saviour—the repose of a weary head on the bosom of an Almighty Friend. Cast away all idea of work, or merit, or doing, or performing, or paying, or giving, or buying, or labouring, in the act of believing on Christ. Understand that faith is not giving, but taking—not paying, but receiving—not buying, but being enriched.

Seeking analogies, Ryle likened faith to a sick person drinking medicine or a drowning person grabbing a rope thrown to him or her. He exhorted his Helmingham congregation: "We rejoice to see you coming regularly to hear the Gospel. We rejoice to see an orderly, well-behaved congregation of worshippers. But faith, faith, faith—is the grand result we long to see in your souls."[42]

Ryle explored at length the relationship between faith and repentance in his contribution to a series of evangelistic addresses at London's Exeter Hall in the summer of 1858. Under the auspices of Lord Shaftesbury, these special weekly services, led by evangelical clergy from across the country, aimed to reach the "working classes" of the metropolis with the Christian gospel. Ryle had taken part in the first series in 1857 and was invited back

---
[41] Ryle, *Are You Free?*, 18–20, 22.
[42] Ryle, *Where Are Your Sins?*, 22–24.

the following year. The initiative was strongly opposed by local London clergyman Augustin Gaspard Edouart (1817–1905), in whose parish Exeter Hall was situated, who complained to the bishop of London that the intrusion of uninvited preachers into his territory was irregular, illegal, and reminiscent of the Puritans. Although Edouart threatened legal action and managed temporarily to halt the work in November 1857, it was restarted in July 1858.[43] Ryle's address was a highlight, hailed by the London press. The *Morning Herald* reported that his "great popularity . . . attracted an immense congregation." When Exeter Hall opened, it was filled in less than ten minutes by over five thousand people, and the doors had to be closed "to prevent more pressing into the building." Ryle delivered "a most eloquent and impressive sermon, which was listened to with breathless attention."[44] The *St James's Chronicle* agreed. It praised his preaching as "plain, earnest, home-striking, full of saving truth, and rich in pointed illustration. Although the sermon on Sunday occupied a full hour and a half it was listened to throughout with the most intense attention."[45]

Ryle's text at Exeter Hall was Jesus's warning in Luke 13:3, "Except ye repent, ye shall all likewise perish." He argued that this might sound stern, but Jesus's words in fact conveyed "tender love," alerting people to danger—like a father who sees his son tottering toward the edge of a cliff and shouts sharply, "Stop, stop!"; or a mother who sees her child about to eat a poisonous berry and cries out, "Stop, stop! Put that down!"; or someone who roughly wakes a neighbor at midnight by yelling "Fire! Fire!" and thus saves the neighbor's life.[46] Repentance, or turning from sin, is one of the foundation stones of Christianity, Ryle exclaimed, and it always has "a blessed companion," faith in Christ. He refused to "waste time splitting theological hairs" about whether repentance comes before faith or faith before repentance, insisting only that they belong side by side.[47] Repentance is a universal necessity. This was not merely a subject for thieves, drunkards, and fornicators, Ryle told his audience. Christ's summons to repentance embraced the full range of society, from Queen Victoria in her palace to her poorest subject, the pauper in the workhouse; both the master of the household sitting in his drawing room and his lowest-ranked

---

[43] *The Exeter Hall Services: Copy of a Correspondence Between the Bishop of London and the Rev. A. G. Edouart, in Reference to These Services* (London, 1858).
[44] "The Exeter Hall Services," *Morning Herald*, August 30, 1858, 5.
[45] "The Exeter Hall Services," *St James's Chronicle*, August 31, 1858, 1.
[46] Ryle, "Repentance," 103.
[47] Ryle, "Repentance," 107.

servant, the scullery maid in the kitchen; both the science professor at the university and the uneducated farm boy who spent his days following the plow—"all, all without exception, are born in sin, and all must repent and be converted if they would be saved."[48]

Ryle was careful to emphasize that sins are washed away by the blood of Christ, not by tears of repentance, and it is "bad divinity" and "wretched theology" to say otherwise. Nonetheless, it is also true that Christians must hate and forsake their sins. Some theologians dismissed this doctrine as a form of "legalism," which undermined salvation by grace alone. But Ryle insisted: "All justified people are penitent people. . . . The Lord Jesus Christ desires not to see the sinner come to him cleaving to his sins, and hugging in his arms the enemies which brought Christ to his cross." Ryle declared that a gospel void of a call to forsake sin "is not the Gospel at all; it is rank antinomianism, and nothing else. . . . Christ is a Saviour *from* sin, not a Saviour for man *in* sin."[49]

To the gathered crowd at Exeter Hall, Ryle suggested that only repentance leads to true happiness. Many who appear "merry" when partying among their friends in fact feel "wretched" when alone and simply drown their sorrows in new entertainments. Addiction to opium (or "laudanum"), supplied by the Indo-Chinese opium trade, was a growing problem in early Victorian Britain, and the drug's seductive powers were popularized by Thomas De Quincey's autobiographical *Confessions of an English Opium-Eater* (1821), republished in 1856.[50] Ryle borrowed the image: "Just as the opium-eater needs a larger dose every year he goes on eating opium, so does the man that seeks happiness in anything except in God need greater excitement every year that he lives, and after all is never happy." For his next illustration, the preacher drew attention to the clock at St Paul's Cathedral, just a mile from Exeter Hall, and its famous hour bell, "Great Tom"—the largest bell in London until surpassed in 1859 by "Big Ben" at the Houses of Parliament. He likened it to the voice of conscience summoning the impenitent person to repent.[51]

Ryle acknowledged that repentance is a spiritual battle and that the devil is prowling around like a "roaring lion" seeking to devour his prey

---

[48] Ryle, "Repentance," 109.
[49] Ryle, "Repentance," 109–10, 112.
[50] Virginia Berridge and Griffith Edwards, *Opium and the People: Opiate Use in Nineteenth-Century England* (Allen Lane, 1981); Barry Milligan, *Pleasures and Pains: Opium and the Orient in Nineteenth-Century British Culture* (University Press of Virginia, 1995).
[51] Ryle, "Repentance," 112–13.

Sin and Salvation

(1 Pet. 5:8). To drive home the point, he turned to another popular attraction in the metropolis, the London Zoo at Regent's Park, opened to the public in 1847. "I saw a lion once at the Zoological Gardens being fed. I saw his meal cast down before him. I saw the keeper try to take that meal away—I remember the lion's roar, his spring, his struggle to retain his food." In the same way, Ryle observed, the devil would never allow someone to repent without a fight.[52] Therefore, he ended his sermon with a direct evangelistic summons:

> Yes, you, who have come to Exeter Hall tonight—you who have come partly from curiosity; you, who have come because some one has asked you to come; you, who have come knowing you are not yet at peace with God.... I say to you, in my Master's name, Repent, repent, repent this very night, and that without delay.[53]

Ryle then quoted the opening verses of "Just As I Am," published in 1836 by Anglican evangelical hymnwriter Charlotte Elliott (1789–1871). It began:

> Just as I am, without one plea,
> But that Thy blood was shed for me,
> And that Thou bidst me come to Thee,
> O Lamb of God, I come![54]

This hymn—later popularized by twentieth-century evangelists, most notably at Billy Graham's rallies—summarized the heart of Ryle's message: total dependence on Christ, especially his atoning death, and the urgent need to respond to Christ's call.

---

[52] Ryle, "Repentance," 116.
[53] Ryle, "Repentance," 122, 124.
[54] Ryle, "Repentance," 126.

CHAPTER 3

CONVERSION

The precise circumstances of Ryle's Christian conversion, toward the end of his time as an Oxford undergraduate in 1837, are obscure. Like all students and dons at the university in the early nineteenth century, he was a member of the Church of England and had to subscribe to the Thirty-Nine Articles of Religion as a condition of matriculation. Daily attendance at college chapel was obligatory. Nevertheless, Ryle recalled in his autobiography, "My character underwent a thorough and entire change, in consequence of a complete alteration in my views of religion, both as to my belief and practise." This change was "extremely great," with "a sweeping influence over the whole of my life ever since." Looking back, Ryle concluded that until he was twenty-one years old, despite his Anglican credentials he had "really no true religion at all." Although he attended church and professed to be a Christian, he was "perfectly careless, thoughtless, ignorant, and indifferent about my soul, and a world to come," never praying or reading the Bible.

> I never plunged into the immoralities that many young men do, because I had no natural taste for them. I was never led into drunkenness, gambling, theatre-going, race-going, betting, or other things into which young men run.... But I really was altogether without God in the world, and though many thought me a very proper, moral, respectable young man, I was totally unfit to die.[1]

---

[1] *Bishop J. C. Ryle's Autobiography: The Early Years*, ed. Andrew Atherstone (Banner of Truth, 2016), 61–62.

Ryle went on to explain that the circumstances leading to his conversion were "very many and very various." "It was not a sudden immediate change but very gradual. I cannot trace it to any one person, or any one event or thing, but to a singular variety of persons and things. In all of them I believe now the Holy Ghost was working though I did not know it at the time."[2] Among these influences, Ryle mentioned the witness of Christian friends, the impact of listening to evangelical preaching at home in Macclesfield, and a severe illness that confined him to bed in Oxford with inflammation of the lungs shortly before his final exams in November 1837. He described the last six months of that year as a "turning point" in his life, nothing less than "conversion" and "regeneration." Alluding to Ephesians 2, he concluded: "Before that time I was dead in sins, and on the high road to hell, and from that time, I became alive, and had a hope of heaven. And nothing to my mind can account for it, but the free sovereign grace of God."[3]

After Ryle's death, an alternative conversion narrative began to circulate, recounted by his friend Canon Alfred Christopher (1820–1913), an Oxford clergyman. Christopher claimed that he had been told it by Ryle himself. "God opened his eyes to the Gospel in a very simple way. Not by a sermon, a book, a tract, a letter, or a conversation, but by a single verse of His Word impressively read by a clergyman unknown to him." According to this version of the story, Ryle attended a parish church in Oxford (probably Carfax Church in the city center, later demolished) one Sunday afternoon, where he heard Ephesians 2 read with deliberate pauses in verse 8: "By grace are ye saved—through faith—and that not of yourselves—it is the gift of God." In his obituary of Ryle for *The Record* newspaper, Christopher explained: "That verse, read so that each clause might sink into the mind by itself, showed the undergraduate the Gospel. . . . How much can God do by one verse of His Word!"[4] It is surprising that Ryle made no mention of this memorable occasion when dictating his autobiography, if it really was so decisive in his spiritual awakening, though a close reading suggests that Christopher's account is compatible with Ryle's own version of events.[5]

Ryle himself encountered similar apparent contradictions when researching the ministry of Daniel Rowlands (ca. 1711–1790), the evangelical revivalist at Llangeitho in Wales whom Ryle called one of the "greatest

---

[2] *J. C. Ryle's Autobiography*, 67–68.
[3] *J. C. Ryle's Autobiography*, 70, 73.
[4] "Canon Christopher's Reminiscences," *The Record*, June 15, 1900, 572.
[5] For analysis, see Andrew Atherstone, "Canon Christopher on Ryle's Conversion," in *J. C. Ryle's Autobiography*, 199–213.

spiritual champions" of the eighteenth century.[6] There were varying accounts of Rowlands's spiritual awakening in biographies by two Victorian clergymen, John Owen and Edward Morgan, both published in 1840. According to Owen, Rowlands was converted when listening to a sermon by the prominent Welsh clergyman Griffith Jones of Llanddowror.[7] However, according to Morgan, Rowlands had earlier begun to adopt evangelical doctrines after noticing the effectiveness of a local Dissenting minister who drew large congregations.[8] Yet Ryle was unperturbed by the apparent conflict in these chronologies.

> I do not attempt to reconcile the two accounts. I can quite believe that both are true. When the Holy Ghost takes in hand the conversion of a soul, he often causes a variety of circumstances to concur and co-operate in producing it. This, I am sure, would be the testimony of all experienced believers. Owen got hold of one set of facts, and Morgan of another. Both happened probably about the same time, and both probably are true.[9]

Ryle believed that the work of the Holy Spirit in conversion is often gradual and multifaceted. Provided that spiritual rebirth is authentic, the precise contextual circumstances are immaterial.

Dead or Alive?

The radical, supernatural nature of Christian conversion was a frequent theme in Ryle's writings. *Living or Dead?*, his tract for New Year 1849, expounded another verse from his own putative conversion text, "You hath he quickened, who were dead" (Eph. 2:1). Human beings by nature are "dead," Ryle argued. He saw this as the true explanation for the paucity of Christian devotion evident throughout Britain, even among professing believers who regularly attended church.

> It is not in churchyards alone where the dead are to be found. There are only too many inside our churches, and close to our pulpits—too many on the benches, and too many in the pews. . . . There are dead souls in all

---
[6] J. C. Ryle, *The Christian Leaders of the Last Century; or, England a Hundred Years Ago* (London, 1869), 180.
[7] John Owen, *A Memoir of the Rev. Daniel Rowlands* (London, 1840), 54–55.
[8] Edward Morgan, *Ministerial Records; or Brief Accounts of the Great Progress of Religion*, part 1, *The Rev. D. Rowlands, of Llangeitho* (London, 1840), 11–13.
[9] Ryle, *Christian Leaders*, 183–84.

our parishes, and dead souls in all our streets. There is hardly a family in which all live to God. There is hardly a house in which there is not some one dead.

Christian conversion is therefore not merely a matter of "a little mending and alteration—a little cleansing and purifying—a little painting and patching—a little turning over a new leaf." It is altogether more radical, "the planting within us a new nature—a new being—a new principle—a new heart." Searching for appropriate analogies of radical change, Ryle pictured a block of quarried marble now carved into a beautiful statue, or a wild wasteland transformed into a flower garden, or a lump of ironstone melted down and forged into the springs of a pocket watch. Yet none of these analogies fitted the nature of conversion, Ryle insisted, because they all involved creating a new shape from the same old substance. The spiritual change required in human beings is of an entirely different order, "a change as great as a resurrection from the dead," nothing less than being "born again, born from above, born of God."[10] In his tract *Regeneration* (1850), Ryle likewise observed that the change needed is not the mere restraint of evil nature, like chaining up a raging tiger, nor superficial renewal, like a snake shedding its old skin, but the birth of a new creature, like a butterfly rising from the body of a caterpillar.[11]

This need for conversion is true of every person on the face of the globe, in every culture, Ryle declared, because human hearts "are all alike at the bottom, all stony, all hard, all ungodly, all needing to be thoroughly renewed." In 1841, New Zealand became a British colony, annexed by the Crown a year after British sovereignty had first been proclaimed over the islands following the Treaty of Waitangi with Māori chiefs. British merchants and missionaries established pioneer settlements, and the Church of England dispatched George Selwyn (1809–1878) as the first bishop of New Zealand. Ryle built upon this wave of colonial excitement. He argued that despite the great disparity in Christian heritage and education between the two nations, as to their spiritual needs, "the Englishman and the New Zealander, stand on the same level in the matter. Both are naturally dead, and both need to be made alive."[12] Evangelistic missions were therefore equally essential in England, because without conversion,

---
[10] J. C. Ryle, *Living or Dead? A Question for 1849* (Ipswich, 1849), 7–9.
[11] J. C. Ryle, *Regeneration: A Tract for the Times* (Ipswich, 1850), 19–20.
[12] Ryle, *Living or Dead?*, 11.

"there is no life in us at all. We may be living Churchmen, but we are dead Christians."[13]

New birth cannot be self-generated, Ryle instructed his readers. Nor can the clergy produce conversions in their congregations by more energetic ministrations. Conversion requires nothing less than the supernatural intervention of the Holy Spirit, and therefore Ryle exhorted: "Pray for a great out-pouring of the Spirit. He alone can give edge to sermons, and point to advice, and power to rebukes, and cast down the high walls of sinful hearts. It is not better preaching, and finer writing that is wanted in this day, but more of the presence of the Holy Ghost."[14] In earthly affairs, people wisely plan ahead by arranging life and property insurance. Why not also attend to spiritual business with the same seriousness, Ryle reasoned in *Living or Dead?*, rather than putting it off for another year? "The next time the daisies bloom, it may be over your grave.... You know not what a day might bring forth, much less a year." Therefore, he prayed: "Others may think it enough to mourn over dead bodies. For my part, I think there is far more cause to mourn over dead souls.... Oh! that this year might be a year of life to your souls! Oh! that the Spirit might come down upon your hearts and make you new men."[15] Ryle issued this conversion call with a sense of heightened eschatological urgency. During 1848—the so-called "year of revolutions"—an unprecedented wave of revolutionary fervor had been sweeping across Europe, encompassing many nations, from Italy to Denmark, via France and Austria.[16] "The latter days have fallen upon us," Ryle concluded. "The kingdoms of the earth are shaking, falling, crashing, and crumbling away.... The King Himself is close at hand."[17]

Similar themes recurred in *Wheat or Chaff?*, Ryle's New Year tract for 1851. Its central argument was that all of humanity falls into two categories—converted or unconverted, sheep or goats, wise or foolish, wheat or chaff. National excitement in 1851 was fixed upon the opening of the Great Exhibition at the specially constructed Crystal Palace, in London's Hyde Park. It became a cultural icon of the optimism and prowess of the early Victorian age, drawing over six million visitors (almost a fifth of the British population) to its magnificent displays of modern industry and invention

---

[13] Ryle, *Living or Dead?*, 15.
[14] Ryle, *Living or Dead?*, 22.
[15] Ryle, *Living or Dead?*, 25, 27–28.
[16] Christopher Clark, *Revolutionary Spring: Fighting for a New World, 1848–1849* (Allen Lane, 2023).
[17] Ryle, *Living or Dead?*, 30.

from Britain and its global empire.[18] "But the eye of the Lord," Ryle declared, "will only see two companies thronging that large palace of glass—wheat and chaff." He warned that professing Christians, even if they loved attending church and listening to preachers, would be found on the same side as famous atheists if they lacked saving faith in Christ. "From Paine and Voltaire to the dead churchman who can think of nothing but outward ceremonies—from Julian and Porphyry to the unconverted admirer of sermons in the present day—all, all are standing in one rank before God; all, all are chaff."[19]

Ryle acknowledged that this way of dividing the world, between converted and unconverted, was unpopular because it smacked of extremism. Many wanted to invent a third category—"a quiet, easy-going, moderate kind of Christianity," neither too sinful nor too serious—where most English people would naturally be found, attending church but not born again. Yet Ryle denounced this idea of a third way as "an immense and soul-ruining delusion. . . . It is as vain an invention as the Pope's purgatory. It is a refuge of lies—a castle in the air—a Russian ice-palace—a vast unreality—an empty dream." A "Russian ice palace" was an exotic idea to British readers. The most famous was built at Saint Petersburg during the winter of 1739–1740 on the orders of Empress Anna Ivanovna, to celebrate victory in the Russo-Turkish War. It was constructed from large blocks of ice from the Neva River but melted by the following summer and became synonymous with delusory fantasy. Everything hinged, Ryle insisted, upon faith in Christ. Natural gifts without the converting grace of the Holy Spirit, he suggested, are like a long row of zeros with no digit at the front—"they look big, but they are of no value." "You may sway kingdoms by your counsel, move millions by your pen, or keep crowds in breathless attention by your tongue," but without submission to Christ it counts for nothing.[20]

Ryle further unpacked the relationship between nature and grace in *Are You an Heir?* (1852). He challenged the widespread notion that every human being is a child of God, even the person who lacks faith in Christ. Not pulling his punches, Ryle called this a "vile heresy," a "delusive notion," and a "wild theory," not consonant with Scripture. "It is a perilous dream, with which many are trying to soothe themselves, but one from which

---

[18] Jeffrey Auerbach, *The Great Exhibition of 1851: A Nation on Display* (Yale University Press, 1999); Auerbach and Peter Hoffenberger, eds., *Britain, the Empire, and the World at the Great Exhibition of 1851* (Ashgate, 2008); Geoffrey Cantor, *Religion and the Great Exhibition of 1851* (Oxford University Press, 2011).
[19] J. C. Ryle, *Wheat or Chaff? A Question for 1851* (Ipswich, 1851), 5, 7.
[20] Ryle, *Wheat or Chaff?*, 6–8.

there will be a fearful waking up at the last day."[21] On the contrary, Ryle insisted, no one has a natural right to call God his or her Father. According to the Church of England's catechism in the Book of Common Prayer, human beings are "by nature born in sin, and the children of wrath," a verdict with which Ryle concurred.[22] He observed that sin is hereditary for all Adam and Eve's descendants, but grace is not, as proved by the fact that many Christian parents do not produce Christian children. Only when the Holy Spirit leads someone to put faith in Jesus Christ does that person become a child of God.[23]

Ryle acknowledged that God as Creator of the universe is, in one sense, "the universal Father of all mankind." Yet this sonship by creation "belongs to stones, trees, beasts, or even to the devils, as much as to us" and is no guarantee of heaven. Ryle celebrated that God's love and compassion extend to every human being, but he nevertheless maintained that it is impossible to approach God as a pardoning Father without the mediating work of Jesus Christ. "Where there is no faith in Christ, it is drivelling folly to say that a man may take comfort in God as his Father. God is a reconciled Father to none but the members of Christ." The promises of the gospel are extremely wide, but come with a condition: "Believe on the Lord Jesus Christ, and thou shalt be saved" (Acts 16:31). Therefore, Ryle argued, it is absurd for those who resist Jesus to call themselves children of God. "God is to be their Father—but on their own terms! Christ is to be their Saviour—but on their own conditions! What can be more unreasonable? What can be more proud? What can be more unholy, than such a doctrine as this?" Ryle warned his readers that this idea, growing in popularity in the 1850s, "sounds beautiful and charitable in the mouths of poets, novelists, sentimentalists, and tender-hearted women" but is unscriptural.[24] He therefore concluded his tract by interrogating his readers: "Whose child are you? Are you the child of nature or the child of grace? Are you the child of the devil or the child of God? You cannot be both at once. Which are you? . . . Oh! that you would never rest till the question is settled!"[25]

Ryle often returned to these themes, which were central to his evangelistic motivations. His tract for New Year 1864 asked a blunt question:

---

[21] J. C. Ryle, *Are You an Heir? A Question for Everybody* (Ipswich, 1852), 6–8.
[22] Catechism (1662), in *The Book of Common Prayer: The Texts of 1549, 1559, and 1662*, ed. Brian Cummings (Oxford University Press, 2011), 429.
[23] Ryle, *Are You an Heir?*, 6.
[24] Ryle, *Are You an Heir?*, 8–10.
[25] Ryle, *Are You an Heir?*, 30.

Are You Converted? He defined conversion as "a mighty turning of heart, opinion, and life, towards God" and gave a string of historical examples, from Augustine of Hippo and Martin Luther to eighteenth-century Church of England evangelicals, former slave trader John Newton, and Thomas Scott, author of the spiritual autobiography *The Force of Truth* (1779).[26] "Any one may get to heaven without money, rank, or learning," Ryle reasoned. "No one, however wise, wealthy, noble, or beautiful, will ever get to heaven without conversion."[27] The heart of the unconverted person is like "a brick or a stone" toward the Christian gospel. As evidence, he pointed to a typical English Sunday congregation, where the majority attended "for fashion and form's sake" but showed little interest in the worship of God:

> Observe how listless, and apathetic, and indifferent, they evidently are about the whole affair. It is clear their hearts are not there! They are thinking of something else, and not of religion. They are thinking of business, or money, or pleasure, or worldly plans, or bonnets, or gowns, or new dresses, or amusements. Their bodies are there, but not their hearts. And what is the reason? What is it they all need? They need conversion.[28]

For this reason, Ryle always preached evangelistically to his own congregation. He rejoiced that, because of the supernatural power of the Holy Spirit, "the age of spiritual miracles is not yet past. Dead souls in our congregations can yet be raised. Blind eyes can yet be made to see. Dumb prayerless tongues can yet be taught to pray." So he ended his tract, as always, with a direct appeal: "Repent, and be converted. Rest not, rest not, rest not, till you know and feel that you are a converted man."[29]

Holy Spirit Intervention

The converting work of the Holy Spirit was central to Ryle's understanding of radical spiritual change. For example, in *The Garden Inclosed* (1869), he explained that the Spirit gives followers of Christ "new hearts, new minds, new tastes, new desires, new sorrows, new joys, new wishes, new pleasures, new longings . . . new eyes, new ears, new affections, new opinions." It is a "new existence," by the transforming power of the Holy Spirit.[30] This

---

[26] J. C. Ryle, *Are You Converted? A Question for 1864* (London, 1864), 8.
[27] Ryle, *Are You Converted?*, 3.
[28] Ryle, *Are You Converted?*, 10.
[29] Ryle, *Are You Converted?*, 14, 21.
[30] J. C. Ryle, *The Garden Inclosed: A Parable for All Who Love Flowers* (London, 1869), 10.

emphasis was expounded more fully in *Have You the Spirit?*, Ryle's tract for New Year 1854, in which he asked his readers what "experimental acquaintance" they had with the Holy Spirit. He described the Spirit as the distinguishing proof that Christians belong to God. Borrowing familiar illustrations from agriculture and jewelry, he called the Spirit "the shepherd's mark on the flock of the Lord Jesus . . . the goldsmith's stamp on the genuine sons of God."[31] Conversely, those who lack the Spirit are not genuine believers, Ryle insisted, even if they are baptized and regularly attend church. "Sacraments, and services, and sermons may produce outward formality, and clothe us with a skin of religion, but there will be no life," because only the power of the Spirit "can make true Christians." "Reader, let this also be written in your memory, and never forgotten. No Holy Spirit—no true Christianity! You must have the Spirit *in* you, as well as Christ *for* you, if you are ever to be saved." Many of Ryle's contemporaries dismissed this doctrine as "enthusiasm" or "fanaticism," but he was resolved: "I take my stand on the plain teaching of the Bible."[32]

Although conversion is always the Spirit's work, Ryle observed that the Spirit uses many different means in "awakening the soul," and it is therefore "a most grievous mistake" to think that every Christian must share the same testimony or one type of experience. "With some He uses a sermon, with others the Bible, with others a tract, with others a friend's advice, with others a sickness or affliction, with others no one particular thing, that can be distinctly traced."[33] Nevertheless, only the Spirit can bring true conviction of sin and the need for redemption: "Ministers may alarm us for a little season. Sickness may break the ice on our hearts. But the ice will soon freeze again, if it is not thawed by the breath of the Spirit."[34] Evangelistic tracts, church schools, and well-oiled missionary enterprise were powerless without the Spirit. Therefore, Ryle called upon his readers to join him in praying that 1854 "may be a year in which the Spirit may be poured out from on high more abundantly than He ever has been yet," across the whole world, not least for the conversion of Jews, Muslims, "heathen," and Roman Catholics, "especially in Italy and Ireland."[35] Yet Ryle's primary concern was closer to home. It was easy for ministers to despair at their own poor abilities, or at the unresponsiveness of their

---
[31] J. C. Ryle, *Have You the Spirit? A Question for 1854* (Ipswich, 1854), 3, 5.
[32] Ryle, *Have You the Spirit?*, 9–10.
[33] Ryle, *Have You the Spirit?*, 17.
[34] Ryle, *Have You the Spirit?*, 20.
[35] Ryle, *Have You the Spirit?*, 32.

congregations, who seemed "as hard and insensible as the nether millstone." And yet, he proclaimed, "we believe the power of the Holy Ghost," who "can come down like fire and melt the hardest hearts.... And so we preach on."[36]

Three years later, Ryle returned to the subject at St Ann's Church, in the center of Manchester, as part of a series of nineteen sermons from prominent Anglican evangelical clergymen, including such luminaries as Hugh Stowell (1799–1865) and Hugh McNeile (1795–1879).[37] The preaching series was designed to coincide with the Manchester Art Treasures Exhibition, an ambitious Victorian enterprise opened by Prince Albert that ran between May and October 1857 and attracted over 1.3 million visitors. Unlike the Great Exhibition of 1851, which had paraded Britain's industrial and technological prowess, the Manchester Exhibition displayed over sixteen thousand works of fine art, including ten thousand decorative items. Many were from private collections, never before seen in public, from old masters to Pre-Raphaelites and encompassing portraits, watercolors, photographs, engravings, and sculptures. This unprecedented event took place in a vast, purpose-built venue, the Art Treasures Palace, constructed from iron and glass on a three-acre site, Manchester's answer to the Crystal Palace.[38]

Ryle's subject in Manchester was the work of the Holy Spirit, and his sermon was quickly published as a tract, *None of His!* (1857), an exposition of Romans 8:9, "If any man have not the Spirit of Christ, he is none of His." He quoted with approval the Puritan Thomas Goodwin, who observed in *The Worship of the Holy Ghost* (1704) that Christians often focus on God the Father and God the Son but have "almost lost this Third Person" from their thoughts and prayers, failing to give the Holy Spirit the glory and honor due to him.[39] Ryle insisted that the Bible assigns a prominent place to the Holy Spirit for the entirety of Christian discipleship. "In a word, all that believers have from grace to glory—all that they are from the first moment they believe to the day they depart to be with Christ—all, all, all may be traced to the work of God the Holy Ghost." "Settle it in your

---
[36] Ryle, *Have You the Spirit?*, 28.
[37] *"Things That Accompany Salvation": Nineteen Sermons, Preached in St Ann's Church, Manchester, During the Season of the Manchester Art Treasures' Exhibition, 1857* (London, 1858).
[38] Helen Rees Leahy, ed., "Art, City, Spectacle: The 1857 Manchester Art Treasures Exhibition Revisited," *Bulletin of the John Rylands University Library of Manchester* 87, no. 2 (2005); Elizabeth A. Pergam, *The Manchester Art Treasures Exhibition of 1857: Entrepreneurs, Connoisseurs and the Public* (Ashgate, 2011).
[39] J. C. Ryle, *None of His! A Tract on the Work of the Holy Ghost, Being Thoughts on Rom viii. 9* (Ipswich, 1857), 5.

minds," he continued, "that the work of all three Persons in the blessed Trinity, is absolutely and equally needful to the salvation of every saved soul."[40]

Ryle reiterated that without the intervention of the Holy Spirit, no one can ever turn to God in repentance and faith. The organizers of the Manchester Exhibition deliberately imbued their initiative with spiritual significance, and a line from Alexander Pope was written in large letters in the Art Treasures Palace: "To wake the soul by tender strokes of art." Although the exhibition had captured the public imagination, Ryle laid down a direct theological challenge: "Intellectual training and secular education alone make no true Christians. Acquaintance with fine arts and science leads no one to heaven. Pictures and statues never brought one soul to God. The 'tender strokes of art' never prepared a soul for the judgment day." Ryle observed that Ancient Greece also had many accomplished painters and sculptors, such as Zeuxis, Parrhasius, Phidias, and Praxiteles, "masters as great in their day as any in modern times. Yet the Greeks knew nothing of the way of peace with God. They were sunk in gross idolatry. They bowed down to the works of their own hands." Without the Holy Spirit, conversion is impossible.[41]

Even Christian preaching and biblical apologetics are ineffective in producing conversions without the Holy Spirit's intervention, Ryle observed. "The most zealous efforts of ministers alone make no true Christians. The ablest scriptural reasoning has no effect on the mind. The most fervent pulpit eloquence will not move the heart. The naked truth alone will not lead the will." Clergy knew this only too well "by painful experience," and from his own Suffolk ministry Ryle could think of many specific examples of unconverted parishioners "sitting under our pulpits year after year, and hearing hundreds of sermons, full of Gospel truth, without the slightest result." Year after year, such a hearer remained

> unaffected and unmoved by every scriptural argument—cold as the stones on which he treads as he enters our church—unmoved as the marble statue which adorns the tomb against the wall—dead as the old dry oak of which his pew is made—feelingless as the painted glass in the windows, through which the sun shines on his head.[42]

---
[40] Ryle, *None of His!*, 9.
[41] Ryle, *None of His!*, 11–12.
[42] Ryle, *None of His!*, 12.

What was required was nothing less than "new birth," a supernatural act of creation by the Holy Spirit. Without this new birth, Ryle insisted, there can be no salvation.

The work of the Holy Spirit is often mysterious, Ryle acknowledged. Why is one person in a family converted but not other relatives? Why did Saul become an apostle but not other Pharisees? Why did John Newton become an evangelical preacher but not other slave-ship captains? Why was England a Christian nation but not China? Nothing could explain this, Ryle believed, except the sovereign action of the Holy Spirit.[43] Those who had received the Spirit—convicting them of sin, drawing them to Christ, and giving them a love for the Bible and prayer—should therefore rejoice with gratitude at these supernatural desires. "Did these things come of nature? Oh! no! Did you learn these things in the schools of this world? Oh! no! no! They are all of grace. Grace sowed them. Grace watered them. Grace began them. Grace has kept them up."[44]

Ryle again ended his Manchester tract by calling his readers to pray for God to pour out the Spirit abundantly. He observed that there were far more Christian preachers in the 1850s than there had been in the early church, and yet, proportionately, they had far less spiritual impact. Therefore he urged, "We want more of the presence of the Holy Ghost—more in the pulpit, and more in the congregation—more in the pastoral visit, and more in the school." The Spirit brings life, growth, and fruitfulness, but without the Spirit "all will be dead, tame, formal, sleepy, and cold."[45] Decades later, in 1891, as bishop of Liverpool, Ryle became president of the Daily Prayer Union, an Anglican society founded in 1879 to promote daily prayer for the work of the Holy Spirit throughout the world. Its quarterly journal, *Pentecostal Power*, praised Ryle for his leadership in seeking "a great outpouring of the Holy Ghost."[46]

Revivals and Revivalists

Ryle's tracts were always direct in seeking conversion. For example, in *Never Perish* (1855) he called upon his readers to repent and follow Christ immediately: "And why not today? Why not this very night? Why not with-

---
[43] Ryle, *None of His!*, 17.
[44] Ryle, *None of His!*, 29.
[45] Ryle, *None of His!*, 30.
[46] Quoted in "The Rev. Henry Law Harkness," *The News: A National Fireside Journal and Review*, October 30, 1891, 55.

out delay seek Christ and live? Oh! reader, answer me, if you can."[47] Nevertheless, in the same tract, he spoke of the importance of discriminating between true and false conversion. Some naive Christians were too quick to interpret an emotional response or moral reform as proof of conversion if they saw someone weeping during a sermon or forsaking swearing and drinking. But Ryle reminded his readers, "A new coat of paint does not make an old door new." Conversion, he insisted, is "no such cheap and easy and common thing as many seem to fancy. It is a mighty work on the heart which none but He who made the world can effect." There is a vital distinction between feelings and faith.[48]

In *Never Perish*, Ryle claimed that "the history of all revivals proves that there may often be a great quantity of seemingly religious impression without any true work of the Spirit."[49] He read especially deeply into the story of the eighteenth-century Evangelical Revival, and his earliest historical lecture focused on George Whitefield (1714–1770). It was delivered in January 1852 to the Church of England Young Men's Society for Aiding Missions at Home and Abroad, at Freemasons' Hall (headquarters of the United Grand Lodge of England), a popular central London venue often rented by nonmasonic groups, including evangelical missionary societies.[50] Ryle sought to rehabilitate Whitefield's reputation, praising him as one of the greatest ministers the Church of England had ever known.[51] Next, he began to investigate Whitefield's contemporaries. This research bore fruit in popular journalism with pen portraits of eleven prominent revival clergy, published in monthly installments from February 1866 to January 1868 in *The Family Treasury of Sunday Reading*, which were then collected together as a single volume, *The Christian Leaders of the Last Century; or, England a Hundred Years Ago* (1869). Canon Christopher praised it as "one of the most stirring, minister-moving books I have ever seen" and urged parishioners to gift it to their clergy.[52]

In *Christian Leaders*, Ryle portrayed pre-revival England as a land enveloped by "a gross, thick, religious and moral darkness." The clergy were

---
[47] J. C. Ryle, *Never Perish: Being Thoughts on Final Perseverance* (Ipswich, 1855), 32.
[48] Ryle, *Never Perish*, 22.
[49] Ryle, *Never Perish*, 22.
[50] Robert Soames, "The Non-Masonic Uses of Freemasons' Hall, 1775–1885," *Ars Quatuor Coronatorum* 136 (2023): 1–15.
[51] J. C. Ryle, "George Whitefield," in *Lectures Delivered Before the Church of England Young Men's Society for Aiding Missions at Home and Abroad, at Freemason's Hall, January and February, 1852* (London, 1852), 31–75.
[52] Alfred Christopher, letter to the editor, *The Record*, December 28, 1868.

ignorant, the churches were empty, and the state of British morality, Ryle claimed, was revealed by William Hogarth's notorious cartoons. Into that landscape of degradation and sloth stepped the evangelical revivalists, whom Ryle praised in a repeated refrain as "spiritual heroes," "spiritual champions," and "spiritual giants." According to his narrative, they transformed the nation by their sacrificial ministries, especially their bold biblical preaching, and were models for the evangelical "standard bearers" in the modern day.[53] Nevertheless, *Christian Leaders* contained little reflection on the nature of genuine conversions and revivals. It was primarily a study in ministerial usefulness, focusing on the power of evangelical preaching, and offered an almost entirely positive account.

In one area—the Evangelical Revival's ecstatic phenomena—Ryle was more circumspect. He hailed the preaching of John Berridge (1716–1793) of Everton, Bedfordshire, for its "immense" spiritual impact leading to the "awakening" of thousands of people, but also acknowledged that Berridge's ministry was sometimes associated with "very curious physical effects." "Some of his hearers cried out aloud hysterically, some were thrown into strong convulsions, and some fell into a kind of trance or catalepsy, which lasted a long time." Ryle defended Berridge, arguing that the revivalist never encouraged this demonstrative behavior. Ryle claimed that "such phenomena will sometimes appear in cases of strong religious excitement . . . they are peculiarly catching and infectious, especially among young women . . . even the most scientific medical men are greatly puzzled to explain them." Furthermore, Ryle argued that "many calm and sober-minded witnesses" had recently testified to similar happenings associated with the Ulster revival of 1859. Drawing a discreet veil over the controversy, he concluded that, like "demoniacal possession," it was a "very deep and mysterious" subject. "But a minister ought certainly not to be put down as a fanatic because people go into convulsions under his preaching."[54]

While celebrating the eighteenth-century revival, Ryle was far more critical of Victorian revivalism. For example, in *Is It Real?* (1862), he asserted that much "revivalist religion" in the mid-nineteenth century was "utterly unreal." Many people claimed to be suddenly convicted of sin and "overwhelmed with joys and ecstasies of soul" but then returned to their old ways as soon as the excitement had worn off. Their Christian profession

---

[53] Ryle, *Christian Leaders*, 12–14.
[54] Ryle, *Christian Leaders*, 228–29.

was deceptive, "base metal from the devil's mint" and "worthless in God's sight."[55] Ryle examined this question in more detail in *What Does It Cost?*, his tract for New Year 1866. He gave examples from Scripture of those who, like Demas, fell away from the Christian faith, and he drew contemporary lessons for modern revivalism. "For want of counting the cost the hearers of powerful evangelical preachers often come to miserable ends," Ryle lamented. Although they were "stirred and excited" temporarily, "hundreds of professed converts, under religious revivals, go back to the world after a time, and bring disgrace on religion." Often this was because they had been misled about the nature of true Christianity, as if discipleship meant "nothing more than a so-called 'coming to Christ'" without realizing that it also involved trials.[56]

All "true revivals" should be celebrated, Ryle made clear, no matter in what section of the church they originated or under what preacher. Nevertheless, he warned that the modern "revival movement" was promoting a theological system that was "defective and mischievous in the extreme." In Ryle's judgment, it was guilty of an incessant overemphasis on three theological truths to the exclusion of all else: instantaneous conversion, the invitation for unconverted sinners to come to Christ, and the possession of inward joy and peace as the proof of conversion. "Instantaneous conversion, no doubt, ought to be pressed on people," he agreed. "But surely they ought not be led to suppose that there is no other sort of conversion, and that unless they are suddenly and powerfully converted to God, they are not converted at all!" Likewise, it is "the very corner-stone of Gospel preaching" to urge hearers to come to Christ immediately, "just as we are." But they also needed to hear about their sin and guilt before God outside of Christ. Peace and joy should be proclaimed, but not as if they were essential to justification; otherwise people were misled by revivalist preachers into assuming that "true faith" always brought "triumphant feelings." This teaching was deeply damaging, Ryle warned. On the one hand, it discouraged Christians who did not experience the emotional heights being pressed upon them. On the other hand, it misled non-Christians who were "deluded" into thinking themselves converted "under the pressure of animal excitement, and temporary feelings." The fundamental mistake of the revivalists was to overlook the sovereignty of the Holy Spirit in saving

---
[55] J. C. Ryle, *Is It Real? A Question for the Times* (Ipswich, 1862), 12–13.
[56] J. C. Ryle, *What Does It Cost? A Question for 1866* (London, 1865), 11–12.

sinners. Many revivalists, Ryle suggested, "talk as if conversions could be manufactured at man's pleasure."[57]

The antidote to these revivalist errors was to teach "all the counsel of God" in scriptural proportion, not allowing two or three doctrines to overshadow all the rest. Repentance must be taught as fully as faith. The variety of the Holy Spirit's methods must be explained. And people needed to understand that following Christ involved "warfare as well as peace, a cross as well as a crown." Ryle concluded that "unhealthy excitement is above all things to be dreaded in religion, because it often ends in fatal, soul-ruining reaction and utter deadness." In particular, he doubted the genuineness of mass conversions, whether on the mission field in New Zealand or during citywide "revivals" in Britain. "God's ordinary plan," he declared, "is to call in individuals one by one." Therefore, Ryle was always doubtful when he heard of large numbers suddenly being converted together. He recommended that revivalists preach frequently on two Gospel texts—the parable of the sower and Jesus's command to "count the cost."[58]

> Offer them salvation, ready, free, full, immediate salvation. Press Christ and all His benefits on their acceptance. But in all your work tell the truth, and the whole truth. Be ashamed to use the vulgar arts of a recruiting serjeant. Do not speak only of the uniform, the pay, and the glory. Speak also of the enemies, the battle, the armour, the watching, the marching, and the drill. Do not present only one side of Christianity.[59]

Gospel preaching, Ryle insisted, must speak not only of the cross of redemption on which Christ died but also of the cross of self-denial that every Christian must carry.

In other contexts, Ryle continued to drive home this point. For example, in *Are We Sanctified?* (1874), he welcomed the increased prevalence of mission services and "revival meetings" that were helping to animate the Church of England. Yet he warned that these initiatives brought dangers as well as advantages, because the devil always sowed tares among the wheat. Many people, he lamented, "appear moved and touched and roused under the preaching of the Gospel, while in reality their hearts are not changed at all." They were driven merely by "the contagion of seeing others weep-

---

[57] Ryle, *What Does It Cost?*, 12–14.
[58] Ryle, *What Does It Cost?*, 14–15.
[59] Ryle, *What Does It Cost?*, 17.

ing, rejoicing, or affected" without genuine repentance and faith in Christ. "I know no state of soul more dangerous," Ryle concluded, "than to imagine we are born again and sanctified by the Holy Ghost, because we have picked up a few religious feelings."[60] Likewise, preaching to undergraduates at Cambridge University in 1879, he warned against a Christianity of "spasmodic and hysterical excitement." "It may suit weak and sentimental minds for a little season; but it rarely lasts."[61] One of the chief proofs of authentic conversion is the continuance of the convert as a disciple of Jesus Christ through all the highs and lows of the Christian life.

---

[60] J. C. Ryle, *Are We Sanctified? A Question for 1874, Being Thoughts on John xvii. 17 and 1 Thess iv. 3* (London, 1874), 18–19.
[61] J. C. Ryle, *Looking unto Jesus: A Thought for Christmas, 1879* (London, 1879), 4.

CHAPTER 4

SOVEREIGN GRACE

In December 1868, the United Kingdom was abuzz with general election fever, the first parliamentary election since the passing of the Second Reform Act. Following the substantial extension of the franchise, 2.3 million votes were cast, compared with just 855,000 at the previous general election in 1865—though most working-class men, and all women, were still excluded.[1] William Gladstone swept to power, defeating his rival Benjamin Disraeli to secure the keys to 10 Downing Street.[2] Ryle threw himself into this national excitement with *Your Election! A Tract for the Times* (1868). It began by lamenting the partisan passions, quarrels, lies, intimidation, flattery, and broken promises stoked by the election season, and warned that the public should never expect too much of their elected representatives. After this political commentary, Ryle segued into his theological theme:

> But, reader, there is another Election, which is of far higher importance than any election to Parliament—an Election whose consequences will abide when Queen, Lords and Commons have passed away—an Election which concerns all classes, the lowest as well as the highest, the women as well as the men. . . . Whether you are in Parliament or not, whether you vote or not, whether you are on the winning side or not, all this will matter very little a hundred years hence. But it will matter greatly whether you are in the number of "God's Elect."

[1] Colin Rallings and Michael Thrasher, eds., *British Electoral Facts, 1832–1999* (Ashgate, 2000), 10–11.
[2] Dick Leonard, *The Great Rivalry: Gladstone and Disraeli* (Tauris, 2013).

The rest of the tract was a lively exposition of the doctrine of election, which Ryle defined succinctly: "God has been pleased from all eternity to choose certain men and women out of mankind, whom by His counsel secret to us, He has decreed to save by Jesus Christ. None are finally saved except those who are thus chosen." The Holy Spirit works in the elect to convict them of sin, lead them to Christ, bring them to repentance and faith, renew them, sanctify them, keep them from falling away, and ultimately bring them safely to heaven. "In short God's eternal Election is the first link in that chain of a sinner's salvation of which heavenly glory is the end. None ever repent, believe, and are born again, except the Elect."[3]

This doctrine was widely disputed and reviled, Ryle admitted, even among Christians. Indeed, he noted, perhaps from painful personal experience, that simply mentioning the word *election* was enough to provoke "anger, ill-temper, and passion" in some quarters.[4] Yet he insisted it was part of scriptural revelation and so must be humbly believed. Some of Ryle's Anglican opponents rejected the doctrine as "a mere piece of Calvinism," suitable only for Presbyterians and other disciples of the Genevan Reformer.[5] But in reply, Ryle simply quoted Article 17 of the Thirty-Nine Articles—one of the official formularies of the Church of England—which teaches that the doctrine of predestination, or election in Christ, is "full of sweet, pleasant, and unspeakable comfort" to Christian believers.[6] He rejoiced in Article 17 as the best statement of the doctrine outside the Bible.[7]

Nevertheless, Ryle admitted that the scriptural doctrine of election was frequently misunderstood and must be taught cautiously. "It is one of Satan's chief devices to make the Gospel odious by tempting men to distort it. Perhaps no part of Christian theology has suffered so much damage in this way as the doctrine of personal Election." Wrongly interpreted, it can drive people to despair, or to antinomianism and licentiousness, if they come to believe that they are not elect. God's sovereign decrees do not dissolve personal responsibility for one's actions and response to the gospel message, Ryle insisted. The Bible addresses human beings "not as mere logs, and bricks, and stones" but as "free-agents" who are accountable to God.

---
[3] J. C. Ryle, *Your Election! A Tract for the Times* (London, 1868), 5–7.
[4] Ryle, *Your Election!*, 7.
[5] Ryle, *Your Election!*, 11.
[6] Article 17 ("Of Predestination and Election"), in *The Book of Common Prayer: The Texts of 1549, 1559, and 1662*, ed. Brian Cummings (Oxford University Press, 2011), 678.
[7] Ryle, *Your Election!*, 12.

The Bible never says that sinners miss heaven because they are not Elect, but because they neglect the great salvation, will not repent, and will not believe. The last judgment will abundantly prove that it is not the want of God's Election, so much as laziness, the love of sin, unbelief, and unwillingness to come to Christ, that ruined the souls that are lost.

Nor should the doctrine of election prevent preachers from broadcasting a full and free offer of salvation to all their hearers.

We know not who are God's Elect, and whom He means to call and convert. Our duty is to invite all. To every unconverted soul without exception we ought to say, "God loves you, and Christ has died for you." To everyone we ought to say, "Awake—repent—believe—come to Christ—be converted—turn—call upon God—strive to enter in—come—for all things are ready."

Some Calvinists argued that because only the elect would be saved, it was wrong to offer salvation to everyone, but Ryle dismissed this line of reasoning as "simply absurd." "We will invite all, in the firm belief that the invitation will do good to some. We will prophesy to the dry bones, if God commands us."[8] Ryle believed this was the apostolic method. He therefore concluded *Your Election!* as he did all his tracts, with an evangelistic summons. He urged his readers not to allow quibbles and disputes about predestination to prevent them from coming to Christ without delay. Faith in Christ is always primary. Quoting the sixteenth-century martyr John Bradford, Ryle observed that before training in "the great University" of election and predestination, Christians need to be firmly established in "the little Grammar School" of repentance and faith.[9]

Parliamentarians were condemned to a life of disappointment, Ryle reflected, even under the extended franchise in an expanding British democracy. Their hard-fought election victories in 1868 would be short-lived and fundamentally unsatisfying. Their seats in the House of Commons, and around the cabinet table, could be held for only a few years and must soon be relinquished to others. "But he that is one of God's Elect has a treasure which can never be taken from him," Ryle celebrated, "and a place from which he can never be removed. Blessed is that man who sets his heart on this Election! There is no election like the Election of God!"[10]

---

[8] Ryle, *Your Election!*, 13–15.
[9] Ryle, *Your Election!*, 20.
[10] Ryle, *Your Election!*, 22.

Salvation Belongs to the Lord

The sovereign grace of God in salvation was a repeated theme throughout Ryle's *Expository Thoughts on the Gospels*. For example, commenting on John 6:44 ("No man can come to me, except the Father . . . draw him"), he described it as a "very humbling truth." "The favourite notion of man is that he can do what he likes, repent or not repent, believe or not believe, come to Christ or not come—entirely at his own discretion. In fact, man likes to think that his salvation is in his own power." On the contrary, Ryle observed, human nature since Adam's fall is so "corrupt and depraved" that no one will come to Christ and believe in Christ without the grace of God "inclining his will, and giving him a disposition to come." Preaching and moral persuasion alone are powerless. The sinner must be supernaturally "drawn" to Christ by grace. "Man never of himself begins with God. God must first begin with man."[11] Likewise, commenting on John 15:16 ("Ye have not chosen me, but I have chosen you"), Ryle proclaimed: "Christ must first choose us and call us by His Spirit, or else we shall never choose Christ. . . . Our song to all eternity will be that which fell from the lips of Jonah: 'Salvation is of the Lord.'"[12]

As an example of the "sovereignty of God in saving sinners," Ryle pointed to the two criminals crucified alongside Jesus. Both went through the same experience, and both witnessed Jesus's final hours at close quarters. "Yet one died in his sins, as he had lived, hardened, impenitent and unbelieving. The other repented, believed, cried to Jesus for mercy, and was saved." The sovereign choice of God is inscrutable, Ryle emphasized. It is impossible to explain why the gospel is hidden from one person but revealed to another, or why the same Sunday sermon can leave one parishioner in "perfect indifference" but send another home converted. Faced with these inexplicable facts, the right response is to pray in humility, "Even so, Father: for so it seemed good in thy sight" (Matt. 11:26).[13] "One account only can be given of all this," Ryle concluded. "All is ordered by the sovereign hand of God."[14]

The doctrine of electing grace is closely linked to the doctrine of "human impotence," which Ryle argued is "the uniform teaching of the

---
[11] J. C. Ryle, *Expository Thoughts on the Gospels, for Family and Private Use: St John*, vol. 1 (London, 1865), 388–89.
[12] J. C. Ryle, *Expository Thoughts on the Gospels, for Family and Private Use: St John*, vol. 3 (London, 1873), 126.
[13] J. C. Ryle, *Expository Thoughts on the Gospels, for Family and Private Use: St Luke*, vol. 2 (Ipswich, 1859), 470.
[14] J. C. Ryle, *Expository Thoughts on the Gospels, for Family and Private Use: St Luke*, vol. 1 (Ipswich, 1858), 122.

Bible" and of every Reformation confession of faith. For example, Article 10 ("Of Free Will") of the Thirty-Nine Articles begins, "The condition of man after the fall of Adam is such, that he cannot turn and prepare himself by his own natural strength and good works to faith and calling on God." This turning to God is impossible, Article 10 continues, without prevenient grace—that is, the prior grace of God that initiates salvation.[15] This doctrine was offensive to many people because it denies innate human goodness and capability, but Ryle found it confirmed by ministerial experience: "The longer ministers of the Gospel live, the more do they find that there is something to be done in every heart which neither preaching, teaching, arguing, exhorting, or means of grace can do. When all has been done, God must 'draw,' or there is no fruit." Furthermore, "many who profess to deny man's impotence in theory, often confess it in their prayers and praises, almost in spite of themselves. Many people are very low Arminians in print or in the pulpit, but excellent Calvinists on their knees."[16]

Ryle held the sovereign grace of God to be "irresistible," though he acknowledged this to be a subject "on which good men differ greatly." He admitted there is sometimes "a great fight and struggle" between the sinner and God when the work of conversion is initiated, but "when grace once begins it always wins the victory at last." Commenting on John 6:37 ("All that the Father giveth me shall come to me"), Ryle wrote: "All who are given to Christ shall come to Him. No obstacle, no difficulty, no power of the world, the flesh, and the devil, can prevent them. Sooner or later they will break through all, and surmount all. If 'given,' they will 'come.' To ministers the words are full of comfort." Nevertheless, Ryle explained that this drawing by God is never in violent opposition to the person's own will, like "the drawing of a prisoner to a jail, or of an ox to the slaughterhouse." Instead, God works through the person's will, transforming heart and desires by "the unseen agency of the Holy Ghost" so that he or she wants to respond to Christ.[17]

Ryle emphasized that because God is sovereign in salvation, God can save anyone of his choosing, in any way of his choosing. At the same time, however, God has appointed "means of grace," especially gospel preaching and prayer, through which he normally chooses to act. This is a fundamental principle, Ryle insisted—that "God ordinarily draws through

---
[15] Article 10 ("Of Free Will"), in Cummings, *The Book of Common Prayer*, 676.
[16] Ryle, *St John*, 1:389.
[17] Ryle, *St John*, 1:377, 389, 391.

the instrumentality of His Word. The man that neglects the public preaching and private reading of God's Word, has no right to expect that God will draw him. The thing is possible, but highly improbable."[18] He pointed to the example of the blind man at Jericho (Luke 18:35) who did not "sit lazily at home, and wait for relief to come to him," but placed himself by the roadside where he might encounter Jesus. Although it is true that "God will have mercy on whom he will have mercy" (Rom. 9:15), it is also true that mercy normally comes to those who use the means of grace. Although Jesus is sometimes found by those who do not seek him (Rom. 10:20), Jesus is always found by those who do seek him. Ryle's application was inherently practical: "To expect grace to be put into our hearts, if we sit idling at home on Sundays, and go to no place of worship, is presumption and not faith. . . . The Sabbath breaker, the Bible neglecter, and the prayerless man are forsaking their own mercies and digging graves for their own souls."[19]

God's Love Toward Sinners

In his New Year tract for 1861, entitled *Do You Believe?*, Ryle expounded the famous gospel text "God so loved the world" (John 3:16). He argued passionately that God's love extends to the whole of humanity—to "the world," not just to "the elect." God loves everything he has made, even those who are in rebellion against him. Ryle urged: "Let us resist to the death the unscriptural doctrine of universal salvation. It is not true that all mankind will be finally saved. But let us not fly into the extreme of denying God's universal compassion." Although Ryle identified as an evangelical Calvinist, he wanted to distance himself from a form of Victorian hyper-Calvinism he viewed as unscriptural and unhealthy. He agreed that God's elect are "loved with a special love, and will be loved to all eternity," yet he also affirmed that God loves every person. This divine love is not a vague or abstract idea, Ryle explained, but is manifested tangibly in the person and work of Jesus Christ.[20]

The efficacy and extent of Christ's atonement had been a major focus of theological dispute since the seventeenth century. The Synod of Dort in 1618–1619 articulated what later became known as the "five points of Calvinism," including the concept of "particular redemption" (sometimes

---

[18] Ryle, *St John*, 1:391.
[19] Ryle, *St Luke*, 2:284–85.
[20] J. C. Ryle, *Do You Believe? A Question for 1861* (Ipswich, 1860), 5, 7–8.

Sovereign Grace

called "definite" or "limited" atonement), that Christ died only for the elect. This doctrine was popularized by Puritan authors like John Owen in his *Salus Electorum, Sanguis Jesu: or, The Death of Death in the Death of Christ* (1648), though it was rejected by his fellow Puritan Richard Baxter. Ryle stood in the Puritan tradition and often championed Owen's works but is best understood (like Baxter) as a "four-point," not a "five-point," Calvinist. Concerning the extent of the atonement, Ryle was out of step with the Calvinist mainstream.

Ryle wanted to claim the language of "particular redemption," but by this he meant an atonement limited in efficacy, not limited in sufficiency or scope. In *Do You Believe?*, he wrote:

> I confess, boldly, that I hold the doctrine of particular redemption, in a certain sense, as strongly as any one. I believe that none are effectually redeemed but God's elect. They and they only are set free from the guilt, and power, and consequences of sin. But I hold no less strongly, that Christ's work of atonement is sufficient for all mankind. There is a sense in which He has tasted death for every man, and has taken upon Him the sin of the world.[21]

For Ryle, this was fundamentally a question of scriptural integrity. Elsewhere, he resisted what he called "an extreme view of particular redemption," though it was in fact the standard Calvinist view. He believed it to be flatly contradicted by Jesus's statement that he came "to save the world" (John 12:47). Some Calvinist commentators argued that "the world" means "the elect" from all the nations of the globe, Gentiles as well as Jews, but Ryle again dismissed this interpretation as "an evasion of the plain meaning of words."[22]

Ryle frequently returned to this question in his *Expository Thoughts*, especially when addressing Johannine teaching about "the world." For example, the Lamb of God "taketh away the sin of the world" (John 1:29). A chief implication, Ryle argued, is that because of Christ's death, all people are "salvable," though not all will in the end be saved. "I dare not confine the intention of redemption to the saints alone. Christ is for every man. . . . In the work of the Father in election, and of the Spirit

---
[21] Ryle, *Do You Believe?*, 12.
[22] J. C. Ryle, *Expository Thoughts on the Gospels, for Family and Private Use: St John*, vol. 2 (London, 1869), 429.

in conversion, I see limitation in the Bible most clearly. But in the work of Christ in atonement I see no limitation." In defense of his views, he quoted a range of theologians, including Augustine of Hippo and John Calvin himself.[23]

As evidence of "Christ's infinite willingness to save," Ryle quoted from apostolic texts like 2 Peter 3:9, "The Lord is . . . not willing that any should perish, but that all should come to repentance," and 1 Timothy 2:4, "[God] will have all men to be saved, and to come unto the knowledge of the truth." Yet he lamented that this gospel principle "sorely perplexes narrow-minded and shallow theologians."[24] He warned his hyper-Calvinistic readers not to be "more systematic" than the Bible and that "idolatrous veneration of a system" would result in grave theological error. By restricting God's love to the elect, they presented a "harsh and narrow" view of God's character, as if God were cruel, unjust, and uncompassionate. God's love for the world is "a love of pity and not of approbation or complaisance. But it is not the less a real love," Ryle insisted. In support of this interpretation, he also claimed the Calvinist theologian John Davenant (1572–1641), one of the Church of England's delegates to the Synod of Dort.[25] Ryle was always at pains to show that many of the great Reformed theologians were on his side of the argument.

In further defense of this position, Ryle pointed to Jesus's tender compassion for the Galilean crowds. Although Jesus had a "special love" for his believing people, he also had a "general love" even for "the faithless, the graceless, the followers of this world."[26] Reflecting on Jesus's tears over the city of Jerusalem, Ryle again observed: "His compassion extends to every man, woman, and child on earth. . . . Hardened sinners are fond of making excuses for their conduct. But they will never be able to say that Christ was not merciful, and was not ready to save." For these reasons, Ryle rejected the doctrine of "reprobation," or "double predestination," which teaches that some people are predestined to exclusion from God's saving grace. "There is no necessity that anyone should be lost," he declaimed. "There is no such thing as decreed damnation in the Bible." "Christ loves and pities all, even those who are His open enemies. None are hated, though none but believers are finally saved."[27]

---

[23] Ryle, *St John*, 1:61–63.
[24] Ryle, *St Luke*, 2:140.
[25] Ryle, *St John*, 1:158–59.
[26] J. C. Ryle, *Expository Thoughts on the Gospels, for Family and Private Use: St Mark* (Ipswich, 1857), 154.
[27] Ryle, *St Luke*, 2:314, 318, 470.

Evangelism, Not Metaphysics

Ryle's conception of the sovereign grace of God in salvation, and the breadth of God's love, had direct implications for his preaching ministry. He noticed how frequently Jesus in the Gospels offered pardon and grace not just to "the elect" but to vast crowds of "carnal-minded and unconverted" people. Ryle saw this as a mandate for preachers to make "a wide, broad, full, free, unlimited offer of Christ to all mankind without exception."[28] Likewise, commenting on the Great Commission to "go ye into all the world, and preach the gospel to every creature" (Mark 16:15), Ryle celebrated the importance of global missions. The glad tidings of Jesus should be proclaimed to everyone, everywhere, without exception. Christians should never shrink from telling everyone, "God is full of love to you, Christ is willing to save you."[29]

"Nothing can happen, in heaven or in earth, without God's knowledge and permission," Ryle acknowledged. "But sinners are always addressed by God as responsible, and as free agents."[30] Divine sovereignty and human responsibility, even if apparently incompatible, are both taught by Scripture. Therefore, no one who misses out on heaven can blame God's election.

> It is not any decree of God. It is not God's unwillingness to receive. It is not any limitation of Christ's redeeming work and atonement. It is not any want of wide, broad, free, full invitations to repent and believe. It is simply and entirely man's own fault—his want of will. . . . Man's salvation, if saved, is entirely of God. Man's ruin, if lost, is entirely of himself.[31]

Ryle attempted to hold these scriptural truths together and sharply criticized hyper-Calvinistic ministers for being unbalanced and one-sided in their doctrines. He accused them of twisting the "glorious truths" of election into an unbiblical system and, thus, of spoiling the gospel "by cramping and limiting it." Hyper-Calvinists ignored the full teaching of Jesus, Ryle complained.[32]

Since the names of the elect are known only to God, Ryle considered it the preacher's responsibility "to invite everyone, without exception, to

---
[28] Ryle, *St John*, 1:356, 367.
[29] Ryle, *St Mark*, 363.
[30] Ryle, *St Luke*, 2:402.
[31] Ryle, *St John*, 1:320.
[32] Ryle, *St John*, 1:356.

come to Christ, and to tell men that everyone who does come to Christ shall be received and saved."[33] This policy of ministerial agnosticism shaped Ryle's approach to the mysteries of salvation. In his tract *Do You Believe?*, he protested:

> I will not waste time in trying to explain what cannot be explained, and unravel what cannot be unravelled. I will not attempt to show metaphysically in what way an unconverted man *can* look to Christ, or repent, or believe. But this I know, that it is my plain duty to bid every unbeliever to repent and believe.

Ryle was more concerned for practical evangelism than for philosophical dispute and insoluble doctrinal conundrums. He therefore concluded the tract with a summons: "Reader, trust Christ, look to Christ, cry to the Lord Jesus Christ. . . . Awake and cry to Jesus about your soul! Whatever difficulties there may be about believing, one thing at least is abundantly clear—no man ever perished and went to hell from the foot of the cross."[34]

Safe and Secure

Ryle testified that in his many years of parish ministry, the "most hopeless and painful deathbeds" he had attended were those of "backsliders," who had previously professed Christ but then "fallen away."[35] He lamented that "spiritual shipwrecks" were "deplorably numerous," even among church leaders, and warned all Christians to be on their guard: "None is so holy, but that he may fall—not finally, not hopelessly, but to his own discomfort, the scandal of the church, and the triumph of the world."[36] Yet, at the same time, Ryle taught the perseverance of the saints, a natural corollary of the sovereign grace of God in salvation. This doctrine emphasizes that none of those given to Christ by the Father will be lost (John 6:39), and Ryle summarized the idea in his *Expository Thoughts*:

> Weak as they are, they shall all be saved. Not one of them shall be lost and cast away: not one of them shall miss heaven. If they err, they shall be brought back: if they fall, they shall be raised. The enemies of their souls

---
[33] Ryle, *St John*, 1:378.
[34] Ryle, *Do You Believe?*, 29.
[35] Ryle, *St Luke*, 2:173.
[36] J. C. Ryle, *Beware! A Warning Against Unsound Doctrine, Being Thoughts on Matt. xvi. 6* (Ipswich, 1857), 4, 6.

may be strong and mighty, but their Saviour is mightier; and none shall pluck them out of their Saviour's hands.[37]

As he explained further in *Your Election!*, "A work that was planned before the foundation of the world, by an Architect of almighty power and perfect wisdom, is a work which will never be allowed to fail and be overthrown."[38]

In *Wheat or Chaff?*, Ryle asserted that at the last day the followers of Christ will be found safe: "Sleeping or waking, quick or dead, mouldering in the coffin or standing at the post of daily duty—believers shall be secure and unmoved." If Christ loved his people enough to die for them on the cross, he will surely never let them be cast away. Expanding on New Testament metaphors, Ryle rejoiced: "I do not believe the Lord Jesus will ever lose one of His flock. He will not let Satan pluck away from Him so much as one sick lamb. He will not allow one bone of His mystical body to be broken. He will not suffer one jewel to fall from His crown." Next, he turned to the contemporary metaphor of a Victorian shipwreck, a familiar sight along the Suffolk coast in the 1850s. He invited his readers to imagine witnessing a shipwreck and plunging into the waves to save a drowning child at risk to their own lives. They would not then leave the child shivering and unconscious on the beach, thinking they had done enough by rescuing him or her from the ocean, but would carry the child in their arms to the warmth of the nearest house and would not leave until full recovery was ensured. "And can you suppose the Lord Jesus Christ is less merciful and less compassionate?" Ryle asked. Surely, he argued, Christ as the perfect Savior would not leave salvation uncertain. Ryle acknowledged that it is possible to fall from "false grace," but never from "true grace." Even if believers sin in devastating ways through adultery or apostasy, like King David or the apostle Peter, they will be brought back. The power and promises of the Holy Trinity will preserve and protect them. "The election of God the Father shall not be fruitless—the intercession of God the Son shall not be ineffectual—the love of God the Spirit shall not be labour in vain."[39]

These privileges belong to all believers, Ryle proclaimed, including the weak in faith. Infants in a family are loved as much as older siblings. Vulnerable seedlings in a garden are tended as diligently as sturdy trees. Lambs in a flock are watched over by the shepherd as carefully as old sheep.

---
[37] Ryle, *St John*, 2:230.
[38] Ryle, *Your Election!*, 19.
[39] J. C. Ryle, *Wheat or Chaff? A Question for 1851* (Ipswich, 1851), 18–20.

"Oh! rest assured it is just the same in Christ's family, in Christ's garden, in Christ's flock. All are loved. All are tenderly thought of. All are cared for. And all shall be found in His garner at last."[40] "If you have committed your soul to Christ," Ryle concluded, "Christ will never allow that soul to perish." The omnipotent love of Christ makes it a certainty. "The everlasting arms are round about you. Lean back in them and know your safety. The same hand that was nailed to the cross is holding you. The same wisdom that framed the heavens and the earth is engaged to maintain your cause. . . . Ah! reader, they are well kept whom Christ keeps."[41]

Ryle returned to similar themes in *Never Perish* (1855), an exposition of the promise of Jesus, the good shepherd, concerning his sheep: "I give unto them eternal life; and they shall never perish, neither shall any man pluck them out of my hand" (John 10:28). "Once in Christ, they shall always be in Christ," Ryle affirmed. "In a word, every man, woman, and child on earth that receives saving grace, shall sooner or later receive eternal glory. Every soul that is once justified and washed in Christ's blood, shall at length be found safe at Christ's right hand in the day of judgment."[42] Ryle was at pains to emphasize that this doctrine was taught by the New Testament "1400 years before Calvin was born."[43] In its defense, he offered a list of forty-four scriptural texts and left it to "the honest common sense" of every Bible reader to reach a verdict. Anyone who would explain away "such plain texts" might as well also dispute all the leading themes of the gospel, Ryle quipped. He suggested that if the question were tried in a court of law by "an unprejudiced, intelligent jury," the verdict would go in favor of final perseverance, because it "is so deeply founded on scriptural grounds, that so long as the Bible is the Judge, it cannot be overthrown."[44] Ultimately for Ryle, it was a matter of submitting to the authority of Jesus: "Yes! reader, Jesus has spoken it, and Jesus meant it to be believed."[45]

Furthermore, Ryle calculated that the perseverance of the saints was taught by all the Church of England's leading bishops and theologians at the time of the Reformation, including Hugh Latimer, John Hooper, John Jewel, John Whitgift, and John Davenant.[46] Indeed, Article 17 of the Thirty-

---

[40] Ryle, *Wheat or Chaff?*, 21–22.
[41] Ryle, *Wheat or Chaff?*, 30–31.
[42] J. C. Ryle, *Never Perish: Being Thoughts on Final Perseverance* (Ipswich, 1855), 5.
[43] Ryle, *Never Perish*, 10.
[44] Ryle, *Never Perish*, 15, 17–18.
[45] Ryle, *Never Perish*, 34.
[46] Ryle, *Never Perish*, 38.

Nine Articles affirms that the elect shall "at length by God's mercy attain to everlasting felicity."[47] Therefore, as an Anglican clergyman, bound by his subscription to the Thirty-Nine Articles, Ryle deemed it his public duty to uphold this teaching. As a pastor concerned for the spiritual health of his Suffolk parishioners, he also emphasized that final perseverance was a matter of great practical importance. To reject it was to undermine the joy and confidence of Christian disciples.

> Once admit that the saints of God may perish, and you seem to me to tear from the Gospel crown its brightest jewel. We are hanging on the edge of a precipice. We are kept in awful suspense until we are dead. . . . Where is the good news in all this? What becomes of the glad tidings? Verily such doctrine seems to me to cut up the joy of the Gospel by the roots.

By contrast, final perseverance guarantees "solid peace" and "solid comfort" for believers, not just for the present but also for the eternal future. It places the burden of salvation on Christ, not on the quality of their Christian discipleship. It fixes the believer's feet on rock, not on quicksand.[48] It is the best antidote to spiritual anxiety and hesitancy to know that every believer "is fenced, walled, protected, guarded by the Almighty power of Father, Son, and Holy Ghost. . . . This is strong consolation."[49] As always in Ryle's tracts, he had little interest in merely debating theories. The "doctrines of sovereign grace" were, to him, inherently practical, intended not for philosophical argument but for everyday application to Christian life and growth.

---

[47] Article 17 ("Of Predestination and Election"), in Cummings, *The Book of Common Prayer*, 678.
[48] Ryle, *Never Perish*, 26–28.
[49] Ryle, *Never Perish*, 30.

CHAPTER 5

HEART RELIGION

One of the keynotes of Victorian evangelical piety was "heart religion." It aimed to be experiential, personal, and emotionally engaged, set in contrast to Christian legalism, nominalism, formalism, and barren orthodoxy. The movement drew deeply from the language of the "heart" that pervades the Book of Common Prayer, and from Puritan devotional literature, as well as from famous Evangelical Revival texts, such as Jonathan Edwards's *A Treatise Concerning Religious Affections* (1746) and John Newton's *Cardiphonia: or the Utterance of the Heart* (1781), which were republished in multiple editions during the nineteenth century.[1] These ideas blossomed in evangelical hymnody, poetry, preaching, devotional aids, evangelistic tracts, and conversion narratives. Ryle stood within this affective tradition and frequently brought a heart-centered emphasis to his writings.

Heart religion was a central motif, for example, in Ryle's tract *Lot's Wife* (1855). He suggested that the religious participation of Lot's wife was "kept up for fashion's sake and not from feeling. It was a cloak worn for the sake of pleasing her company, but not from any sense of value." Outwardly, she conformed to her husband's faith and "allowed herself to be passively towed along in his wake. But all this time her heart was wrong in the sight of God. The world was in her heart, and her heart was in the world." Ryle warned that, like Lot's wife, someone can enjoy many spiritual privileges

---
[1] John Corrigan, *Business of the Heart: Religion and Emotion in the Nineteenth Century* (University of California Press, 2002); Phyllis Mack, *Heart Religion in the British Enlightenment: Gender and Emotion in Early Methodism* (Cambridge University Press, 2008); John Coffey, ed., *Heart Religion: Evangelical Piety in England and Ireland, 1690–1850* (Oxford University Press, 2016).

and yet remain unconverted. "The same fire which melts the wax hardens the clay. . . . Nothing so hardens the heart of man as a barren familiarity with sacred things." His readers might have been raised by Christian parents and taught the gospel from infancy, or be members of evangelical congregations with excellent preaching, or be employed as servants by Christian families "in a house where the fear of God reigns" and household prayers were conducted daily. Yet these spiritual advantages counted for nothing without a changed heart. "After all, what have you got in your heart?" he asked. "Have you yet received the Holy Ghost? If not, *you are no better than Lot's wife*."[2]

This theme was expounded at greater length in *Is Thy Heart Right?*, Ryle's annual address for New Year 1860. Like many of his tracts, it was marketed for wide distribution, priced at one shilling and six pence per dozen (that is, one and a half pence each), to be bought in bulk.[3] "I do not ask about your head," he began. "You may know the whole truth as it is in Jesus, and consent that it is good. You may be clear, correct, and sound in your religious opinions." Nor was he enquiring about his readers' outward behavior. "It may be moral, decent, respectable, in the eyes of men. Your minister, and friends, and neighbours, may see nothing very wrong in your general conduct. But all this time you may be hanging on the brink of everlasting ruin."[4] What God demands, first and foremost, Ryle insisted, is the heart: "We may give God a bowed head and a serious face, our bodily presence in His house, and a loud amen. But until we give God our heart, we give Him nothing at all."[5]

For analogies, Ryle turned first to modern technology. A pocket watch might be expensive and beautiful—with skillfully designed face and hands—but it would not work if the mainspring was broken. A steam engine might be expertly built—with every joint, crank, and rod in the correct place—but it would not operate if the furnace was cold. Next, Ryle turned to the Old Testament idea of a "stony heart" (Ezek. 11:19), approaching the metaphor from different angles.

First, a stone is hard. He spoke of the granite rocks on the Cornish coast, pummeled by the waves of the Atlantic Ocean for thousands of years but standing unbroken. "It is just the same with the natural heart. Afflic-

---

[2] J. C. Ryle, *Lot's Wife: Being Thoughts on Luke xvii. 32* (Ipswich, 1855), 6–8.
[3] "Rev J. C. Ryle's Annual Addresses for Christmas and the New Year," advertisement, *British Standard*, December 16, 1859, 1.
[4] J. C. Ryle, *Is Thy Heart Right? A Question for Everybody* (Ipswich, 1860), 3.
[5] Ryle, *Is Thy Heart Right?*, 6.

Heart Religion

tions, mercies, losses, crosses, sermons, counsels, books, tracts, speaking, writing—all, all are unable to soften it. Until the day that God comes down to change it, it remains unmoved."[6]

Second, a stone is cold. Helmingham parish church where Ryle was rector is a small building dominated by impressive memorial statues to the Tollemache family of Helmingham Hall. Next to the pulpit is a monument to the first baronet, Sir Lionel Tollemache (1562–1612), knighted by James I, and his three Tollemache predecessors, each portrayed in a formal pose, kneeling in a row, wearing beards and ruffs, and swords at their hips. Immediately opposite the pulpit is a statue of the second baronet, another Sir Lionel Tollemache (1591–1640), a member of Parliament during the reign of Charles I, portrayed lying on his side, in his armor, with his head resting on his hand and a fixed gaze. Ryle observed:

> The old marble statues in Helmingham church have heard the substance of every tract I have ever written. Yet they never show any feeling. Not a muscle of their marble faces ever shrinks or moves. It is just the same with the natural heart. It is utterly destitute of spiritual feeling. It cares less for the story of Christ's death on the cross, than it does for the last new novel, or the last debate in Parliament, or the account of a railway accident, or a shipwreck, or an execution. Until God sends fire from heaven to warm it, the natural heart of man has no feeling about religion.

Third, a stone is barren. Turning to agriculture, Ryle reminded his East Anglian audience that farmers could reap a good harvest from Norfolk sands, Cambridgeshire fens, or Suffolk clay but would never manage to grow crops on the summit of Mount Snowdon or Ben Nevis, the highest mountains in Wales and Scotland. "You will never reap wheat on granite or slate—on lime-stone or trap-stone—on oolite or sandstone—on flint or on chalk." It is the same with the natural heart, Ryle explained, bearing no fruit.[7]

Fourth, a stone is dead, without growth or movement. Ryle pointed to Bass Rock, an uninhabited volcanic island in Scotland's Firth of Forth, and to Mont Blanc in the Alps, unchanged for thousands of years. In the same way, the natural heart "has not a spark of spiritual life about it. Until God plants the Holy Ghost in it, it is dead and motionless about real religion."[8]

---
[6] Ryle, *Is Thy Heart Right?*, 7, 9–10.
[7] Ryle, *Is Thy Heart Right?*, 10.
[8] Ryle, *Is Thy Heart Right?*, 11.

He urged in conclusion: "You may go to the best church on earth, and hear the best of preachers. You may be the best of churchmen, or the soundest member of a chapel. But all this time if your heart is not right in the sight of God, you are on the high road to destruction."[9]

Counterfeit Faith

Ryle explicitly linked conversion of the heart with religious integrity. "There is nothing about it of falsehood, hypocrisy, or part-acting," he observed in *Is Thy Heart Right?* "Its religion will be real, genuine, thorough, and sincere."[10] This particular aspect of heart religion was the focus of Ryle's tract for New Year 1862, entitled *Is It Real?* Piling up synonyms, he warned against a Christianity that was "base, and hollow, and formal, and false, and counterfeit, and sham, and nominal."

> Real religion is not mere show, and pretence, and skin-deep feeling, and temporary profession, and outside work. It is something inward, solid, substantial, intrinsic, living, lasting. You know the difference between base coin and good money—between solid gold and tinsel—between plated metal and silver—between real stone and plaster imitation.

Ryle suggested that the 1860s in British culture was "universally an age of base metal and alloy," full of cheap imitations.[11] As he protested in another tract: "We live in an age of shams, cheats, deceptions, and impositions . . . of white-wash, varnish, lacquer, and veneer . . . of plaster, compo, plating, gilding, and electrotyping . . . of adulterated food, paste diamonds, false weights and measures, unsound timber, and shoddy clothing."[12] This wider Victorian phenomenon had also infiltrated the churches, Ryle believed. "If we measure the religion of the age by its apparent quantity, there is much of it. But if we measure it by its quality, there is very little indeed. On every side we want MORE REALITY."[13]

Reflecting on Jesus's rebukes to the scribes and Pharisees despite their external moral behavior, Ryle emphasized "the exceeding abominableness of false profession and mere outward religion in God's sight. Open profligacy and wilful obedience to fleshly lusts are no doubt ruinous sins, if

---

[9] Ryle, *Is Thy Heart Right?*, 16.
[10] Ryle, *Is Thy Heart Right?*, 14.
[11] J. C. Ryle, *Is It Real? A Question for the Times* (Ipswich, 1862), 3–4.
[12] J. C. Ryle, *Are You Converted? A Question for 1864* (London, 1864), 6–7.
[13] Ryle, *Is It Real?*, 4.

not given up. But there seems nothing which is so displeasing to Christ as hypocrisy and unreality."[14] He asserted that in every age of the Christian church, since the days of Judas Iscariot and Simon Magus in the New Testament, there had been "a vast amount of unreality and mere nominal religion among professing Christians." There was abundant evidence of this in the mid-nineteenth century, he suggested. Beginning with his own denomination, the Church of England, Ryle lamented that for many parishioners their religion was not "real Christianity" but "Churchianity." "They are baptized at her fonts, married at her communion rails, buried in her churchyards, preached to on Sundays by her ministers," but the great doctrines of apostolic Christianity as laid down in the Book of Common Prayer and the Thirty-Nine Articles had no influence on their lives. Turning next to Nonconformity, he likewise maintained that for many their religion was mere "Dissentianity." "Their Christianity is as sapless and fruitless as a dead tree, and as dry and marrow-less as an old bone." He lamented that Victorian Nonconformists were often "utterly destitute" of the "experimental and practical piety" of their famous Puritan predecessors like John Owen, Thomas Manton, Thomas Goodwin, Richard Baxter, and Robert Traill.[15]

The same was true of particular theological traditions in the Church of England. Ryle rebuked Tractarianism—revised to "Ritualism" in the compilation version of his tract[16]—for breeding unreality: "You will sometimes see men boiling over with zeal about vestments, and gestures, and postures, and church decorations, and daily services, and frequent communions, while their hearts are manifestly in the world." Their Christianity was false, "a mere name." Yet Ryle reserved his fiercest strictures for evangelicalism. He lamented that although evangelicals professed "great affection for the pure 'Gospel,'" they often did that gospel great damage:

> They will talk loudly of soundness in the faith, and have a keen nose for heresy. They will run eagerly after popular preachers, and applaud protestant speakers at public meetings to the very echo. They are familiar with all the phrases of evangelical religion, and can converse fluently about its leading doctrines. . . . And yet these people in private will sometimes do things of which even some heathens would be ashamed.

---
[14] Ryle, *Is It Real?*, 7.
[15] Ryle, *Is It Real?*, 9–11.
[16] J. C. Ryle, "Reality," in *Practical Religion: Being Plain Papers on the Daily Duties, Experience, Dangers, and Privileges of Professing Christians* (London, 1878), 54.

Ryle criticized the dishonesty, injustice, anger, selfishness, pride, and unkindness often revealed in evangelical circles. "And is such Christianity as this real? It is not. It is a miserable imposture, a base cheat and caricature." When surveying contemporary Christianity, he concluded sorrowfully that "the abounding want of reality . . . is to be seen on every side."[17]

Genuine Christian faith, Ryle argued, is rooted in the heart. It must not be merely intellectual: "You may know the truth, and assent to the truth, and believe the truth, and yet be wrong in God's sight." Nor merely verbal: "You may repeat the creed daily. You may say 'amen' to public prayer in church, and yet have nothing more than an outward religion." Nor merely emotional: "You may weep under preaching one day, and be lifted to the third heaven by joyous excitement another day, and yet be dead to God." The ultimate test is the Christian's heart.

> Your religion, if it is real, and given by the Holy Ghost, must be in your *heart*. It must occupy the citadel. It must hold the reins. It must sway the affections. It must lead the will. It must direct the tastes. It must influence the choices and decisions. It must fill the deepest, lowest, inmost seat in your soul.[18]

Unreal Christianity, Ryle declared, is particularly abhorrent to God. It would therefore be preferable "to be found an ignorant heathen at the last day, than to be found with nothing better than a nominal religion." "Cease from all trifling and playing with religion," he urged his readers; "become honest, thorough-going, wholehearted followers of the Lord Jesus Christ."[19]

Formalism

In Ryle's analysis, one of the most virulent expressions of counterfeit faith was formalism. Twelve months after *Is It Real?*, he tackled the topic in a pair of tracts published in December 1862—*Do You Love Christ?*, an address for Christmas, and *Form or Heart?*, an address for New Year 1863. "Formality is not Christianity," he wrote in the Christmas tract. "Ignorant lip-worship is not true religion. . . . All are not true Christians who are members of the visible church of Christ."[20]

---
[17] Ryle, *Is It Real?*, 11–13.
[18] Ryle, *Is It Real?*, 14.
[19] Ryle, *Is It Real?*, 19.
[20] J. C. Ryle, *Do You Love Christ? A Question for All!* (London, 1862), 5.

Heart Religion

The New Year tract unpacked this idea at greater length. Ryle reckoned that since the birth of Christianity, there had never been "so much formality and false profession" as in the mid-nineteenth century. The Worcestershire Puritan Thomas Hall, who was thrown out of the Church of England at the "Great Ejection" of 1662, had written in his *Practical and Polemical Commentary* (1658), "Formality, formality, formality is the great sin of England at this day, under which the land groans." Yet Ryle believed that the situation had grown much worse two centuries later. He lamented that many people's Christianity was "a mere matter of form, or fashion, or custom" without any influence on their hearts and lives. Some were regularly at public worship, keeping up the sacraments and ceremonies of the church, but knew nothing of "experimental Christianity." Others knew the gospel in theory, professing "to delight in Evangelical doctrine" and trumpeting the "soundness" of their theology, but displayed no evidence of "practical godliness." All of these, Ryle asserted, were Christians in name only, not in substance. Their religion was "an empty form" and an offense to God.[21]

Ryle exhorted his readers to flee from religious formalism as they would from open sin. "Formalism may take your hand with a smile, and look like a brother, while sin comes against you with sword drawn, and strikes at you like an open enemy. But both have one end in view. Both want to ruin your soul; and of the two, formalism is far the most likely to do it." To attend public worship and join in prayer and praise without heartfelt engagement is spiritually deadening, Ryle warned. It is possible to deceive fellow worshipers, but impossible to deceive God. Moreover, religious formalism is of no spiritual value. "A painted fire cannot warm, and a painted banquet cannot satisfy hunger, and a formal religion cannot bring peace to the soul."[22]

Once again, Ryle returned to the central theme of the heart. "It is not enough that a man holds a correct creed of doctrine, and maintains a proper outward form of godliness. What is his heart? That is the grand question. This is what God looks at.... When the heart is wrong, all is wrong in God's sight." Some congregations delighted in beautiful liturgies with beautiful singing in beautiful buildings, but without "converted, renewed, broken, penitent hearts," all was spoiled.[23] Conversely, Ryle argued, if the heart of the people was right, then God would overlook their paltry and defective

---
[21] J. C. Ryle, *Form or Heart? A Question for Everybody* (Ipswich, 1863), 3–6.
[22] Ryle, *Form or Heart?*, 8–9.
[23] Ryle, *Form or Heart?*, 10, 12–13.

forms of worship. Many Christians around the globe gathered in unattractive surroundings. "They meet in miserable dirty chapels, so-called, or in wretched upper-rooms and cellars," he wrote. "They sing unmusically. They hear feeble prayers, and more feeble sermons. And yet the Holy Ghost is often in the midst of them!" Because their hearts wanted to honor God, they were blessed by God, and God's kingdom prospered more there than in many gorgeous cathedrals. "Settle it down firmly in your minds that formal religion is not saving religion," Ryle repeated, "and that heart-religion is the only religion that leads to heaven."[24]

Ryle proposed that formal religion was perennially popular in British society because it demanded very little of its recruits. "Only say your prayers—and go to church with tolerable regularity—and receive the sacrament occasionally—and the vast majority of Englishmen will set you down as an excellent Christian." Heart religion, on the other hand, was often met with mockery and contempt. Ryle suggested that the scribes and Pharisees in the first century would have welcomed a messiah who encouraged formalism and ceremonialism, but they could not tolerate a religion of "humiliation and sanctification of heart." Meanwhile Ryle's heroes from church history—the Reformers, Puritans, and evangelical revivalists—were all "hated" because they preached against formalism and for a salvation that requires "repentance, faith, regeneration, and holiness of heart."[25] In Victorian Britain, Christians who promoted heart religion were still a derided minority, Ryle maintained. However, his tract targeted not only the more ceremonial forms of Christianity. Turning his guns on his home base, he exclaimed, "There is no formalism so dangerous as Evangelical formalism."[26]

These themes recurred frequently in Ryle's teaching in later decades. For example, preaching in Derby in 1882 on the priest and the Levite who "passed by on the other side" of the Jericho road when they saw someone in need (Luke 10), he observed, "Barren formality will save no man's soul, however high his office, if his heart is not right in the sight of God." Of all sins denounced by Jesus, Ryle suggested, "none drew down such severe reproof from His lips as hypocrisy, part-acting, and mere external religion." Ryle was particularly alarmed by the growing trend he discerned in Victorian culture toward emphasizing religious externals, such as church

---
[24] Ryle, *Form or Heart?*, 15.
[25] Ryle, *Form or Heart?*, 18–20.
[26] Ryle, *Form or Heart?*, 23.

architecture and ceremonial—robes, processions, banners, music, ritual, posture, and decorations. He noted, for example, that "enormous sums" of money were being spent in the 1880s on flowers and ferns to beautify church buildings, whereas comparatively little was spent on evangelism. Ryle dismissed these externals as "sensuous religion" and "pernicious trifles," which were "suspicious symptoms of inward disease."[27]

Intellectualism

Ryle was a competent scholar, with a first-class degree from the University of Oxford, and a voracious reader of historical theology, with a large personal library. Nevertheless, he insisted that it is wrong to put confidence in theological learning. Writing in 1856, he observed that in the medieval church, Scholastic theologians like Thomas Aquinas, Duns Scotus, and Peter Lombard had been highly admired. "But what is the most learned man, if he be not taught by the Holy Ghost?" Ryle queried. "Vast knowledge of books and great ignorance of God's truth may go side by side." He suggested that the *Memoir* (1844) and *Sermons* (1847) of Robert Murray M'Cheyne (1813–1843), an evangelical minister in the Church of Scotland, had done more spiritual good than any folio ever written by the patristic theologians Origen of Alexandria or Cyprian of Carthage, and that although the Bedfordshire Puritan John Bunyan (1628–1688) was ignorant of Greek and Latin, his *Pilgrim's Progress* (1678) had benefitted the world more than all the writing of the medieval Scholastics put together. Ryle concluded: "Learning is a gift that ought not to be despised. It is an evil day when books are not valued in the church. But it is amazing to observe how vast a man's intellectual attainments may be, and yet how little he may know of the grace of God."[28]

Ryle frequently applied this principle to Christian discipleship in his preaching and tracts. Addressing a predominantly evangelical readership, he was especially concerned at the prevalence of a barren and intellectualized orthodoxy within Victorian Christianity. "The clearest head-knowledge will save no man," he urged. "The most correct and orthodox views will not prevent a man perishing by the side of the most ignorant heathen if he is not born again."[29] Doctrinal accuracy is never sufficient.

---
[27] J. C. Ryle, *"Go, and Do Thou Likewise" (Luke x. 37): Thoughts on a Much-Neglected Duty* (London, 1883), 9–11.
[28] J. C. Ryle, *St Peter at Antioch: A Tract for the Times* (Ipswich, 1856), 11–12.
[29] J. C. Ryle, *Never Perish: Being Thoughts on Final Perseverance* (Ipswich, 1855), 31.

Personal, experiential relationship with Christ is essential. In *Do You Believe?*, Ryle proclaimed:

> A believer's religion does not consist in mere intellectual assent to a certain set of propositions and doctrines. It is not a mere cold belief of a certain set of truths and facts concerning Christ. It consists in union, communion, and fellowship with an actual living Person, even Jesus the Son of God.[30]

Likewise, in *Do You Love Christ?*, he noted: "There are myriads of Christians who know every article of the Athanasian, Nicene, and Apostolic Creeds, and yet know less of real Christianity than a little child who knows that he loves Christ."[31] "True saving Christianity," Ryle repeated, "is not the mere believing a certain set of opinions, and holding a certain set of notions." Its essence is "knowing, trusting, and loving" Jesus. New Testament Christians like Phoebe and Philemon probably understood little dogmatic theology, Ryle speculated, but they all loved Jesus.[32]

In 1869, at the height of the antiritualist controversies, Ryle warned the Church Association not to confuse orthodoxy with conversion. No one will get to heaven with "mere head-knowledge of Protestantism," he exclaimed, or by rehearsing the correct doctrinal answers in a theological debate. "It is the possession of grace in the heart, and not the intellectual knowledge of it, that saves the soul," he insisted.[33] Elsewhere he lamented that Christians too often appeared satisfied with "a mere 'otiose assent' to certain theological propositions" and "a cold, tame assent to creeds." Yet the antidote was close at hand. Ryle appealed to his audience: "If there was more real living faith on earth, I suspect there would be less unbelief. Scepticism, in many a case, would shrink, and dwindle, and melt away, if it saw faith more awake, and alive, and active, and stirring."[34]

True experiential religion therefore embraces not just the intellect but also the affections and emotions. "Feelings are, no doubt, very deceitful," Ryle wrote. "But where there are no inward religious feelings there is no faith. A man who knows nothing of an inward, spiritual, experimental

---
[30] J. C. Ryle, *Do You Believe? A Question for 1861* (Ipswich, 1860), 25.
[31] Ryle, *Do You Love Christ?*, 10.
[32] Ryle, *Do You Love Christ?*, 17–18.
[33] J. C. Ryle, *"Be Not Carried About!" A Caution for 1870, Being Thoughts on Hebrews xiii. 9* (London, 1870), 23.
[34] J. C. Ryle, *Tried by Its Fruits: A Thought for 1884* (London, 1884), 28.

religion, is not yet a believer."[35] Ryle's doctrinal expositions were often couched in the language of affective love. He viewed feelings as one of the proofs of authentic conversion by the Holy Spirit, a point he drove home in *What Is Your Hope?*, a tract for New Year 1857: "The cold marble of a Grecian statue may well be unimpassioned. The dried mummy from Egypt may well look stiff and still. The stuffed beast in a museum may well be motionless and cold. They are all lifeless things. But where there is life, there will always be feeling."[36] Just as Ryle wanted Christians to embrace the intellect while eschewing intellectualism, he rejected emotionalism but refused to neglect the emotions in healthy Christian discipleship.

Zeal

One of the ways in which heart religion is exhibited, according to Ryle's theological framework, is through serious, earnest, zealous investment in Christian faith. Writing in 1850, he observed that it was easy to excite people with the latest news from New York and New Zealand, or with the latest literary sensations, like Lord Macaulay's multivolume *History of England* (1848) and Charles Dickens's *David Copperfield* (1850). Yet, concerning the great themes of the Bible, the same people were completely unmoved, as if these eternal truths did not concern them personally at the deepest level. They sat in church "like spectators in a theatre or court of law," disconnected from the proceedings. "Oh! that men were wise, and would lay these things to heart!," Ryle cried. "Oh! that they would not trifle, dally, linger, live on half-and-half Christians, meaning well, but never acting boldly, and at last awake when it is too late."[37]

The Colonial Church and School Society was created in 1851 through the amalgamation of two earlier mission agencies, with a focus on Christian education of the poor in the British colonies by sending out evangelical clergymen, catechists, and school teachers. Ryle was a firm supporter of this missionary initiative, joining deputations on its behalf at venues across England. In May 1852 he preached the society's annual sermon in London at St Dunstan-in-the-West, Fleet Street, and took as his subject the need for Christian zeal. "I want to strike a blow at the lazy, easy, sleepy Christianity of these latter days," he announced. He wanted Christians to

---
[35] Ryle, *Do You Believe?*, 25.
[36] J. C. Ryle, *What Is Your Hope? A Question for 1857* (Ipswich, 1856), 15.
[37] J. C. Ryle, *Wheat or Chaff? A Question for 1851* (Ipswich, 1851), 28–29.

be people with "a burning desire to please God, to do His will, and to advance His glory in the world in every possible way" through hard work and self-sacrifice.[38] This was characteristic of the apostles and the Reformers, Ryle suggested, as well as modern missionaries like William Carey in India, Henry Martyn in Persia, Robert Morrison in China, Adoniram Judson in Burma, and Henry Williams in New Zealand.[39]

Zeal is essential to the health of the church, Ryle insisted: "There is little danger of there ever being too much zeal for the glory of God. God forgive those who think there is!" Therefore, Christian zeal should always be actively cultivated and encouraged. "Try to blow up the fire in your own heart, and the hearts of others, but never, never check it. Beware of throwing cold water on zealous souls, whenever you meet with them. Beware of nipping in the bud this precious grace when first it shoots." He acknowledged that zealous Christians sometimes made mistakes, and like elephants deployed on the battlefield in classical antiquity, they sometimes injured their own side. "But zeal does not need damping in a wretched, cold, corrupt, miserable world like this."[40] Ryle especially criticized the bishops of the Church of England for demoralizing and excluding keen Christians. "The greatest mistake the rulers of a Church can make, is to drive zealous men out of its pale. By so doing they drain out the life-blood of the system, and hasten on ecclesiastical decline and death."[41]

Ryle lamented that too many professing believers were "rich in wet blankets, but poor in anything like Christian fire." They were quick to raise objections, but slow to take decisive action. He contrasted this with wider society, where zeal was conspicuous among barristers at Lincoln's Inn and parliamentarians at Westminster, and among bankers, businessmen, accountants, and shopkeepers. Many were energetically pursuing gold in California and Australia, while others were zealously attempting to "rescue Franklin from thick ribbed ice."[42]

The ill-fated expedition led by Sir John Franklin had captured the national imagination. His party sailed from England in 1845 on board *HMS Erebus* and *HMS Terror*, aiming to navigate the Northwest Passage in the Canadian Arctic, but they disappeared after becoming icebound and abandoning their ships. After a campaign by Lady Franklin, the British Admi-

---

[38] J. C. Ryle, *Be Zealous: Thoughts on Galatians iv. 18* (Ipswich, 1852), 4.
[39] Ryle, *Be Zealous*, 6–9.
[40] Ryle, *Be Zealous*, 24–25.
[41] Ryle, *Be Zealous*, 20.
[42] Ryle, *Be Zealous*, 28.

ralty launched a series of search and rescue missions, beginning in 1848, all of which failed to find the explorers. The last and largest rescue attempt, led by Admiral Sir Edward Belcher with five ships, set off in 1852 but itself became icebound. Two years later, the members of Franklin's expedition were officially declared dead, presumed to have frozen or starved, though most of their bodies were never recovered.[43] Ryle admired the zeal of these intrepid adventurers and urged his congregation at St Dunstan-in-the-West to adopt a similarly wholehearted approach to Christian discipleship. "Try to live so as to be missed," he encouraged. As motivation to sacrificial action, Ryle recommended meditation on Christ's sufferings. "What are you doing for Him? Oh! resolve that for the time to come you will spend and be spent for Christ."[44]

As his sermon reached its rousing conclusion, Ryle proclaimed: "Beware of cooling down. You have only to be lazy, and to sit still, and you will soon lose all your warmth. . . . It may be very true that wise young believers are very rare. But it is no less true that zealous old believers are very rare also." The indefatigable French Roman Catholic theologian Antoine Arnauld (1612–1694)—praised by Ryle as "that noble-minded Jansenist"—had famously replied when encouraged to rest: "Rest! Have we not all eternity to rest in!" Ryle called upon his evangelical audience to take these words to heart, even if their zeal provoked a backlash and they were called fanatics or fools. "Care not for the praise or frown of man. There is but one thing worth caring for, and that is the praise of God. There is but one question worth asking about our actions, 'How will they look in the day of judgment?'"[45] Ryle's teaching on the Christian life was frequently shaped by this eschatological expectation. Judgment day would reveal not just the true value of human actions but the true state of human hearts.

---

[43] Russell A. Potter, *Finding Franklin: The Untold Story of a 165-Year Search* (McGill-Queen's University Press, 2016); Russell A. Potter, "Sir John Franklin and the Northwest Passage in Myth and Memory," in *The Cambridge History of the Polar Regions*, ed. Adrian Howkins and Peder Roberts (Cambridge University Press, 2023), 207–28.
[44] Ryle, *Be Zealous*, 29–30.
[45] Ryle, *Be Zealous*, 30–31.

CHAPTER 6

FRUITS OF FAITH

The Thirty-Nine Articles of Religion, the Church of England's confessional statement, provided a crucial framework for Ryle's understanding of the Christian life. He first studied them as a schoolboy when competing for the Newcastle Scholarship at Eton College in the early 1830s. They "insensibly prepared my mind to receive Evangelical principles, when my heart first began to turn to think of religion," he recalled.[1] The Articles distilled Reformation doctrine into very succinct form and deeply shaped Ryle's theological world. He celebrated that they offered an incomparable combination of theological "fulness, boldness, clearness, brevity, moderation, and wisdom."[2] For example, they carefully navigated the contested realm of faith and works. Article 12 describes a Christian's "good works," which follow justification, as "the fruits of faith." Good works cannot put away sins, but they are pleasing to God "and do spring out necessarily of a true and lively faith, insomuch that by them a lively faith may be as evidently known, as a tree discerned by the fruit."[3]

In his tracts, Ryle frequently expounded this idea of faith made visible. In *Living or Dead?* (1849), he exclaimed: "An indwelling of the Spirit that does not show itself by outward fruits, and a grace that men's eyes cannot discover, are both to be viewed with the utmost suspicion. Believe me if you have no other proof of spiritual life but your baptism, you are yet a dead soul." He therefore exhorted Christian believers to distinctive living: "Are

---
[1] *Bishop J. C. Ryle's Autobiography: The Early Years*, ed. Andrew Atherstone (Banner of Truth, 2016), 71.
[2] J. C. Ryle, *Who Is the True Churchman? or, the Thirty-Nine Articles Examined* (London, 1872), 12.
[3] Article 12 ("Of Good Works"), in *The Book of Common Prayer: The Texts of 1549, 1559, and 1662*, ed. Brian Cummings (Oxford University Press, 2011), 677.

you alive? Then see that you prove it by your actions." This includes bearing a "consistent witness," where words and works match up, and lively Christian discipleship—not a "poor torpid life, like that of a tortoise or a sloth," but an "energetic stirring life, like that of a deer or bird."[4]

Likewise, in *Have You the Spirit?* (1854), Ryle taught that the indwelling of the Holy Spirit will always result in practical evidence. He again argued that this was standard Church of England doctrine, pointing to the authorized *Homily for Whitsunday*, which proclaims that "as the tree is known by his fruit, so is also the Holy Ghost."[5] Ryle gave several agricultural illustrations from everyday life very familiar to his readers. The wind on a stormy day was evidenced by its powerful effects, as "when I see the clouds driven before it, and the trees bending under it—when I hear it whistling through doors and windows, or howling round the old chimney tops." The dew on a summer evening fell down imperceptibly but was witnessed "when I go forth in the morning after a cloudless night, and see every leaf sparkling with moisture, and feel every blade of grass damp and wet." Walking through cornfields in July—a familiar experience in rural Suffolk—the rich ears of grain were proof that a sower had been at work with plow and harrow. Turning next to three technological illustrations, Ryle explained that magnetic fields are invisible, but he could see the iron of the compass needle always turning north. The mainspring of a watch is hidden behind its face, but he could see the hands moving. Or when he stood on a pier on the Suffolk coast and watched a ship on the horizon steering its course toward the harbor, he knew there must be someone at the helm guiding its movements. In the same way, Ryle insisted, there will always be outward evidence of the Spirit's presence in the life of the Christian, and it is a "dangerous and unscriptural delusion" to think otherwise.[6] He listed several visible "marks of the Spirit," including love for the Scriptures, for prayer, for fellow believers, and for holy living. The essential thing is ongoing evidence of indwelling by the Holy Spirit, not whether someone can point to a datable conversion experience in the past. "Remember, I do not ask you to tell me the day or month when the Spirit began His work in you. Enough for me if fruit trees bear fruit, without inquiring the precise time when they were planted."[7]

---

[4] J. C. Ryle, *Living or Dead? A Question for 1849* (Ipswich, 1849), 24, 28.
[5] "An Homily Concerning the Coming Down of the Holy Ghost and the Manifold Gifts of the Same: For Whitsunday," in *The Books of Homilies: A Critical Edition*, ed. Gerald Bray (James Clarke, 2015), 440.
[6] J. C. Ryle, *Have You the Spirit? A Question for 1854* (Ipswich, 1854), 13–14.
[7] J. C. Ryle, *Have You the Spirit?*, 25.

The same subject appeared frequently in other tracts. In *None of His!* (1857), Ryle reiterated that the Holy Spirit's invisible actions always lead to visible results. The presence of the Holy Spirit in someone's life was not evidenced by having his or her name in the parish's baptism register or a seat in the family pew.[8] Church membership and receiving the sacraments are no proofs of conversion. Indeed if any professing Christian lacks the five "grand marks" of the Spirit—deep conviction of sin, lively faith in Jesus Christ, holiness of character and conduct, earnest private prayer, and love and reverence for the Bible—then "we have just cause to be afraid about a man's soul."[9] Similarly, in *Do You Love Christ?* (1862), Ryle argued that the existence of such love is proved by the Christian's desire to please Christ, to honor his name, to read his word, and to enjoy the company of his friends. "Love to the Lord Jesus Christ, is no hidden, secret, impalpable thing. It is like light—it will be seen. It is like sound—it will be heard. It is like heat—it will be felt. Where it exists it cannot be hid. Where it cannot be seen you may be sure there is none."[10]

Are You Converted? (1864) hammered home the same theme. Ryle lamented that many people turned away from Christianity "in disgust" when they saw the wicked behavior of professing Christians. But these professions of faith were false, he insisted, generated merely because "their animal feelings were excited" or because they "fancied that a few spasmodic sensations and convictions were the true grace of God." On the contrary, genuine faith always leads to a visible change in a person's character and conduct. Ryle proclaimed:

> Never, never, will I allow that the blessed Spirit can be in a man's heart, when no fruit of the Spirit can be seen in his life. A conversion which allows a man to live in sin, to lie, and drink, and swear, is not the conversion of the Bible. It is a counterfeit conversion, which can only please the devil, and will lead the man who is satisfied with it, not to heaven but to hell.[11]

"Grace that cannot be seen is no grace at all," he reiterated in *Evangelical Religion* (1868), "and nothing better than Antinomianism. In short, we believe that where there is nothing *seen*, there is nothing possessed."[12]

---

[8] Ryle, *None of His! A Tract on the Work of the Holy Ghost, Being Thoughts on Rom viii. 9* (Ipswich, 1857), 19.
[9] Ryle, *None of His!*, 26.
[10] J. C. Ryle, *Do You Love Christ? A Question for All!* (London, 1862), 17.
[11] J. C. Ryle, *Are You Converted? A Question for 1864* (London, 1864), 18–20.
[12] J. C. Ryle, *Evangelical Religion: What It Is, and What It Is Not* (London, 1868), 10.

Renouncing Worldliness

One of the visible fruits of faith is growth in "godliness" and renunciation of "worldliness," a theme addressed in a pair of Ryle's tracts, *Remember Lot* (1849) and *Lot's Wife* (1855). These two Old Testament character studies drew lessons from Lot, who "lingered," and Lot's wife, who "looked back" (Gen. 19:16, 26).

Ryle portrayed Lot as "a true believer—a real child of God—a justified soul—a righteous man." Yet, like many of God's people, Lot was "slow when he should have been quick—backward when he should have been forward—trifling when he should have been hastening—loitering when he should have been hurrying—cold when he should have been hot." He was always trying to "keep in with the world," inventing excuses for maintaining "questionable friendships."[13] In an expanded version of the tract, republished as a chapter in *Holiness*, Ryle lamented:

> One day you are told of their attending a Bible reading: the next day perhaps you hear of their going to a ball. One day they fast, or go to the Lord's table and receive the sacrament: another day they go to the race-course in the morning, and the opera at night. One day they are almost in hysterics under the sermon of some sensational preacher: another day they are weeping over some novel.[14]

Ryle described Britain in the mid-nineteenth century as a generation when "a lingering, Lot-like religion abounds. The stream of profession is far broader than it once was, but far less deep in many places." Certain types of Christianity had become "almost fashionable," such as belonging to a church party, talking about the latest religious controversy, buying popular Christian books as soon as they were published to display ostentatiously, subscribing to religious societies, debating the merits of different preachers, and following the latest Christian trends. But this sort of Christian behavior required very little sacrifice, Ryle warned: "To walk closely with God—to be really spiritually-minded—to behave like strangers and pilgrims—to be distinct from the world in employment of time, in conversation, in amusements, in dress—to bear a faithful witness for Christ in all places . . . these are still rare things."[15]

---
[13] J. C. Ryle, *Remember Lot* (Ipswich, 1849), 4, 6, 8.
[14] J. C. Ryle, "Lot: A Beacon," in *Holiness and Other Kindred Subjects* (London, 1877), 347–48.
[15] Ryle, *Remember Lot*, 20–21.

"Lingering is the sure destruction of a happy Christianity," Ryle proclaimed. "Come and consider Lot's lingering, and be wise."[16] Lot focused too much on the world, not on eternity. He made the mistake of settling in the city of Sodom, perhaps to gain better profit in his business, or because "his wife liked the town better than the country, for the sake of society," or for his daughters' education. "Make a wrong choice—an unscriptural choice—in life," Ryle warned, "and settle yourself down unnecessarily in the midst of worldly people, and I know no surer way to damage your own spirituality, and to go backward about your eternal concerns." Because of his "needless mingling with worldly people," Lot ended in "a dry, dull, sleepy, barren, heavy, carnal, stupid, torpid state of soul."[17] Furthermore, he wrecked his witness for God among the inhabitants of Sodom. "As a general rule, lingering souls do no good to the world, and bring no credit to God's cause. Their salt has too little savour to season the corruption around them. . . . There is nothing magnetic, and attractive, and Christ-reflecting about their ways."[18]

Ryle sought to apply these lessons to his readers in their own decision-making. First, when choosing a house, they must consider not only location and comfort but also their spiritual welfare. "Is the Gospel preached within an easy distance? . . . Is there a real man of God near, who will watch over your soul?" Second, when choosing a job, they must think not only of salary and career prospects but also of whether it would help them grow as a Christian. Third, when choosing a spouse, it was not enough to look for beauty and affection. "Think of your soul, your immortal soul. Will it be helped upwards, or dragged downwards by the union you are planning? Will it be made more heavenly, or more earthly—drawn nearer to Christ, or to the world?" In particular, Ryle rejected the possibility that a Christian might marry a non-Christian. He quoted the apostolic injunction "Be ye not unequally yoked" (2 Cor. 6:14) and warned that it is naive for a Christian to assume he or she will be able to win an unbelieving spouse for Christ. "Matrimony is nowhere named among the means of conversion," he observed dryly.[19] In a later tract, Ryle used very strong language to shock his readers. He asserted that it was better to die than to marry an unbeliever. For a "praying, Bible-reading, God-fearing, Christ-loving, Sabbath-keeping"

---

[16] Ryle, *Remember Lot*, 9.
[17] Ryle, *Remember Lot*, 11–12.
[18] Ryle, *Remember Lot*, 17.
[19] Ryle, *Remember Lot*, 13–14.

Christian to marry someone who took no interest in "serious religion" was to ensure a lifetime of unhappiness and fixed "a mill-stone round your own neck in running the race towards heaven."[20]

In similar vein, *Lot's Wife* portrayed "worldliness" as her chief sin. Ryle admonished his readers to be alert to this "immense danger" and described it as an "epidemic disease" plaguing the modern church. To illustrate the contemporary need for this message in the 1850s, he identified various groups of people who began strongly in the Christian life before fading away. The fruits of faith proved to be only temporary. For example, he highlighted the spiritual trajectory of children raised in evangelical families, who in their youth could recite abundant Bible texts, enjoyed singing hymns and listening to sermons with their parents, and professed to love Jesus Christ and to long for heaven. Yet, by early adulthood these spiritual convictions evaporated.[21] In 1855, Ryle's eldest son was only a few months old, and Ryle wrote from observing other families. In later years, as a father, he wrote from bitter personal experience.

This teaching was developed further in Ryle's tract *Come Out!* (1878), republished as *Worldly Conformity* (1878), a practical exposition of 2 Corinthians 6:17, "Come out from among them, and be ye separate, saith the Lord." "In every age of the Church," he began, "separation from the world has always been one of the grand evidences of a work of grace in the heart." Conversely, those who claim the name of Christian without the reality always refuse to "come out." Ryle reckoned it was a particularly pressing subject because of a widespread anxiety in the Victorian church "to make things pleasant in religion—to saw off the corners and edges of the cross, and to avoid, as far as possible, self-denial." Many activities deemed harmless by modern Christians would have been considered damaging to people's souls in a previous generation. It was now commonly believed that they could "go anywhere, and do anything, and spend [their] time in anything, and read anything, and keep any company, and plunge into anything, and all the while may be very good Christians."[22] Ryle was alarmed by these trends, and his tract was a passionate warning against the inherent perils. He pillaged the New Testament for texts that showed the spiritual dangers of the cares and pleasures of "the world." Now in his early sixties,

---
[20] J. C. Ryle, *Come Out! A Hint for 1878, Being Thoughts on Separation from the World* (London, 1878), 22.
[21] Ryle, *Lot's Wife*, 11–13.
[22] Ryle, *Come Out!*, 3–4.

he identified this, in particular, as "the great rock on which thousands of young people are continually making shipwreck."[23]

Ryle aimed to clear away misconceptions about separation from the world. It did not mean that Christians should withdraw from society and give up their secular trades or professions. Nor should they refuse to interact with their unconverted friends and relatives. Nor should they stop reading newspapers and avoid nonreligious subjects like science, art, literature, or politics. "Christians who plume themselves on their ignorance of secular things are precisely the Christians who bring religion into contempt." Nor should they seek holiness by isolating themselves like monks, nuns, and hermits, which Ryle dismissed as "one of the crying errors of the Church of Rome" and an "unhappy delusion." On the contrary, he insisted, true believers should be cheerfully invested in the contexts and communities in which God placed them. This was part of their duty as Christians, in obedience to Jesus, and to avoid this responsibility was "lazy cowardly conduct."[24] They should make a positive public contribution as a matter of Christian witness: "Let us never give the world occasion to say that our separation is foolish, senseless, ridiculous, unreasonable, uncharitable, and unscriptural."[25]

Fundamentally, Ryle was concerned about personal behavior. His primary rule was that Christians must be guided by the Scriptures, not by the world's standards of right and wrong. It is foolish, he warned, to follow the moral fashion and "to set your watch by the town clock." The fact that "everybody thinks so, everybody says so, everybody does it, everybody will be there" is irrelevant to the Christian. Ryle urged his readers to choose their companions wisely, because intimate friendships with unconverted people are "very dangerous to the soul," hindering Christian discipleship. God's people should also be careful in spending their leisure time, especially their evenings after work. "Tell me how a man spends his evenings," he suggested, "and I can generally tell what his character is."[26]

Ryle was unafraid to offer pastoral guidance on specific activities, though he did so with some diffidence, acknowledging that in many scenarios it is difficult to come to a right judgment about Christian involvement. Every Christian needs to make up his or her own mind, Ryle advised,

---

[23] Ryle, *Come Out!*, 8.
[24] Ryle, *Come Out!*, 10–12.
[25] Ryle, *Come Out!*, 14.
[26] Ryle, *Come Out!*, 15–16, 21.

in accordance with conscience. He agreed that, generally speaking, recreation is healthy. "In a world of wear and tear . . . occasional unbending and relaxation are good for all. Body and mind alike require seasons of lighter occupation, and opportunities of letting off high spirits, and especially when they are young." Therefore, he approved of sports such as cricket, rowing, running, "and other manly athletic recreations."[27] Ryle himself was a cricketer in his youth. His earliest surviving letter—now in the archives of the Marylebone Cricket Club in central London—dates from 1834, when he was captain of the Eton Eleven, challenging his opposite number at Harrow School to a match at Lord's Cricket Ground, part of an annual cricketing tradition continued into the twenty-first century.[28] Ryle was also captain of the Oxford University cricket team and took ten wickets in the victory over Cambridge University at Lord's in 1836. During the summers at Oxford, he played cricket "incessantly," from noon until dusk every day. He gave up the sport when he was ordained, not because he thought it was sinful but because he now had new ministerial priorities.[29] In *The Christian Leaders of the Last Century*, he drew particular attention to the fact that his "spiritual hero," Henry Venn (1725–1797), likewise renounced cricket a few days before his ordination in 1747.[30] Ryle also approved of games of skill, like chess. "Anything which strengthens nerves, and brain, and digestion, and lungs, and muscles, and makes us more fit for Christ's work, so long as it is not in itself sinful, is a blessing, and ought to be thankfully used." The danger, rather, was excessive investment in these innocent pastimes. They were healthy medicine when taken in moderation but "downright poison when swallowed down in huge doses." The Christian who enjoyed them "must know when to stop, and how to say Hold! Enough! Do they interfere with his private religion? Do they take up too much of his thoughts and attention? Have they a secularizing effect on his soul?"[31]

However, other types of recreation must always be avoided, Ryle insisted. In particular, he highlighted the spiritual dangers of attending horse-races and theaters. He admitted that it was "perfectly harmless" to watch galloping horses and that William Shakespeare's plays were impres-

---

[27] Ryle, *Come Out!*, 19.
[28] *J. C. Ryle's Autobiography*, 36–38.
[29] *J. C. Ryle's Autobiography*, 52, 59, 81.
[30] J. C. Ryle, *The Christian Leaders of the Last Century; or, England a Hundred Years Ago* (London, 1869), 260–61.
[31] Ryle, *Come Out!*, 20.

Fruits of Faith 93

sive productions. Yet he argued that, in England in the 1870s, horse racing and theaters had become "inseparably bound up with things that are downright wicked," especially gambling, drunkenness, and fornication. To sanction such amusements was to encourage sin.[32] Nevertheless, Ryle held back his opinion on three other popular pastimes—ballroom dancing, cards, and field sports—for an appendix to his tract, partly because they were predominantly upper-class pursuits and his tract was aimed at a wider readership. He admitted that there was nothing morally wrong with "the mere bodily act of dancing." King David "danced before the LORD with all his might" (2 Sam. 6:14), and King Solomon taught that there is "a time to dance" (Eccl. 3:4). Ryle observed:

> Just as it is natural to lambs and kittens to frisk about, so it seems natural to young people, all over the world, to jump about to a lively tune of music. If dancing were taken up for mere exercise, if dancing took place at early hours, and men only danced with men, and women with women, it would be needless and absurd to object to it.

Yet ball-going in the 1870s involved "very late hours, extravagant dressing, and an immense amount of frivolity, vanity, jealousy, unhealthy excitement, and vain conversation. Who would like to be found in a modern ball-room when the Lord Jesus Christ comes the second time?" In his youth in the 1830s, Ryle himself had often gone to balls—in his words, "before I knew better"—so he spoke from personal experience when he warned that they had "a most dissipating effect on the mind, like opium-eating and dram-drinking on the body" (though there is no evidence that he ever tasted opium or whisky). Parents who urged their sons and daughters to attend balls were "risking great injury to their children's souls," he reckoned.[33]

Ryle's judgment on card-playing was similarly frank. He agreed that it was "nonsense" to claim that there was "positive wickedness in an innocent game of cards, for diversion, and not for money." Many frail older people, in particular, benefited from cards in the evenings, to keep them awake and alert. Yet the risks were great, especially if the habit was picked up by the working classes. "If masters and mistresses once begin to play cards in the parlour, servants are likely to play cards in the kitchen;

---
[32] Ryle, *Come Out!*, 18.
[33] Ryle, *Come Out!*, 30–31.

and then comes in a whole train of evils," including the likelihood of "desperate gambling."[34] Concerning field-sports, however, Ryle was reluctant to lay down such strict guidance. He acknowledged that it was not sinful to go "galloping across country, or shooting grouse, partridges, or pheasants, or catching salmon or trout." Indeed, he knew many people for whom "violent out-door exercise" was necessary for their physical and mental health. But, as with alcohol, he urged moderation in hunting, shooting, and fishing, which could too easily become wholly absorbing and carried to sinful excess. At the same time, Ryle also recognized the need to be cautious when criticizing other people's recreations. "The man who can neither ride, nor shoot, nor throw a fly, is hardly qualified to speak dispassionately about such matters. It is cheap and easy work to condemn others for doing things which you cannot do yourself, and are utterly unable to enjoy!"[35]

Practical Religion

Ryle entitled one of his compilation volumes *Practical Religion*, a central theme in his theology of the Christian life. This was another dimension of the fruits of faith. For example, in *Have You Charity?*, a tract for New Year 1865, Ryle began: "There are many high-flying Christians, in this present day, who almost refuse to look at anything *practical* in Christianity. They can talk of nothing but two or three favourite doctrines. . . . The Bible contains much about practice as well as about doctrine."[36] It is not sufficient, he declared, to be able to quote biblical texts or defend theological opinions: "Remember that the knowledge which is barren of practical results in life and temper, is a useless possession."[37] In this he explicitly built upon the apostle Paul's warning that "though I . . . understand all mysteries, and all knowledge . . . and have not charity, I am nothing" (1 Cor. 13:2).

"Charity," Ryle explained, means practical neighborly love. Yet it should not be reduced simply to philanthropic gifts to the poor: "It is easy to spend a fortune in giving away money, and soup, and wine, and bread, and coals, and blankets, and clothing, and yet to be utterly desti-

---

[34] Ryle, *Come Out!*, 31.
[35] J. C. Ryle, *Worldly Conformity: What It Is Not, and What It Is* (London, 1878), 73–75.
[36] J. C. Ryle, *Have You Charity? A Question for the New Year, Being Thoughts on 1 Cor xiii. 13* (London, 1865), 4–5.
[37] Ryle, *Have You Charity?*, 19.

Fruits of Faith

tute of Bible charity."[38] Deep love demonstrated in practical ways is one of the fruits of Christian faith, Ryle maintained, and therefore cannot be separated from gospel teaching. It is impossible to produce the fruit without the root. "I firmly believe, as a general rule, you will not find such charity as the Bible describes, except in the soil of a heart thoroughly imbued with Bible religion. Holy practice will not flourish without sound doctrine." Therefore, Ryle protested against the inconsistency of those who welcomed the practical results of the Christian message but did not care for the message itself. In particular, he criticized parents who wanted their children to grow up unselfish and kind, but who refused to point their children to faith in Jesus Christ. These were illogicalities in Ryle's view, nothing less than a "delusion." Christian behavior cannot be separated from Christian faith.[39]

This was a further reason that Ryle disliked "the vast majority of novels, romances, and tales of fiction"—because this literature in the 1860s was guilty of fixing the divorce between faith and the fruits of faith as a fashionable idea. Fictional heroes and heroines were frequently presented to the reading public as models of perfection, always generous and forgiving, yet without Christian faith. Romantic novels propagated false conceptions of human nature "to a most mischievous degree." Ryle acknowledged that kindness and compassion, to a certain extent, were undoubtedly evident among many who lacked "vital religion." "But the glorious plant of Bible charity, in all its fulness and perfection, will never be found without union with Christ, and the work of the Holy Ghost."[40] Concerning the practical impact of faith in Jesus Christ, he asserted elsewhere, "Nothing called religion, whether Classic heathenism, or Buddhism, or Confucianism, or Mahometanism [Islam], has ever produced effects on consciences and conduct, which can bear comparison for a moment with the effects produced by Christianity."[41]

As a bishop, Ryle frequently taught on these themes to public audiences. For example, in October 1882, he preached at All Saints Church, Derby, at the annual service in support of the Derbyshire General Infirmary, the county's major hospital, founded by local philanthropists in 1810. Among the sizeable congregation was the city's mayor, Abraham Woodiwiss, with

---
[38] Ryle, *Have You Charity?*, 7.
[39] Ryle, *Have You Charity?*, 14–15.
[40] Ryle, *Have You Charity?*, 15–16.
[41] J. C. Ryle, *"What Canst Thou Know?" (Job xi. 7, 8): A Question for the Times* (London, 1884), 15–16.

his regalia and retinue, alongside aldermen, councillors, and the high sheriff. The "handsome sum" of £207 was pledged to the hospital, according to the *Derby Daily Telegraph*, one of the highest amounts ever raised at the event.[42] Ryle chose as his text Luke 10:37, "Go, and do thou likewise," from the parable of the good Samaritan. "Christianity is eminently a practical religion," he began. "That salvation is only by grace—that justification is by faith without the deeds of the law—both these are foundation verities, cardinal truths of the Gospel. But it is no less true that saving faith will always be known by its fruits." Therefore, he urged the congregation to pattern their lives on the practical kindness and self-sacrifice of the Samaritan. "Be not content with mere thinking, feeling, talking, and intending. 'Go, and do.'"[43]

Ryle lamented that "selfish indifference" was characteristic of the late-Victorian age, with many hospitals, schools, and missions hindered through lack of funds. "Where are the Samaritans, we may well ask, in this land of Bibles and Testaments? Where are the men who love their neighbours, and will help to provide for dying bodies and souls?" Within the booming British economy, millions of pounds were spent every year on recreational pursuits, yet comparatively little "for the cause of Christ." Ryle observed that basic Christian principles of generosity seemed to have been largely forgotten. Turning to classical antiquity, he likened wealthy Victorians to Croesus, the king of Lydia in the sixth century BC whose name was synonymous with abundant riches. Yet, despite their financial resources, the Victorians often gave no more than a guinea to philanthropic causes. Likewise, Ryle decried the new phenomenon of church and charity fundraising bazaars—increasingly popular in the 1880s—designed to persuade people to give money by getting something in return, "as children in badly-managed families are bribed and tempted to be good by sugar-plums" (candied sweets). These were all signs that Britain was devoid of a good-Samaritan spirit.[44]

Ryle exhorted his Derbyshire hearers toward "active, practical love" as a New Testament duty. Nevertheless, he was clear that a "little spasmodic philanthropy," such as donating food to the poor, was insufficient. He argued that deep love for others springs only from "experimental union with Christ. . . . True charity and love to our neighbour will never be really

---

[42] "Anniversary of the Derby Infirmary: Sermon by the Bishop of Liverpool," *Derby Daily Telegraph*, October 27, 1882, 3.
[43] J. C. Ryle, *"Go, and Do Thou Likewise" (Luke x. 37): Thoughts on a Much-Neglected Duty* (London, 1883), 3–4.
[44] Ryle, *Go, and Do Thou Likewise*, 13–14.

Fruits of Faith 97

learned except in the school of Christ." Acts of philanthropy separated from Christian faith were like cut flowers in a vase compared with the beauties of a summer garden. Only those with deep conviction of sin and thankfulness to Christ, Ryle argued, "will long, and strive, and burn to be like your Master, and will be always trying to do good, and to leave the world a better world than it was when you were born."[45]

Practical actions, springing from Christian faith, should not be restricted to people's spiritual needs, Ryle declared. Preaching in Liverpool Cathedral in July 1883 to the British Medical Association at the opening of their annual conference, he emphasized the importance of the human body in Christian theology. While pagan philosophers might regard the body with contempt, as a spiritual hindrance, at the heart of Christianity are the bodily incarnation, atonement, resurrection, and ascension of Jesus. Ryle proclaimed:

> Whatever students and book-worms and philosophers may please to say, there is an indissoluble connection between the bodies and minds and souls of mankind. You cannot separate them. Not one of the three can be safely neglected. The Church which only cares for saving souls, and the State which only cares for educating minds, are both making a vast mistake.[46]

Christians should therefore be deeply concerned with promoting bodily health, Ryle exhorted the gathered medics. This included initiatives to promote better sanitation throughout Britain, with access to clean air and water, well-built homes, and affordable food. He claimed that the Christian church had always done much more to care for the sick than non-Christian societies had done, whether in ancient Greece or Rome, or in nineteenth-century India, China, and Japan. This was part of Ryle's regular apologetic. As he told the British Medical Association, "The infidel, the sceptic, and the agnostic may sneer at Bible religion if they please, but they cannot get over the fact that medical and surgical knowledge have always advanced side by side with the Gospel of Christ."[47]

Two months later, preaching in Southport in September 1883 to the British Association for the Advancement of Science, Ryle built on this

---
[45] Ryle, *Go, and Do Thou Likewise*, 17–18, 20.
[46] J. C. Ryle, *The Beloved Physician: A Sermon Preached (by Request) in Liverpool Cathedral, at the Opening of the Annual Conference of the British Medical Association in Liverpool, on July 31st, 1883* (London, 1883), 11.
[47] Ryle, *The Beloved Physician*, 15.

theme. His sermon was published as *Tried by Its Fruits* (1884)—republished in one of his compilation volumes as "The Best Evidences of Christianity"—and continued this apologetic thrust. He noted that many politicians and social reformers in the late nineteenth century were calling for the nation's ancient institutions, such as universities, corporations, colleges, and schools, to be tested by their results. He urged that Christianity should be subjected to the same scrutiny. Many commentators were dismissing Christian faith as "effete and worn out," utterly unsuited to the modern age, like last year's almanac, now worthless and deserving to be thrown away. It might suit the uneducated and the poor but was said to be "unworthy of the notice of intellectual men." Yet Ryle asserted that it was dishonest for skeptics and agnostics to ignore the incalculable good that Christianity had done for the world.[48]

Ryle suggested that classical civilization during the Augustan Age (immediately before the arrival of Christianity) may have excelled in literature, art, and architecture, but religiously and morally it was a period of "thick darkness" and "debasing idolatry." "The greatest philosophers, such as Socrates, groped, as in the night."[49] The preacher then outlined the enormous impact of Christianity in raising the moral standards of the world concerning respect for human life, women, children, servants, the poor, and property, and in the pursuit of justice, equality, decency, purity, and charity. In support, he pointed to recent publications like C. L. Brace's *Gesta Christi: or, A History of Humane Progress Under Christianity* (1882) and W. G. Blaikie's *Christianity and Secularism Compared in Their Influence and Effects* (1883). Ryle acknowledged that there were periods in the history of the church when the fruits of Christianity had been "miserably scanty and poor, and the tree which bore them has seemed rotten and only fit to be cut down." He had in mind especially the "corruption" of faith in the so-called Dark Ages, in the centuries before the Reformation. Nevertheless, he insisted that the public blessings of Christianity had mammoth consequences in shaping modern society for the better. Many secularists who despised Christianity in the 1880s were oblivious to the "enormous debt" they owed to the long-term effects of "Bible religion."[50]

---

[48] J. C. Ryle, *Tried by Its Fruits: A Thought for 1884* (London, 1884), 3–4; republished as Ryle, "The Best Evidences of Christianity," in *Principles for Churchmen: A Manual of Positive Statements on Doubtful or Disputed Points* (London, 1884).
[49] Ryle, *Tried by Its Fruits*, 6.
[50] Ryle, *Tried by Its Fruits*, 13, 15.

Ryle argued that, judged simply by tangible results, "modern unbelief and scepticism, and free thought" could not compete with the great blessings that "simple, old-fashioned" Christianity had brought to the world.[51] Authentic Christian life and faith, he insisted, is always transformative and always visible in practical ways.

---

[51] Ryle, *Tried by Its Fruits*, 24.

CHAPTER 7

FIGHTING FOR HOLINESS

Military metaphors were one of Ryle's favorite ways to illustrate the nature of the Christian life. His own military experience was perfunctory: serving for five years in his early twenties, from 1836 to 1841, as a captain in the Macclesfield branch of the Cheshire Yeomanry, his county's volunteer cavalry regiment, which involved little more than ten days in Liverpool each year for parades and exercises.[1] It was an era of peace, and he never saw active combat. Nevertheless, in the second half of the nineteenth century, warfare was a constant feature of British life, as Queen Victoria's armies were engaged in battles across the world, extending and protecting the empire. Closer to home, two international conflagrations embroiled the nations of Europe, and Ryle saw both as opportunities to teach evangelical theology. During the Crimean War of 1853–1856, he published his tract on justification *Have You Peace?* (1855). During the Franco-Prussian War of 1870–1871, he turned the question in a different direction in a tract on sanctification entitled *Are You Fighting?* (1871).

Ryle recognized that battles were front-page news and always fascinating to the public. Some were fixed in national folklore and taught in schools, like the great Battle of Waterloo in 1815, which brought an end to the Napoleonic Wars, or more recent contests like the Battles of Balaclava and Inkerman in Crimea in 1854, or the Siege of Lucknow during the Indian Rebellion in 1857. *Are You Fighting?*, written in late 1870, highlighted the alarming news reaching England from the Continent, where the

---

[1] *Bishop J. C. Ryle's Autobiography: The Early Years*, ed. Andrew Atherstone (Banner of Truth, 2016), 80.

Prussian armies had routed the French Emperor Napoleon III at the Battle of Sedan, starved and bombarded Metz and Strasbourg into submission, and besieged Paris, leading quickly to the surrender of the French capital in January 1871. This conflict presaged the Great War of the early twentieth century. In his tract, Ryle announced:

> We meet each other at a critical period of the world's history. Men's minds are full of "wars and rumours of wars." Men's hearts are full of fear while they look at the things which seem coming on the earth. On every side the horizon looks black and gloomy. Who can tell when the storm will burst?[2]

Nevertheless, Ryle used the opportunity to direct his readers' attention to spiritual concerns: "But, reader, there is another warfare of far greater importance than any war that was ever waged by man. It is a warfare which concerns not two or three nations only, like France, Prussia, and Bavaria, but every Christian man and woman born into the world." This spiritual fight, Ryle asserted, concerned their very souls. Like any warfare, it involved hand-to-hand combat, wounds, guards, exhaustion, sieges, assaults, defeats, victories, and tremendous consequences.[3] There was a key contrast with earthly battles, however. Although Ryle enjoyed military metaphors, he was careful not to glorify or romanticize war. He agreed that war was sometimes necessary "to procure the liberty of nations, to prevent the weak from being trampled down by the strong," but it still involved awful bloodshed and destruction and was "an immense and incalculable evil." However, one type of war is not evil but good, Ryle observed—the "good fight" (1 Tim. 6:12), the fight of the soul.[4]

Are You Fighting? expounded this theme from multiple angles. Genuine biblical Christianity, Ryle asserted, is "a struggle, a fight, and a warfare."[5] Indeed, this is one of the chief ways to distinguish true Christians from nominal Christians, he explained. Nominal Christians attend church or chapel every Sunday, but "you never see any 'fight' about their religion!" The true Christian, by contrast,

> is called to be a soldier, and must behave as such from the day of his conversion to the day of his death. He is not meant to live a life of religious

---
[2] J. C. Ryle, *Are You Fighting? A Question for 1871, Being Thoughts on 1 Timothy vi. 12* (London, 1871), 4.
[3] Ryle, *Are You Fighting?*, 3–4.
[4] Ryle, *Are You Fighting?*, 19.
[5] Ryle, *Are You Fighting?*, 9.

ease, indolence, and security. He must never imagine for a moment that he can sleep and doze along the way to heaven, like one travelling in an easy carriage.

Christians must constantly wage war against their "never-dying foes"—the world, the flesh, and the devil—struggling daily against sin and wrestling in prayer.[6]

During the Napoleonic Wars, the Duke of Wellington reputedly stated that the worst mistake a nation could make was to underrate its enemy and wage merely a "little war"—that is, literally, *guerrilla* warfare, rather than major combat. Ryle applied this Wellingtonian aphorism to the Christian life.[7] Every Christian, he insisted, must "carry arms and go to war." None can "plead exemption, or escape the battle." The fight against sin is relentless, with no opportunity for breathing space, armistice, or truce. Therefore, paradoxically, Ryle encouraged his readers that any who found the Christian life a struggle should take comfort, because it was meant to be a struggle. If they found the battle against sin difficult, they should rejoice: "Thank God for it! It is a good sign. . . . Anything is better than apathy, stagnation, deadness, and indifference."[8] He especially praised those who testified to their faith in difficult circumstances, including (in a sudden shift from metaphor to real life) Christian army officers who "displayed a banner for Christ even at the regimental mess-table," like the Victorian military heroes Captain Hedley Vicars (1826–1855), killed during the Siege of Sevastopol, and Major-General Sir Henry Havelock (1795–1857), who died at the Siege of Lucknow.[9]

As Ryle's tract reached its finale, he continued to quarry his military illustrations. Christians fight under "the best of generals," Jesus Christ. The "commissariat," supplying daily provisions to Christian troops, is overseen by the Holy Spirit.[10] They will win the victory as "more than conquerors" (Rom. 8:37). Their conflict against sin brings benefit not only to Christians themselves but also to their local neighborhoods by raising the standards of morality.

> All other wars have a devastating, ravaging, and injurious effect. The march of an army through a land is an awful scourge to the inhabitants. Wherever

---
[6] Ryle, *Are You Fighting?*, 5–6.
[7] Ryle, *Are You Fighting?*, 8.
[8] Ryle, *Are You Fighting?*, 11, 13.
[9] Ryle, *Are You Fighting?*, 18.
[10] Ryle, *Are You Fighting?*, 20–21.

it goes it impoverishes, wastes, and does harm. Injury to persons, property, feelings and morals invariably accompanies it. Far different are the effects produced by Christian soldiers. Wherever they live they are a blessing.[11]

Nor will any Christian be lost in the spiritual battle. During the Crimean War, the "Brigade of Guards"—consisting of the combined battalions of the Grenadier Guards, the Coldstream Guards, and the Scots Guards—suffered heavy casualties. A memorial in their honor was unveiled in central London in 1861, designed by sculptor John Bell, using metal from captured Russian cannons.[12] Ryle described how the Guards "marched out of London to the Crimean campaign a magnificent body of men; but many of the gallant fellows laid their bones in a foreign grave, and never saw London again." In the spiritual war, however, none will perish. Every Christian will survive the combat, protected by God to eternity.

> No soldiers of Christ are ever lost, missing, or left dead on the battlefield. No mourning will ever need to be put on, and no tears to be shed for either private or officer in the army of Christ. The muster roll, when the last evening comes, will be found precisely the same that it was in the morning.[13]

Furthermore, soldiers were rewarded with medals, pensions, peerages, and national honor. Some even received grand estates—like Blenheim Palace in Oxfordshire, gifted to the Duke of Marlborough in 1705 for his triumph against the Franco-Bavarian army in the War of the Spanish Succession, and Stratfield Saye House in Hampshire, gifted to the Duke of Wellington in 1817 for his triumph at Waterloo. Yet even the bravest generals eventually die, Ryle observed, and cannot enjoy these prizes beyond the grave. By contrast, soldiers of Christ usually win little public honor in this life, but are rewarded with an enduring "crown of glory" in the next (1 Pet. 5:4). Therefore, it is foolish to judge by appearances, Ryle concluded. "Reader, settle it in your mind that the Christian fight is a good fight, really good, truly good, emphatically good."[14] Although the struggle against sin is deeply difficult and lifelong, it is ultimately the path to glory.

Ryle picked up similar themes when preaching at the University of Cambridge in March 1879, in a sermon published as *Are We Overcoming?* (1880).

---
[11] Ryle, *Are You Fighting?*, 23.
[12] "The Guards' Memorial in Waterloo Place," *Illustrated London News*, April 13, 1861, 330.
[13] Ryle, *Are You Fighting?*, 22.
[14] Ryle, *Are You Fighting?*, 24.

He highlighted the baptism liturgy in the Book of Common Prayer, where the candidate is signed with the cross as a reminder not to be ashamed "to confess the faith of Christ crucified" and is exhorted "manfully to fight under his banner, against sin, the world, and the devil, and to continue Christ's faithful soldier and servant" to the end of life.[15] This was a Christian obligation, Ryle insisted, and his Cambridge hearers must not succumb to the temptation "to desert your colours, to slink away to the rear, and refuse to fight."[16] During the 1870s, British internationalism was shaped by a pragmatic policy of "masterly inactivity," or deliberate nonintervention, whether in the Franco-Prussian War or in Afghanistan's civil war, in keeping with the imperial strategy of Sir John Lawrence (viceroy of India).[17] Such neutrality might be suitable in diplomatic affairs, Ryle told his Cambridge audience, "but it is utterly impossible in that conflict which concerns the soul. . . . We must fight or be lost. We must conquer or die eternally."[18]

He drew further illustration from Elizabeth Thompson's painting *The Roll Call*, which was first exhibited at the Royal Academy in 1874 and quickly became a national sensation. It depicts a bedraggled group of Grenadier Guards, gathered in the snow on a bleak morning after a Crimean battle, worn out and wounded. It toured Britain, attracting large crowds, and was bought by Queen Victoria for the Royal Collection.[19] Ryle said that it was impossible to view the painting without "deep emotion." In warfare, he reiterated, the morning muster was often "a sorrowful sight." Yet, in Christ's victorious army none will be missing.[20] Ryle developed these metaphors further in a sermon to the Church Pastoral Aid Society, published as *Soldiers and Trumpeters* (1883). Christian warfare is a subject of "vast importance," Ryle declared. Indeed, he viewed it as "one of the essentials of saving religion."[21]

Growth and Progress

During the 1870s a new group of teachers rose to prominence within Victorian evangelicalism, promoting holiness without effort, or "sanctification

---

[15] Baptism (1662), in *The Book of Common Prayer: The Texts of 1549, 1559, and 1662*, ed. Brian Cummings (Oxford University Press, 2011), 412.
[16] J. C. Ryle, *Are We Overcoming? A Question for 1880* (London, 1880), 13.
[17] Christopher Wallace, "'Masterly Inactivity': Lord Lawrence, Britain and Afghanistan, 1864–1879" (PhD thesis, King's College London, 2014).
[18] Ryle, *Are We Overcoming?*, 13–14.
[19] Catherine Wynne, *Lady Butler: War Artist and Traveller, 1846–1933* (Four Courts Press, 2019), 57–76.
[20] Ryle, *Are We Overcoming?*, 21–22.
[21] J. C. Ryle, *Soldiers and Trumpeters: A Word for the Times* (London, 1883), 7.

by faith." They advocated the "higher Christian life," which emphasized resting and abiding instead of struggling and striving. One of the most popular holiness manuals was *The Christian's Secret of a Happy Life* (1875) by Pennsylvanian author Hannah Whitall Smith (1832–1911), who taught that it is as silly to urge a Christian to grow in holiness as to urge a child to grow in height. Conscious effort is unnecessary and even counterproductive.[22] Christians should simply yield themselves to God, without fighting against sin, and let the Holy Spirit do the sanctifying work single-handed. Smith and her husband, Robert Pearsall Smith (1827–1898), traveled around Britain teaching these passivist doctrines, which took root at holiness conventions like that launched in 1875 at Keswick in the Lake District.[23] Ryle responded to the controversy with a new compilation volume entitled *Holiness*, published in 1877 and containing ten of his earlier tracts on sin and sanctification. An expanded edition was published in 1879, double the size, a compilation of twenty tracts. It became Ryle's most famous book.

In the preface to *Holiness*, Ryle protested the tendency of the new holiness teachers to divide conversion from consecration, or normal Christian life from "higher Christian life." He rejected the theory of "a sudden, mysterious transition of a believer into a state of blessedness and entire consecration, at one mighty bound," dismissing it as "a man-made invention."

> Growth in grace, growth in knowledge, growth in faith, growth in love, growth in holiness, growth in humility, growth in spiritual-mindedness— all this I see clearly taught and urged in Scripture, and clearly exemplified in the lives of many of God's saints. But sudden, instantaneous leaps from conversion to consecration I fail to see in the Bible.

Ryle likewise rebuked Keswick devotees who claimed to have attained Christian "perfection" and to have moved beyond hymns like "Just As I Am" (1836) to a higher spiritual experience. They clearly knew very little about the nature of sin or their own hearts, Ryle discerned. Furthermore, he warned that sanctification without personal exertion, simply by yielding to God, was a dangerous revival of the antinomian heresies that had been defeated by Puritans like Richard Sibbes and Thomas Manton in the seventeenth century. "There is an Athenian love of novelty abroad," Ryle

---

[22] Hannah Whitall Smith, *The Christian's Secret of a Happy Life*, enl. ed. (London, 1876), 101.
[23] Melvin Dieter, *The Holiness Revival of the Nineteenth Century* (Scarecrow Press, 1980); David Bebbington, "The Keswick Tradition," in *Holiness in Nineteenth-Century England* (Paternoster, 2000), 73–90.

cried, "and a morbid distaste for anything old and regular, and in the beaten path of our forefathers. . . . There is an incessant craving after any teaching which is sensational, and exciting, and rousing to the feelings. There is an unhealthy appetite for a sort of spasmodic and hysterical Christianity."[24] He lamented that thousands of Christians eagerly crowded into holiness conventions to hear clever new teachers, without the ability to distinguish differences in doctrine. Speaking in January 1878 at the Islington Clerical Conference (an annual gathering of Anglican evangelical clergy in north London), Ryle explicitly criticized the Smiths for their repeated refrain "We do not want theology."[25] He believed that they were contributing to an "epidemic" of "jellyfish Christianity," a wider Victorian religious trend, which privileged "earnestness" over doctrine. Ryle mocked that a jellyfish floating in the sea appears graceful, "contracting and expanding like a little delicate transparent umbrella," but when it reaches the beach, it is "a mere helpless lump," powerless and defenseless.[26]

Are You Fighting? was one of the ten tracts Ryle selected for the first edition of *Holiness*. He retooled it with some extra rhetorical flourishes directed specifically at the new holiness teachers. For example, "If we would be holy we must fight," and "There is no holiness without a warfare," and "All true saints are soldiers."[27] Quoting one of the mottos of the Keswick Convention, Ryle protested, "He that pretends to condemn 'fighting,' and teaches that we ought to sit still and 'yield ourselves to God,' appears to me to misunderstand his Bible, and to make a great mistake."[28] He concluded, "May we never forget that without fighting there can be no holiness while we live, and no crown of glory when we die!"[29]

Ryle struck a similar chord in *What Does It Cost?*, also repurposed for *Holiness*. It was an exposition of Jesus's command that his disciples must "count the cost" (Luke 14:28). Ryle suggested that to be "a mere outward Christian" is "cheap and easy work," simply attending church twice on Sunday and living an average moral life without self-denial or self-sacrifice. But to be "a real Christian" is quite different. "Conversion is not putting a man in an armchair and taking him easily to heaven. It is the beginning of

---

[24] J. C. Ryle, *Holiness and Other Kindred Subjects* (London, 1877), xxiii–xxvii.
[25] J. C. Ryle, *Dogma: A Paper for the Times, Being Thoughts on the Importance of Distinct and Definite Views of Religious Truth* (London, 1878), 10.
[26] Ryle, *Dogma*, 12–13.
[27] J. C. Ryle, "The Fight," in *Holiness and Other Kindred Subjects*, 139, 146, 149.
[28] Ryle, "The Fight," 145.
[29] Ryle, "The Fight," 170.

a mighty conflict in which it costs much to win the victory." In particular, Christians must "keep up a perpetual war" against their sins. "Our sins are often as dear to us as our children. We love them, hug them, cleave to them, and delight in them. . . . Christ is willing to receive any sinners. But He will not receive them if they will stick to their sins." Therefore, all Christians must keep a careful watch over their conduct, in private as well as in public, including their time, tongue, temper, and thoughts. "There is nothing we naturally dislike so much as 'trouble' about our religion," Ryle acknowledged. "Anything that requires exertion and labour is entirely against the grain of our hearts. But the soul can have 'no gains without pains.'"[30]

Another tract selected for the first edition of *Holiness* was *Do We Grow?* (1864), concerning progress in the Christian life. Ryle urged his readers to examine themselves at regular intervals for evidence of spiritual growth, especially at birthdays, or on Communion Sundays (typically four times a year in many Church of England parishes), or each week on the eve of Sunday morning worship. "Time is fast flying," he exclaimed. "Life is fast ebbing away. Every returning year finds us twelve months nearer to death, judgment, and eternity." Lest there be any doubt, Ryle emphasized that peace with God is not a matter of degrees or something that can increase or decrease. It is impossible to be more pardoned, more forgiven, or more accepted by God. Justification is a perfect and complete work, to which nothing can be added, and "the weakest saint is as completely justified as the strongest." Nevertheless, it is possible for the Christian to grow, Ryle insisted, in spiritual graces like repentance, faith, hope, love, humility, and zeal. These might be "little or great, strong or weak, vigorous or feeble," and vary within the same person at different stages of life. He explained: "When I speak of a man growing in grace, I mean simply this—that his sense of sin is becoming deeper, his faith stronger, his hope brighter, his love more extensive, his spiritual-mindedness more marked. He feels more of the power of godliness in his own heart."[31]

Ryle criticized especially those "high-flying religionists"—a strike at the holiness teachers—who claimed to have moved beyond "conflict and soul-humiliation," and whose idea of Christianity was "a state of perpetual joy and ecstasy." Furthermore, it was a "grievous delusion" to pretend that spiritual growth is a special gift from God and that believers need only to

---

[30] J. C. Ryle, *What Does It Cost? A Question for 1866* (London, 1865), 4–7.
[31] J. C. Ryle, *Do We Grow? Being Thoughts on Growth in Grace, 2 Peter iii. 18* (London, 1864), 3–6.

Fighting for Holiness

"sit still" and wait to receive it.[32] On the contrary, Ryle taught, growth in the Christian life requires struggle and effort. He chided those who seemed to have made no spiritual progress since their conversions because they were satisfied with "old grace, old experience, old knowledge, old faith, old measure of attainment, old religious expressions, old set phrases." None must be content to stand still in the Christian life. "Go forward! Go on!"[33]

Popular Puritanism

Ryle's doctrine of sanctification was expounded most fully in two tracts selected for the first *Holiness* compilation volume—*Are You Holy?* (1848) and *Are We Sanctified?* (1874). The earlier tract was peppered with quotations from the Puritans, from whom Ryle derived much of his theological framework. It opened with a quotation from a collection of Thomas Brooks's sermons, *The Crown and Glory of Christianity, or Holiness the Only Way to Happiness* (1662), in which Brooks explained that the central purpose of Christian ministry is "making unholy men holy" and "making them that are already holy, to be more and more holy"; "first to beget holiness, and then to nurse up holiness; first to bring souls to Christ, and then to build up souls in Christ."[34] This was also Ryle's ministerial ambition. In a key definition, he linked holiness directly with the Christian's attitude toward the Bible:

> Holiness is the habit of being of one mind with God, according as we find His mind described in Scripture. It is the habit of agreeing in God's opinion and judgment—hating what He hates—loving what He loves—and measuring everything in this world by the standard of His word. He who most entirely agrees with God, he is the most holy man.

The holy person will seek to shun every sin, keep every divine commandment, and strive to be like Jesus Christ. "He knows his own heart is like tinder, and will diligently keep clear of the sparks of temptation."[35]

Nevertheless, Ryle maintained that holiness does not bring an end to "indwelling sin." Echoing Romans 7, he observed that even the mature believer always finds that "the old man is clogging all his movements" and

---
[32] Ryle, *Do We Grow?*, 16–17.
[33] Ryle, *Do We Grow?*, 24, 26.
[34] J. C. Ryle, *Are You Holy? A Question for New-Year's Day 1848* (Ipswich, 1848), 2.
[35] Ryle, *Are You Holy?*, 5, 8.

that sin is perpetually trying to drag him backward. Nor does holiness reach "ripeness and perfection" at one stroke. Sanctification is "always a progressive work" and always imperfect, even in the greatest saints. "The gold will never be without some dross, the light will never shine without some clouds until we reach the heavenly Jerusalem." Therefore, the Christian life is "continual warfare" against sin, and even the holiest Christian sometimes finds himself "not overcoming, but overcome." Yet holiness is vital because it is a scriptural command and the fruit of faith. "We must be holy," Ryle declared, "because this is the only sound evidence that we have a saving faith in our Lord Jesus Christ."[36] The pursuit of holiness is proof that the Christian loves Jesus, obeying his commands. Ryle borrowed this idea from the Puritan William Gurnall (1616–1679), rector of Lavenham in Suffolk, just twenty miles from Ryle's Helmingham parish. In support, he paraphrased Gurnall's *The Christian in Complete Armour* (1655): "Say not that thou hast royal blood in thy veins and art born of God, except thou canst prove thy pedigree by daring to be holy."[37]

Ryle also highlighted the impact of holiness as a witness to the gospel. He described the Christian's life as "a silent sermon which all can read," and added, "It is sad indeed when they are a sermon for the devil's cause and not for God's. . . . You may talk to people about the doctrines of the gospel, and few will listen, and still fewer understand. But your life is an argument that none can escape." Inconsistent Christians therefore do great damage to the gospel cause and are "Satan's best allies," Ryle exclaimed. He gave the example of a local tradesman who rejected Christianity because his Christian customers were always talking about "the gospel, and faith, and election, and the blessed promises," but they tried to cheat him financially: "Oh! brethren, I blush to be obliged to write such things," Ryle lamented. "I fear that Christ's name is too often blasphemed because of the lives of Christians. . . . From murder of souls by inconsistency and loose walking, good Lord deliver us!"[38] He suggested that the vast majority of professing Christians in Britain in the 1840s had "nothing of Christianity but the name." "You must not merely have a Christian name, and Christian knowledge," he insisted; "you must have a Christian character also. You must be a saint on earth, if ever you mean to be a saint in heaven."[39]

---
[36] Ryle, *Are You Holy?*, 10–11, 14.
[37] Ryle, *Are You Holy?*, 16.
[38] Ryle, *Are You Holy?*, 16–18.
[39] Ryle, *Are You Holy?*, 21–23.

Drawing an analogy from Jesus's teaching on marriage (Mark 10:9)—amplified by the Church of England's wedding liturgy in the Book of Common Prayer—Ryle wrote: "God has married together justification and sanctification. They are distinct and different things beyond question, but one is never found without the other. All justified people will be sanctified, and all sanctified are justified. What God has joined together let no man dare to put asunder." In support, he quoted approvingly from the Scottish Puritan Samuel Rutherford (1600–1661), who wrote in *The Trial and Triumph of Faith* (1652), "The way that crieth down duties and sanctification, is not the way of grace. Believing and doing are blood-friends." Christian faith and Christian character belong inseparably together, but Ryle feared this was largely forgotten by the Victorian church. *Are You Holy?*, like so many of Ryle's other tracts, was therefore an exercise in theological retrieval. He suggested that Jesus would have been rejected as a legalist if he had preached the Sermon on the Mount to a modern congregation, as would Saint Paul for his practical instructions on Christian living. It is all very well for Christians to say that they can never throw off sin completely, but this theological truth too often becomes "only a cloak to cover spiritual laziness, and an excuse for spiritual sloth." Ryle urged his readers to seek to be "more spiritual, more holy, more single-eyed, more heavenly-minded, more whole-hearted."[40]

In conclusion, Ryle emphasized that holiness is the Holy Spirit's work. It begins the moment someone turns to Christ in repentance and faith. To attempt holiness without Christ, by turning over a new leaf or making lifestyle changes, is a vain hope. It is like trying to build a wall from sand that collapses as fast as it is built, or trying to bail water out of a leaky ship only to find that the leaks multiply. Once again Ryle turned to the Puritans for help, quoting from the sermons of Robert Traill (1642–1716): "Wisdom out[side] of Christ is damning folly—righteousness out of Christ is guilt and condemnation—sanctification out of Christ is filth and sin—redemption out of Christ is bondage and slavery." The answer, instead, is to flee to Christ, Ryle urged. "Would you be holy? Would you be partakers of the divine nature? Then go to Christ. Wait for nothing. Wait for nobody." He described holiness as the result of "vital union" with Christ, "the fruit of being a living branch of the true vine."[41] As always, Ryle's teaching,

---
[40] Ryle, *Are You Holy?*, 24–26.
[41] Ryle, *Are You Holy?*, 28.

whatever the doctrine, was strongly Christocentric and led naturally to evangelistic appeal.

A quarter of a century later, Ryle revisited these themes in *Are We Sanctified?*, published as his New Year tract for 1874, at a period when a fresh wave of the holiness controversy was sweeping through British evangelicalism. He described it as "a question of the utmost importance to our souls. If the Bible be true, it is certain that unless we are 'sanctified,' we shall not be saved." Indeed, Ryle warned that to focus exclusively on justification and the forgiveness of sins is (however unwittingly) to dishonor Jesus and to make him "only half a Saviour," because Jesus promised not only to justify his people but also to sanctify them.[42] In systematic fashion, Ryle made twelve doctrinal affirmations, in an attempt to clear away confusions:

- Sanctification is the result of union with Christ through faith.
- Sanctification is the consequence of regeneration.
- Sanctification is the only certain evidence of the Holy Spirit's indwelling.
- Sanctification is the only sure mark of God's election.
- Sanctification will always be seen.
- Sanctification is the responsibility of every believer.
- Sanctification grows by degrees.
- Sanctification depends on diligent use of the "means of grace."
- Sanctification does not remove inward spiritual conflict.
- Sanctification cannot justify, yet it pleases God.
- Sanctification will be a witness to Christian character on the day of judgment.
- Sanctification is "absolutely necessary" to train the Christian for heaven.[43]

Ryle expounded these ideas in detail. For example, he insisted that it is possible to grow progressively in holiness throughout the Christian life by walking more closely with God, like climbing from one step of holiness to another. Christians who simply sat still, satisfied with a low degree of sanctification, were rebuked by Ryle as ignorant and deluded. At the same time, he rejected the concepts of "imputed sanctification" and "sinless perfection" as without scriptural warrant. The true Christian life is one of perpetual inward conflict and struggle, as proved by the autobiographies of the most eminent believers. The language of Paul in Romans 7, for example,

---
[42] J. C. Ryle, *Are We Sanctified? A Question for 1874, Being Thoughts on John xvii. 17 and 1 Thess iv. 3* (London, 1874), 3, 5.
[43] Ryle, *Are We Sanctified?*, 6–15.

"does not describe the experience of an unconverted man, or of a young and unestablished Christian; but of an old experienced saint in close communion with God."[44] The Christian life is also a training ground for heaven, a holy place where sanctification is essential. Multiplying memorable illustrations from the natural world, Ryle concluded, "When an eagle is happy in an iron cage, when a sheep is happy in the water, when an owl is happy in the blaze of noonday sun, when a fish is happy on the dry land—then, and not till then, will I admit that the unsanctified man could be happy in heaven."[45]

In the second half of *Are We Sanctified?*, Ryle offered ten visible marks of "genuine sanctification." Emphasizing the need for inward holiness and a change of heart, he criticized formalism and external religiosity. He lamented, for example, that large numbers of professing Christians talked flippantly about conversion and the gospel while still "notoriously serving sin and living after the world."[46] Others engaged in "sensuous" worship and public acts of asceticism, "in self-imposed austerities and petty self-denials," while they were "absorbed in worldliness, and plunge headlong into its pomps and vanities without shame." Ryle likewise observed that it is impossible to evade sin by becoming a hermit in the desert. On the contrary, holiness is to be lived out in the midst of everyday life. "It is not the man who hides himself in a cave, but the man who glorifies God as master or servant, parent or child, in the family and in the street, in business and in trade, who is the scriptural type of a sanctified man." Borrowing another familiar illustration from Victorian society, Ryle suggested that true holiness was not like a village water pump, sending forth water when worked by external pressure in "spasmodical fits" of goodness, but should instead be like a fountain, flowing continually.[47] Turning next to an image from Suffolk agriculture, he lamented that so many Christians seemed content with "a mere round of church-going and chapel-going," without progress in holy living, simply going round in circles like a horse grinding grain at the mill.[48]

Ryle was primarily a popularizer, expressing succinctly in these short tracts for busy Victorian readers what Puritan theologians had expounded at considerable length. He recommended that modern Christians wanting

---

[44] Ryle, *Are We Sanctified?*, 10–13.
[45] Ryle, *Are We Sanctified?*, 16.
[46] Ryle, *Are We Sanctified?*, 17.
[47] Ryle, *Are We Sanctified?*, 19–21.
[48] Ryle, *Are We Sanctified?*, 30.

to study "experimental theology" were much better served by the Puritans than by bestselling spiritual writers from the Roman Catholic and High Anglican traditions, such as Thomas à Kempis's *The Imitation of Christ* (ca. 1420), Lorenzo Scupoli's *The Spiritual Combat* (1589), or Jeremy Taylor's *The Rules and Exercises of Holy Living* (1650) and *The Rules and Exercises of Holy Dying* (1651). For a proper understanding of sanctification, Ryle preferred John Owen's magnum opus *Pneumatologia; or, A Discourse Concerning the Holy Spirit* (1674), alongside Owen's shorter works *Of the Mortification of Sin in Believers* (1656) and *Indwelling Sin in Believers* (1668). Although Owen was widely mocked as a "benighted puritan," and his writings were unfashionable in the 1870s, Ryle asserted that Owen had "more learning and sound knowledge of Scripture in his little finger, than many who depreciate him have in their whole bodies."[49] Elsewhere, Ryle noted sarcastically that if the new breed of holiness teachers were correct, then John Bunyan's Puritan classic *The Pilgrim's Progress* might as well be thrown on the fire. Bunyan's pilgrim did not simply "yield himself to God," but fought, struggled, and wrestled his way to the Celestial City.[50]

---

[49] Ryle, *Are We Sanctified?*, 31.
[50] Ryle, *Holiness and Other Kindred Subjects*, xxvi.

CHAPTER 8

MEANS OF GRACE

During the 1870s, Ryle undertook a major renovation and rebuilding program of his parish church at Stradbroke. He envisaged it as "a complete pattern of what the House of God ought to be in the Reformed Church of England" and did not want to leave any excuse for his successor to introduce ornaments or fittings of "an un-Protestant character."[1] The chancel was completely redesigned, including a higher roof and a new, larger east window. Most Victorian east-end stained-glass windows show Christ as the central figure, crucified or risen, but Ryle viewed such iconography as a form of idolatry. The Stradbroke window therefore has no human figures. Instead, in the upper section, it depicts four parts of the "armor of God"—helmet, shield, sword, and breastplate (Eph. 6:14–17). The lower section depicts four examples of the "means of grace"—prayer desk, pulpit, baptismal font, and Communion cup and plate—representing prayer, preaching, and the two sacraments.

The means of grace figured prominently in Ryle's teaching on the Christian life. For example, in *Strive!* (1855), he urged his readers to take personal responsibility for their salvation and spiritual growth. He warned against the "spirit of slumber," which had fallen upon many professing Christians. They cared greatly about temporal matters, striving for material prosperity, but not about eternity. Reflecting his local agricultural context in rural Suffolk, Ryle lamented: "Pains about wheat, barley, and beans—pains about

---
[1] J. C. Ryle, "The Chancel of Stradbroke Church," in *Whose Word Is This? Being Thoughts About 2 Tim iii. 16: A Question for 1877* (London, 1877), 2.

rent, and wages, and labour, and land—pains about pigs, and allotments, and eating and drinking—pains about such matters I see in abundance. But I see few who take pains about their souls."[2] This was later varied for a more cosmopolitan readership in his compilation volume *Practical Religion*: "Pains about money, and business, and politics—pains about trade, and science, and fine arts, and amusements."[3] Ryle urged: "Do not suppose that it needs some great scarlet sin to bring you to the pit of destruction. You have only to sit still and do nothing, and you will find yourself there at last." The road to hell, he proclaimed, is a "road of spiritual indolence, spiritual laziness, and spiritual sloth." Therefore, it was essential to invest in the means of grace:

> Beware of shortening your prayers, your Bible reading, your private communion with God. Take heed that you do not give way to a carnal, lazy manner of using the public services of God's house. Fight against any rising disposition to be sleepy, critical, and fault-finding, while you listen to the preaching of the Gospel. Whatever you do for God, do it with all your heart and mind and strength. In other things be moderate, and dread running into extremes. In soul matters fear moderation just as you would fear the plague.[4]

Likewise, in *Are We Sanctified?* (1874), Ryle argued that sanctification is greatly dependent upon "a diligent use of scriptural means"—that is, "Bible reading, private prayer, regular attendance on public worship, regular hearing of God's Word, and regular reception of the Lord's Supper." These were "channels through which the Holy Spirit conveys fresh supplies of grace to the soul" and strengthens the Christian.[5]

In Ryle's opinion, there were three common mistakes concerning the means of grace. The first was to dismiss them as unnecessary for the Christian life. The second was to rely upon them instead of relying upon God. Listening to sermons and receiving the sacraments cannot remove sin, he insisted: "All the means of grace in the world will never do you any good, so long as you trust in them as saviours."[6] The third mistake

---
[2] J. C. Ryle, *Strive! Being Thoughts on Luke xiii. 23* (Ipswich, 1855), 14, 16.
[3] J. C. Ryle, "Self-Exertion," in *Practical Religion: Being Plain Papers on the Daily Duties, Experience, Dangers, and Privileges of Professing Christians* (London, 1878), 35.
[4] Ryle, *Strive!*, 17–18.
[5] J. C. Ryle, *Are We Sanctified? A Question for 1874, Being Thoughts on John xvii. 17 and 1 Thess iv. 3* (London, 1874), 11–12.
[6] J. C. Ryle, *Where Are Your Sins? A Question for Everybody* (Ipswich, 1858), 15.

Means of Grace

was to assume that God only works through a limited number of instruments. Ryle commented in his *Expository Thoughts* on the strange way in which Jesus healed a deaf man by putting fingers in his ears, spitting, and touching his tongue (Mark 7:33). This was proof "that the Lord is not tied to the use of any one means exclusively in conveying grace to the soul." Therefore, no single means should be exalted as "an idol," to the disparagement of other ways in which God, in his sovereignty, might choose to work.[7]

Private Prayer

One of Ryle's early tracts, *Do You Pray?* (1852), focused not on public prayer in the church or family prayer in the household but private prayer when no one else is looking. This, Ryle suggested, was a widely neglected duty. Indeed, he believed that the vast majority of professing Christians did not pray privately at all, or did so in a rushed and cursory manner. Many Christians, he lamented, "mutter their prayers over after they have got into bed, or scramble over them while they wash or dress in the morning." Prayers said without heart engagement were not prayers at all, but were "as utterly useless to our souls as the drum-beating of the poor heathen before their idols. . . . There may be lip-work and tongue-work, but there is nothing that God listens to." Many were ashamed to be caught praying. They would prefer to "storm a breach" in battle than admit that they prayed regularly. "To ride well, to shoot well, to dress well, to go to theatres, to be thought clever and agreeable—all this is fashionable, but not to pray."[8]

Private prayer, Ryle declared, is the principal means of growth in the Christian life and "the secret of eminent holiness." He noticed that some Christians never seem to grow after their conversion. "They are born again, but they remain babes all their lives. They are learners in Christ's school, but they never seem to get beyond ABC. . . . Year after year you see in them the same old besetting sins." Meanwhile, other Christians always seem to be deepening in spiritual maturity. "They grow like the grass after rain. . . . Every time you meet them their hearts seem larger, and their spiritual stature bigger, taller, and stronger." What explains this difference? In nineteen cases out of twenty, Ryle asserted, it is because of their different habits in private prayer. Prayer is the means to growth in godliness.

---

[7] J. C. Ryle, *Expository Thoughts on the Gospels, for Family and Private Use: St Mark* (Ipswich, 1857), 150–51.
[8] J. C. Ryle, *Do You Pray? A Question for 1852* (Ipswich, 1852), 9.

"Praying and sinning will never live together in the same heart. Prayer will consume sin, or sin will choke prayer."[9]

Conversely, to neglect prayer is a primary cause of "backsliding" in the Christian life. As usual, Ryle piled up visual images to drive home his point: "A stranded ship, a broken-winged eagle, a garden overrun with weeds, a harp without strings, a church in ruins, all these are sad sights, but a backslider is a sadder sight still." Indeed, he considered it the unhappiest circumstance that ever befalls a Christian, drifting away from God. After years of observation as a parish minister, Ryle concluded that lack of private prayer is often the root cause of this spiritual disaster:

> Bibles read without prayer—sermons heard without prayer—marriages contracted without prayer—journeys undertaken without prayer—residences chosen without prayer—friendships formed without prayer—the daily act of private prayer itself hurried over, or gone through without heart—these are the kind of downward steps by which many a Christian descends to a condition of spiritual palsy, or reaches the point where God allows him to have a tremendous fall.

The public fall of Christians is always long preceded by their spiritual fall in secret, Ryle maintained. "They are backsliders on their knees long before they backslide openly in the eyes of the world."[10] "Most backslidings begin in the closet," Ryle reiterated in *Watch* (1851). "When a tree is snapped in two by a high wind, we generally find there had been some long hidden decay."[11]

Do You Pray? offered many practical hints. Ryle recommended regular hours of prayer, at least every morning and evening, and that it should not be squeezed into leftover time: "Do not give it the scraps and leavings and parings of your day." Prayer should be fervent and earnest, but there is no need to "shout, or scream, or be very loud." It should be bold, but not with "unseemly familiarity." It should be frequent throughout the day. "Even in company, or business, or in the very streets, you may be silently sending up little winged messengers to God." Ideally, private prayer should be extempore, not read from a book. "If we can tell our doctors the state of our bodies without a book, we ought to be able to tell

---
[9] Ryle, *Do You Pray?*, 10, 13–14.
[10] Ryle, *Do You Pray?*, 16–17.
[11] J. C. Ryle, *Watch: A Word in Season, Being Thoughts on the Parable of the Ten Virgins* (Ipswich, 1851), 30.

Means of Grace 119

the state of our souls to God." Although Ryle always used book prayers in his Sunday ministrations, from the Church of England's Book of Common Prayer, he likened book prayers in private devotions to walking with crutches.[12]

Overall, he was keen to emphasize the naturalness and accessibility of prayer. "Prayer is the simplest act in all religion," he urged his readers. "It is simply speaking to God. It needs neither learning, nor wisdom, nor book-knowledge to begin it. . . . The weakest infant can cry when he is hungry. The poorest beggar can hold out his hand for alms, and does not wait to find fine words." "Fear not, because your prayer is stammering," Ryle encouraged. "Jesus can understand you. Just as a mother understands the first babblings of her infant, so does the blessed Saviour understand sinners. He can read a sigh, and see a meaning in a groan."[13]

Concluding his tract, Ryle described prayer as the "spiritual pulse" by which a Christian's spiritual vigor could be tested. It was a "spiritual weather-glass"—like the Victorian barometers used for predicting the weather—by which it was possible to discern the state of a Christian's heart. "Oh! let us keep an eye continually upon our private devotions," Ryle exhorted. "Here is the pith, and marrow, and backbone of our practical Christianity. Sermons, and books, and tracts, and committee meetings, and the company of good men, are all good in their way, but they will never make up for the neglect of private prayer."[14]

The ministry of Jesus as intercessor was another of Ryle's key themes. In *Do You Pray?*, he observed that a Christian's prayers might be poor in themselves, but they are "mighty and powerful in the hand of our High Priest and elder brother."[15] In April 1859, Ryle traveled from Suffolk to Ireland on delegation with the Society for Irish Church Missions, an evangelical agency founded ten years earlier to reach Roman Catholics with the gospel.[16] There he preached at St Thomas's Church, Dublin, a sermon published as *The True Priest* (1859), contrasting Jesus's finished work of atonement with his ongoing work of intercession. Ryle informed the congregation that they had understood only half the gospel if they focused exclusively on Jesus's death on the cross at Calvary. They must celebrate also Jesus's life as "the

---
[12] Ryle, *Do You Pray?*, 25–26, 28.
[13] Ryle, *Do You Pray?*, 20, 23.
[14] Ryle, *Do You Pray?*, 31.
[15] Ryle, *Do You Pray?*, 11.
[16] Miriam Moffitt, *The Society for Irish Church Missions to the Roman Catholics, 1849–1950* (Manchester University Press, 2010).

great high priest," praying continually for his believing people at the right hand of the throne of grace.[17] As a young man in the early 1840s, Ryle had sometimes personally signed banknotes on behalf of Daintry, Ryle & Co., his family's bank in Macclesfield.[18] He observed that a banknote without a signature was a worthless piece of paper, but with a signature it might be worth a fortune. "So it is with the intercession of Christ. He signs, endorses, and presents the believer's petitions, and through His all-prevailing intercession they are heard on high, and bring down blessings upon the Christian's soul." Ryle emphasized especially the compassion and "matchless tenderness" of Jesus, an "unfailing friend" to the anxious and weary Christian.[19] He explored this subject further in his New Year tract for 1872, entitled *Have You a Priest?*, rejoicing in the Christian's friend and mediator, "the God-man Christ Jesus." "Let us glory in His death," Ryle exhorted, "but let us not glory less in His life. . . . Let us be thankful for the precious blood of Christ; but let us not be less thankful for His precious intercession."[20]

Bible Reading

Ryle maintained that the Bible is "the grand instrument" and "the chief means" by which the Holy Spirit miraculously brings people to faith in Christ and then establishes them in the Christian life. This is the Holy Spirit's normal way of operating, Ryle insisted. "The Spirit ordinarily does these things by the written Word; sometimes by the Word read, and sometimes by the Word preached, but seldom, if ever, without the Word."[21] Ryle's *Expository Thoughts on the Gospels* aimed to stimulate the habit of daily Bible reading. Although this resource became a firm favorite for preachers because of its heartwarming Christocentric applications, it was originally designed for "reading aloud" by heads of households, at family prayers with their children and servants, or by district visitors to the sick and poor, in hospitals and cottages.[22] Ryle's comments were therefore deliberately brief, bold, and arresting. He also hoped, as a subsidiary aim, that *Expository Thoughts* might be profitable for private reading by those who had "neither

---

[17] J. C. Ryle, *The True Priest: A Sermon Preached in St Thomas's Church, Dublin, on Sunday, April 10, 1859, on Behalf of the Society for Irish Church Missions to the Roman Catholics* (Dublin, 1859), 10.
[18] *Bishop J. C. Ryle's Autobiography: The Early Years*, ed. Andrew Atherstone (Banner of Truth, 2016), 86.
[19] Ryle, *The True Priest*, 8, 17.
[20] J. C. Ryle, *Have You a Priest? A Question for 1872* (London, 1872), 4, 17.
[21] J. C. Ryle, *How Readest Thou? A Question for 1853* (Ipswich, 1852), 19–20.
[22] J. C. Ryle, *Expository Thoughts on the Gospels, for Family and Private Use: St Matthew* (Ipswich, 1856), iv, vii.

large libraries nor much leisure," and for whom more substantial commentaries were inaccessible.[23]

During the 1850s, Ryle published strong criticisms against the Church of Rome for neglecting the Scriptures, but he brought a similar charge against his fellow Protestants also. There were more Bibles in Britain than ever before. "We see Bibles in every bookseller's shop—Bibles of every size, price, and style—Bibles great, and Bibles small—Bibles for the rich, and Bibles for the poor."[24] Much of this industry was the fruit of the British and Foreign Bible Society, an evangelical mission agency founded in 1804.[25] Nevertheless, owning a Bible was of little use if it was never read, Ryle warned. Often it lay unopened, "stiff, cold, glossy, and fresh as it was when it came from the bookseller's shop," or out of reach on a high shelf, "neglected and dusty, to be brought down only on grand occasions—such as a birth in the family—like a heathen idol at its yearly festival." Even when the Bible was read, it was often in "a heartless, scrambling, formal kind of way," merely as a cold duty, in a hurry, without spiritual appetite. "Here we are, as a nation, pluming ourselves on our Protestantism," Ryle proclaimed, "and yet neglecting the foundation on which Protestantism is built!"[26]

Some professed Christians had given up reading the Bible because it contained too many difficult passages, but Ryle dismissed such objections as "lazy excuses." He compared them to a captain of an Atlantic steamer bound for London who would be rightly rebuked as a "lazy coward" if he refused to enter the English Channel on the feeble grounds that he did not know every parish and village along the south coast of England. There were enough lighthouses to guide the steamer at every stage of its journey through the Channel—at Lizard, Eddystone, the Start, Portland, St Catherine's, Beachy Head, Dungeness, and the Forelands—shining along the whole route from Cornwall to Kent. In a similar way, Ryle suggested, it is not necessary to understand every small part of Scripture in order to grasp its central salvation message, which shines forth "clearly and unmistakeably" from its pages like a sunbeam.[27]

Christians should read the Bible with an earnest desire to understand it, Ryle exhorted, not mindlessly turning over a set number of pages each

---

[23] J. C. Ryle, *Expository Thoughts on the Gospels, for Family and Private Use: St Luke*, vol. 1 (Ipswich, 1858), v.
[24] Ryle, *How Readest Thou?*, 25.
[25] Leslie Howsam, *Cheap Bibles: Nineteenth-Century Publishing and the British and Foreign Bible Society* (Cambridge University Press, 1991).
[26] Ryle, *How Readest Thou?*, 25, 27.
[27] Ryle, *How Readest Thou?*, 21.

day as if their religious duty were merely to move the bookmark forward. "This is turning Bible reading into a mere form. It is almost as bad as the Popish habit of buying indulgences, by saying a fabulous number of avemarias and paternosters." He insisted upon the maxim "A Bible not understood is a Bible that does no good."[28] Bible knowledge can only be gained, he wrote in *Expository Thoughts*, by "hard, regular, daily, attentive, wakeful reading."[29] God's word must be "studied, pondered, prayed over, searched into, and not left always lying on a shelf, or carelessly looked at now and then."[30]

Yet understanding Scripture is a spiritual, not a merely intellectual, exercise. Therefore, Ryle taught that every time Christians open their Bibles, they should pray for the help of the Holy Spirit. Indeed, Ryle maintained that prayer would throw more light on the text than the famous multivolume commentaries by Matthew Poole (1624–1679), Matthew Henry (1662–1714), Johann Albrecht Bengel (1687–1752), and Thomas Scott (1747–1821); or the recent biblical research of Victorian scholars like Dean Henry Alford, Bishop Charles Ellicott, and Professor J. B. Lightfoot; or in fact "all the commentaries that ever were written."[31] *Expository Thoughts* remarked on the fact that when Jesus was among the apostles after the resurrection, he opened their minds "that they might understand the scriptures" (Luke 24:45). "Human commentaries are useful in their way. The help of good and learned men is not to be despised. But there is no commentary to be compared with the teaching of Christ."[32] Ryle reiterated that "wranglers" from the University of Cambridge (those with first-class degrees in the prestigious mathematics tripos, a synonym for fierce intelligence) could not understand the Bible "unless their hearts [were] right as well as their heads." Nor could the most accomplished students in linguistics and literature, because the "highest critical and grammatical knowledge will find it a sealed book without the teaching of the Holy Ghost."[33]

Since the whole of Scripture is profitable to the Christian, Ryle recommended that it be read in an orderly way, chapter by chapter and book by book. He mourned that many Bible readers "know nothing of the habit of reading through the whole sacred book habitually, omitting nothing,

---

[28] Ryle, *How Readest Thou?*, 41.
[29] Ryle, *St Matthew*, 26.
[30] Ryle, *St Mark*, 40.
[31] Ryle, *How Readest Thou?*, 41; Ryle, *Whose Word Is This?*, 38.
[32] J. C. Ryle, *Expository Thoughts on the Gospels, for Family and Private Use: St Luke*, vol. 2 (Ipswich, 1859), 516.
[33] Ryle, *Whose Word Is This?*, 38–39.

skipping nothing." Instead, they tended to read "only certain pet books or pet chapters, or something which suits their own particular spiritual experience."[34] Ryle warned especially against this widespread habit of "perpetual dipping and picking" in Bible reading. His own devotional rule, which he maintained throughout his life, was to begin both the Old and New Testaments together, read each straight through to the end, and then begin again.[35] Nevertheless, whatever the method, every Christian should resolve "to read the Bible more and more every year we live . . . to get it rooted in our memories, and engrafted into our hearts." Believers should open their Bibles eagerly, not "gaping, and yawning, and dozing" while they read, but like a London merchant hungrily studying the financial news in *The Times*, or like a wife reading a letter from her beloved husband in a distant country. Ryle reminded those who felt it did them no benefit that it was a means of grace designed by God for their growth in Christian maturity: "Settle it down in your mind as an established rule, that whether you feel it at the moment or not, you are inhaling spiritual health by reading the Bible, and insensibly becoming more strong."[36]

The Sabbath

Ryle included the "Sabbath"—that is, Sunday—among the "means of grace," a gift from God to promote spiritual health and growth in the Christian life. During the mid-1850s there was a crescendo in public debate concerning legal restrictions on Sunday trade and recreation, including whether trains should run, the post office should deliver, or military bands should play in parks on Sundays. In the summer of 1855 there were riots in Hyde Park against attempts to close public houses and shops on Sundays, and the political theorist Karl Marx (1818–1883), who joined the vast London crowd during the disturbance, believed he was witnessing the beginning of "the English revolution" of the workers against the monied classes.[37] The National Sunday League, founded in 1855 by anti-Sabbatarian radicals, called for better leisure opportunities for laborers by Sunday opening of recreational and educational spaces like the Crystal Palace, the National Gallery, and the British Museum. They were firmly

---
[34] J. C. Ryle, preface to Rudolf Stier, *The Words of the Angels: or, Their Visits to the Earth, and the Messages They Delivered in New Testament Times* (London, 1886), xi.
[35] Ryle, *How Readest Thou?*, 42–43.
[36] Ryle, *How Readest Thou?*, 45–46.
[37] Brian Harrison, "The Sunday Trading Riots of 1855," *Historical Journal* 8, no. 2 (1965): 219–45.

opposed by Christian campaigners like the Lord's Day Observance Society (founded 1831) and the National Lord's Day Rest Association (founded 1857). These disputes over labor and leisure ran hot in Parliament and the press.[38]

Ryle entered the fray with a tract of his own in 1856, entitled *Keep It Holy! A Tract on the Sabbath Day*, a practical exposition of the fourth commandment: "Remember the sabbath day, to keep it holy" (Ex. 20:8). Like the rest of the Decalogue, it was painted at the east end of Ryle's Helmingham church (alongside the Apostles' Creed and the Lord's Prayer) and was rehearsed at every Lord's Supper in the Book of Common Prayer, to which the congregation was taught to respond, "Lord, have mercy upon us, and incline our hearts to keep this law."[39] Ryle believed it to be an immensely important subject:

> It is not too much to say that the prosperity or decay of English Christianity depends on the maintenance of the Christian Sabbath. Break down the fence which now surrounds the Sunday, and our Sunday Schools will soon come to an end. Let in the flood of worldliness and dissipation on the Lord's Day without let or hindrance, and our congregations will soon dwindle away.

For Parliament to withdraw legal protections from "the Lord's Day" would "advance the kingdom of Satan in England," Ryle asserted. "It would be a joy to the infidel. But it would be an insult and offence to God," he added. "As a minister of Christ, a father of a family, and a lover of my country, I feel bound to plead in behalf of the old English Sunday."[40]

Ryle argued that the Sabbath is part of God's eternal law—established in creation, reaffirmed to Moses on Mount Sinai, and upheld by Jesus and the apostles. He dismissed the notion that it was simply part of Old Testament ritual, like animal sacrifice and circumcision, now surpassed by the New Testament. A church that failed to promote Sabbath observance was therefore not a scriptural church: "What saith the Scripture? This is the grand point after all. What railway directors and newspaper writers think matters nothing. We are not going to stand at their bar when we die. He

---

[38] John Wigley, *The Rise and Fall of the Victorian Sunday* (Manchester University Press, 1980); Martin Spence, "Writing the Sabbath: The Literature of the Nineteenth-Century Sunday Observance Debate," in *The Church and Literature*, ed. Peter Clarke and Charlotte Methuen (Boydell, 2012), 283–95.
[39] Communion (1662), in *The Book of Common Prayer: The Texts of 1549, 1559, and 1662*, ed. Brian Cummings (Oxford University Press, 2011), 390.
[40] J. C. Ryle, *Keep It Holy! A Tract on the Sabbath Day* (Ipswich, 1856), 4.

that judgeth us is the Lord God of the Bible. What saith the Lord?"[41] Ryle urged his Sabbatarian readers not to bow to the "ignorant clamour" of columnists in the Victorian press who were agitating for change, nor to heed the abusive epithets thrown at them, like "puritans" and "pharisees." "Fall back on that old book which has stood the test of eighteen hundred years," he repeated, "and of which every word is true. Take your stand on the Bible and hold fast its teaching."[42]

Ryle taught that Sunday should be dedicated to the pursuit of godliness. It was a day for "holy rest" and for "quiet, sober meditation on eternal things."[43] Time focused on God and the gospel should never be gloomy or wearisome, but was likely to be "the brightest, cheerfullest day of all the seven," he rejoiced. "It is not a yoke, but a blessing . . . not a burden, but a mercy."[44] One of the best ways to benefit from the Sabbath, Ryle suggested in an earlier sermon in 1845 to the young men of Helmingham parish, was always to attend gospel preaching and "let your place in church never be empty." "Sabbaths are a foretaste and fragment of heaven," he told them. "The man who finds them a burden, and not a privilege, may be sure that his heart stands in need of a mighty change."[45] Sabbath observance promotes Christian growth, Ryle insisted. Conversely, Sabbath neglect leads to diminution in the Christian life. Indeed, there was an easy flight of downward steps from "no Sabbath" to "no God."[46] He exhorted the young men of Helmingham:

> Once give over caring for the Sabbath, and in the end you will give over caring for your soul. . . . Begin with not honouring God's day, and you will soon not honour God's house—cease to honour God's house, and you will soon cease to honour God's book—cease to honour God's book, and bye and bye you will give God no honour at all.[47]

Likewise, in *Remember Lot* (1849), written at the height of Britain's early railway boom, Ryle warned his readers not to be tempted by the railway companies' offers of regular employment and good pay: "How will your

---

[41] Ryle, *Keep It Holy!*, 5–6.
[42] Ryle, *Keep It Holy!*, 24.
[43] Ryle, *Keep It Holy!*, 17, 26.
[44] Ryle, *Keep It Holy!*, 12, 19.
[45] J. C. Ryle, *Young Men Exhorted: A Sermon to Young Men, Preached in Helmingham Church*, rev. ed. (Ipswich, 1849), 63–64.
[46] Ryle, *Keep It Holy!*, 14.
[47] Ryle, *Young Men Exhorted*, 63.

soul fare, if you serve a railway company that runs Sunday trains? What day in the week will you have for God and eternity? . . . It will profit you nothing to fill your purse, if you bring leanness and poverty on your soul."[48] Sabbath rest was good for bodies and minds, but above all, it was good for souls.

On broader economic principles, Ryle also drew a causal link between regular rest, productivity, and material prosperity. He claimed that the two most prosperous nations in the world—Britain and the United States—were also the two keenest Sabbath-keeping nations. "Where shall we find on the globe so much energy, so much steadiness, so much success, so much public confidence, so much morality, and so much good government as in those two countries? . . . The grand secret of it all has been the observance of the Sabbath." Ryle calculated that over the previous half century, Britain and the United States had both sacrificed seven years of working days for the sake of Sunday, but had nevertheless grown in global dominance during that period. He reckoned that, even leaving religious considerations aside, it would be "an act of suicidal folly" for the nation to abandon the Sabbath.[49]

Ryle acknowledged that Sabbath observance had much improved since the eighteenth century, but nonetheless he diagnosed that there was still "a vast amount of Sabbath profanation which is every week crying against England in the ears of God."[50] He pointed, for example, to the shocking results of the 1851 Religious Census, which revealed that less than half the population attended a church of any sort on Sundays.[51] It was often "a day of worldliness, a day of ungodliness, a day of carnal mirth, and too often a day of sin." For many people, even professing Christians, Sunday was dedicated to "secular" pursuits—visiting friends, throwing dinner parties, going on journeys, studying account books, reading novels, and talking politics—"a day in short for anything rather than the things of God." Ryle especially decried the delivery of letters and newspapers on Sundays, which distracted their recipients from what they had heard in church. He was glad to report that in his own Helmingham parish there was no Sunday delivery, because the inhabitants had petitioned the postmaster general to stop it.[52]

---

[48] J. C. Ryle, *Remember Lot* (Ipswich, 1849), 14.
[49] Ryle, *Keep It Holy!*, 14–15.
[50] Ryle, *Keep It Holy!*, 20.
[51] K. D. M. Snell and Paul S. Ell, *Rival Jerusalems: The Geography of Victorian Religion* (Cambridge University Press, 2000).
[52] Ryle, *Keep It Holy!*, 21, 23.

In larger towns, shops continued to trade on Sundays, while others were tempted by "Sunday trains on railways, Sunday steamboats on the rivers, and excursions to tea gardens and places of public amusement." These Sabbath entertainments were "all wrong, decidedly wrong," Ryle chastised. Some advocates defended such pastimes as spiritually beneficial, but in Ryle's view they did nothing to promote Christian life, which was Sunday's fundamental purpose. With a series of forceful rhetorical questions, he illustrated his concerns: "What soul was ever converted by tearing down to Brighton or dashing down to Gravesend" (popular holiday resorts)? "What heart was ever softened or brought to repentance by gazing at Titians and Vandykes" in the National Gallery? "What sinner was ever led to Christ" by viewing the impressive winged-bull sculptures (Assyrian *lamassu*) recently unearthed in Mesopotamia by Austen Henry Layard and displayed at the British Museum, or by visiting the Pompeian Court at the Crystal Palace, a full-scale recreation of a Pompeii villa?[53] In the reprint of *Keep It Holy!* in his compilation volume *Knots Untied*, Ryle added, "What worldly man was ever turned to God by listening to polkas, waltzes, or opera music?"[54] He answered his own questions: "No! indeed! all experience teaches that it needs something more than the beauties of art and nature to teach man the way to heaven." As evidence, he pointed to the example of Continental Europe, where Ryle claimed that no moral or spiritual benefit had been achieved by the Sunday opening of art galleries in Italy and Germany, or of the gardens at the Palace of Versailles with its statues and fountains. "What advantages have we to gain by making a London Sunday like a Sunday at Paris, or Vienna, or Rome? . . . It would be a change for the worse not for the better."[55]

Furthermore, Sabbath entertainment for some required Sabbath toil by others, which thus inflicted "a cruel injury on the souls of multitudes of people." Sunday excursions by railway train or steamboat necessitated the employment of large numbers of people—"clerks, porters, ticket-takers, policemen, guards, engine drivers, stokers, omnibus drivers." Likewise, the Sunday opening of exhibitions and art galleries required attendants to serve the visitors. "And have not all these unfortunate persons immortal souls? . . . Their life becomes a long unbroken chain of

---

[53] Ryle, *Keep It Holy!*, 22.
[54] J. C. Ryle, "The Sabbath," in *Knots Untied: Being Plain Statements on Disputed Points in Religion, from the Standpoint of an Evangelical Churchman* (London, 1874), 381.
[55] Ryle, *Keep It Holy!*, 22–23.

work, work, unceasing work. In short, what is play to others becomes death to them."[56] Appealing to the working classes directly, Ryle warned that they had the most to lose. If Sunday became a day of amusement, it would soon be turned into a day of labor. Shop owners, farmers, and factory managers, with a concern for profit, would begin to insist that their operations continued around the clock, seven days a week instead of the usual six. But the Sabbath, Ryle declared, was the working man's "best friend." As a practical innovation, he recommended that employees agitate instead for a half-day holiday on Saturdays (as pioneered by some Christian businesses in the 1850s, like the large London brewery Hanbury, Buxton & Co.), to spend on entertainment, rather than eroding the Christian Sunday.[57]

Despite these heartfelt appeals, Ryle concluded that political campaigning was not the right way to promote the nation's Christian life. It was insufficient merely to flood the House of Commons with petitions against Sunday trading, or to establish societies to defend the Lord's Day. Acts of Parliament could not create Christian disciples. Instead, a deliberate campaign of evangelism was needed to reach working people in populous towns and cities like London, Manchester, Liverpool, and Glasgow, where Sabbath breaking was rife. He recommended dividing every parish into a manageable unit of no more than three thousand inhabitants, and supplying each district with a gospel minister and two Christian lay workers, even if it meant disrupting the Church of England's usual regulations: "We must not wait to build a fine church. We must send a man who is able to preach anywhere—in a garret, a coach-house, an alley, or even in the street—and give him abundant liberty to work, unfettered by precedent and routine."[58] Sunday, in Ryle's theology, was not a Victorian cultural relic but a God-given means of grace. Sunday observance was a way to promote Christian life and growth, but that spiritual life always began with gospel proclamation and conversion to Christ.

Public Worship

In his *Expository Thoughts*, Ryle observed how much Saint Thomas missed out by being absent from the apostolic assembly when Jesus appeared to

---

[56] Ryle, *Keep It Holy!*, 23.
[57] Ryle, *Keep It Holy!*, 27–28.
[58] Ryle, *Keep It Holy!*, 30.

them on Easter Day (John 20:24). Ryle took this as a lesson "never to be absent from God's house on Sundays, without good reason—never to miss the Lord's Supper when administered in our congregation—never to let our place be empty when means of grace are going on." Regular participation in public worship is one of the chief ways to become "a growing and prosperous Christian."[59] Ryle focused on this idea in his tract for New Year 1868, entitled *How Do You Worship?* He asked:

> Where is it that sleeping souls are generally awakened, dark souls enlightened, dead souls quickened, doubting souls brought to decision, mourning souls cheered, heavy-laden souls relieved? Where, as a general rule, but in the public assembly of Christian worshippers, and during the preaching of God's Word? ... Next to the Word of God there is nothing which does so much good to mankind as public worship.[60]

True worship, Ryle taught, must be God-focused, scriptural, intelligent, heartfelt, and reverent. He rebuked those who would "call themselves Christians and go to churches and chapels to stare about, whisper, fidget, yawn, or sleep, but not to pray, or praise, or listen. ... To behave before God as they would not dare to behave before a king, is a very grave offence indeed."[61] In Ryle's view, the essential components of public worship are the reading and preaching of Scripture, prayer, praise, and regular use of the two sacraments. He favored liturgy and reckoned the Book of Common Prayer to be "an admirable and matchless manual of public devotion." Public praise must be congregational, not deputized to a choir. "Praise has been truly called the flower of all devotion. It is the only part of our worship which will never die. Preaching and praying and reading shall one day be no longer needed. But praise shall go on for ever." Baptism and Holy Communion should be continually offered to the congregation because they were "ordained by Christ Himself as means of grace."[62]

However, Ryle also discerned three dangers that were multiplying in Victorian public worship in the 1860s. First, "sacramentalism" gave such excessive attention to baptism and Holy Communion that everything else was buried, and the proper proportions of worship were "completely

---

[59] J. C. Ryle, *Expository Thoughts on the Gospels, for Family and Private Use: St John*, vol. 3 (London, 1873), 454.
[60] J. C. Ryle, *How Do You Worship? A Question for 1868* (London, 1868), 7–8.
[61] Ryle, *How Do You Worship?*, 13–14.
[62] Ryle, *How Do You Worship?*, 19–21.

destroyed." "The honour done to the font and the Lord's table, meet you at every turn. All else, in comparison, is jostled out of its place, overshadowed, dwarfed, and driven into a corner." Second, "ceremonialism," with its "gaudy dressing," gorgeous ornaments, and theatrical rituals, undermined the simplicity of New Testament worship. Ryle observed that sinful humanity preferred the visible to the spiritual, but outward ceremonies were useless without "inward grace." Third, "sacrificialism" turned Christian ministers into "sacrificing priests" and mediators between God and humanity, rather than their proper role as pastors and teachers. Ryle warned that these three prevalent errors were unbiblical and would stunt Christian growth. He therefore urged his readers to flee from them: "Let everyone that loves his soul come out from such worship and be separate. Let him avoid it and turn away from it, as he would from poison."[63]

In an earlier tract, *What Is the Church?* (1852), Ryle observed that separating from a local congregation is a very serious step, but sometimes necessary.[64] He urged his readers to be careful about the place of worship they regularly attended and the preaching they regularly heard: "Beware of deliberately settling down under any ministry which is positively unsound. . . . To hear unscriptural teaching fifty-two days in every year is a serious thing. It is a continual dropping of slow poison into the mind." Ryle despaired that in many English parishes the teaching was little better than "popery," more aligned to Rome than to the Reformation, or than "morality," like the philosophical theories of Plato or Seneca, but devoid of Christ. In those circumstances, the congregation should not be content to "sit still" and "take it quietly." For the sake of their spiritual health, they should find biblical worship elsewhere.[65]

The proper test of public worship, Ryle argued, is not the emotions it stirs up in worshipers—"religious feelings are very deceitful things," often mere "animal excitement," stimulated by music or spectacle, with no lasting effect. The proper test is the practical impact worship makes upon Christian life and growth. "The best public worship is that which produces the best private Christianity." False worship is spiritually deadening, but "true spiritual worship, like wholesome food, will strengthen him who uses it, and make him grow inwardly every year. . . . It will annually give

---
[63] Ryle, *How Do You Worship?*, 23–24, 26.
[64] J. C. Ryle, *What Is the Church? A Question for the Times* (Ipswich, 1852), 31–32.
[65] J. C. Ryle, *St Peter at Antioch: A Tract for the Times* (Ipswich, 1856), 16–18.

bone and sinew and muscle and firmness to his religion." True worship is a means of grace, promoting growth in holiness and Christian maturity. In particular, Ryle emphasized, it draws Christians into closer communion with Jesus Christ, making them "hunger and thirst after a sight of the King. . . . The true worshipper will turn instinctively to Christ by simple faith, just as the compass-needle turns to the pole."[66]

---

[66] Ryle, *How Do You Worship?*, 26–29.

CHAPTER 9

PREACHING

Throughout his nearly six decades of public ministry as parish clergyman and diocesan bishop, Ryle was first and foremost a preacher. Many of his tracts began as sermons and retain his pithy, urgent, dramatic style of delivery, which forced congregations (and then millions of readers) to sit up and take notice. Proclamation of the gospel was his greatest joy and his life's work. It was motivated by theological conviction that the word of God has divine power to transform lives, the means by which the Holy Spirit revives and strengthens the church.

As a young man, aged twenty-six, at his ordination to the presbyterate in December 1842 at Farnham Castle, Ryle and his fellow ordinands were exhorted by the bishop of Winchester, in the words of the Book of Common Prayer ordination liturgy, to remember "into how high a dignity, and to how weighty an office and charge ye are called: That is to say, to be messengers, watchmen, and stewards of the Lord." The presbyter's role was to teach the Scriptures as a pastor and evangelist, "to feed and provide for the Lord's family; to seek for Christ's sheep that are dispersed abroad . . . that they may be saved through Christ forever." As the symbol of his new office, Ryle was presented with a Bible and instructed by the bishop, "Take thou authority to preach the Word of God."[1] This was a divine commission he took extremely seriously.

---

[1] Ordinal (1662), in *The Book of Common Prayer: The Texts of 1549, 1559, and 1662*, ed. Brian Cummings (Oxford University Press, 2011), 635–36, 642.

Before his conversion, Ryle had experienced the spiritual detriment of sitting under poor preaching. In his autobiography, he recalled that there had been "no ministry of the gospel" at the two churches his family attended in Macclesfield in the 1820s: "The clergymen were wretched high and dry sticks of the old school, and their preaching was not calculated to do good to anybody. I can truly say that I passed through childhood and boyhood without ever hearing a single sermon likely to do good to my soul."[2] You could sleep as comfortably under their preaching "as you might in your own armchairs, with nothing to wake you up."[3] Likewise, he reckoned the sermons he heard as a pupil at Eton College were "a perfect farce," "a disgrace," and "beneath contempt." It was no better at Oxford, where the sermons he was required to attend as an undergraduate were "exceedingly dry, and lifeless."[4] Therefore, when Ryle himself became a clergyman, he was determined to pioneer a different approach, with lively biblical preaching at its heart. His influential tract ministry had its roots in his pulpit ministry.

The Priority of Preaching

Ryle's tract *What Is Wanted?* (1854) offered an analysis of the Church of England's numerous weaknesses and the corresponding remedies. He warned that many clergy were so absorbed in running their parishes, supervising the schools, and visiting the sick that they neglected preaching, which should have been their chief priority:

> No pastoral labour will ever compensate for inadequate pulpit preparation. A minister's sermons should be incomparably the first thing in his thoughts. He is not ordained to be a schoolmaster, a relieving officer, or a doctor, but to preach the Word; and if he neglects his sermons under the excuse of other work, he has no right to expect God's blessing.

Many preachers, he observed, were stuck in a rut with a narrow range of topics, working "round and round upon them like a horse in a mill" (one of Ryle's favorite agricultural images), rather than preaching the whole

---
[2] *Bishop J. C. Ryle's Autobiography: The Early Years*, ed. Andrew Atherstone (Banner of Truth, 2016), 62–63.
[3] *Abstract of Report and Speeches at the Forty-Fifth Annual Meeting of the Church Pastoral-Aid Society* (May 6, 1880), 8.
[4] *J. C. Ryle's Autobiography*, 35, 66.

counsel of God. Furthermore, their style of delivery left a great deal to be desired: "We are neither plain enough, nor direct enough, nor bold enough, nor discriminating enough. Our sermons are too like essays, flat, pointless, tame, and wearying—unawakening to sinners, and unedifying to saints—blunt swords, and headless arrows." Probably no Protestant ministers in the world, Ryle claimed, were so badly trained in preaching as the clergy of the Church of England—indeed the vast majority had never been trained at all.[5] These were repeated themes in many of his exhortations on preaching.

In Ryle's reading of church history, he noticed that the spiritual high points of the sixteenth-century Reformation and the eighteenth-century Evangelical Revival were both marked by a revival of biblical preaching. Conversely, at the periods when spiritual life was at its lowest ebb, there was a corresponding decline in preaching. Ryle saw a causal link between the two. Lecturing to the London branch of the Church of England Young Men's Society for Aiding Missions at Home and Abroad in February 1853 on the significance of Bishop Hugh Latimer (ca. 1485–1555), he portrayed English medieval religion on the eve of the Reformation as "a period of utter spiritual darkness." The Roman Catholic priests were "profoundly ignorant"; they might have been able to read their breviaries but "knew nothing whatever of the Bible. . . . Preaching there was scarcely any, and what there was, was grossly unscriptural and unedifying." The English people were also, inevitably, "utterly ignorant of true religion. . . . They had neither sound preaching to hear, nor Bibles to read. . . . Thus the blind led the blind, and all wallowed in the ditch together."[6] Similarly, lecturing in 1868 on the martyrdom of Bishop John Hooper (ca. 1495–1555), Ryle declared that before the Reformation, for lack of gospel preaching, there was "a conspicuous absence of all knowledge of true Christianity," and "gross darkness overspread the land."[7]

That parlous situation was redeemed only when the Reformers began to preach Christ, Ryle explained. He agreed with the Reformers, as a matter of theological conviction, that proclamation of the gospel is the means ordained by God to bring spiritual conviction and conversion. He quoted

---

[5] J. C. Ryle, *What Is Wanted? Being Thoughts and Suggestions on Some of the Chief Wants of the Church of England in the Present Day* (Ipswich, 1854), 28–30.
[6] J. C. Ryle, "Bishop Latimer," in *Lectures Delivered Before the Church of England Young Men's Society for Aiding Missions at Home and Abroad, at Freemason's Hall, January and February 1853* (London, 1853), 158, 160.
[7] J. C. Ryle, *John Hooper (Bishop and Martyr): His Times, Life, Death, and Opinions* (London, 1868), 7–8.

approvingly from Latimer's writings: preaching is "the office of salvation, and the office of regeneration"; "take away preaching, and take away salvation"; "this office of preaching is the only ordinary way that God hath appointed to save us all. Let us maintain this, for I know none other."[8] If this was true in the sixteenth century, Ryle believed, it was true in the nineteenth century also. If the Victorian church was to be reformed and revived, the catalyst would be the pulpit. He acknowledged that Latimer's sermons would "not suit modern taste," but he complained that Victorian Christians were very poor judges of good preaching. A typical modern sermon, Ryle chided, was "too often a dull, tame, pointless, religious essay, full of measured round sentences, Johnsonian English, bald platitudes, timid statements, and elaborately concocted milk and water." Latimer's sermons offered "sound Gospel doctrine" combined with "plain Saxon language, boldness, liveliness, directness, and simplicity."[9]

When Ryle surveyed the history of the seventeenth and eighteenth centuries, he noticed the same pattern. Lecturing on the Puritan Richard Baxter (1615–1691) to the Young Men's Christian Association at London's Exeter Hall in 1853, he outlined how the high church revival under Archbishop William Laud (1573–1645) had undermined the Reformation. Evangelical doctrine was despised, Calvinistic bishops were snubbed, Arminian bishops were promoted, the Sabbath was neglected, and Communion tables were railed and "profanely called altars." But the telltale sign of theological declension was the pulpit: "Preaching and lecturing were depreciated, and forms and ceremonies were exalted."[10] By the early eighteenth century the situation was even worse, Ryle asserted in *The Christian Leaders of the Last Century*. His portrayal of pre-revival times was dire: "cold morality," "barren orthodoxy," and sermons that were "little better than miserable moral essays, utterly devoid of anything likely to awaken, convert, or save souls."[11] The parochial clergy were "sunk in worldliness," illustrated again by the decline in preaching. "They hunted, they shot, they farmed, they swore, they drank, they gambled. They seemed determined to know everything except Jesus Christ and him crucified." Their sermons were "so unspeakably and indescribably bad," Ryle lambasted, that their congregations deserted the church. As for theological literature, "inquire at any old

---
[8] Ryle, "Bishop Latimer," 196.
[9] Ryle, "Bishop Latimer," 186.
[10] J. C. Ryle, "Baxter and His Times," in *Lectures Delivered Before the Young Men's Christian Association in Exeter Hall, from November 1852 to February 1853* (London, 1853), 366.
[11] J. C. Ryle, *The Christian Leaders of the Last Century; or, England a Hundred Years Ago* (London, 1869), 14.

bookseller's shop, and you will find there is no theology so unsaleable" as Hanoverian sermons.[12]

But according to Ryle's historical schema in *Christian Leaders*, the method by which the church was revived through the ministry of men like George Whitefield and John Wesley was "the old apostolic weapon of *preaching*." The evangelicals preached everywhere—in parish pulpits, barns, fields, village greens, and market places, standing on tables, benches, or horse blocks, wherever a crowd could be gathered. They preached simply, "not ashamed to crucify their style, and to sacrifice their reputation for learning" in order to be understood. They preached fervently and directly, believing that "you must speak *from* the heart if you wish to speak *to* the heart." And their sermons were "eminently doctrinal, positive, dogmatical, and distinct," full of the gospel and full of Jesus Christ.[13] All Ryle's individual vignettes in *Christian Leaders* focused on their preaching ministries, often with a detailed analysis of their sermons. Whitefield, for example, was celebrated as "the greatest preacher of the gospel England has ever seen." His sermons were said to be packed with gospel truth—remarkably lucid, bold, and earnest—and delivered with immense pathos and feeling.[14] Likewise, the Methodist leader John Fletcher (1729–1785), during his ministry at Madeley in Shropshire, was "always doing one and the same thing—always preaching, always teaching, always trying to awaken sinners, always trying to build up saints."[15]

Many Victorian clergy had succumbed to the wrong set of priorities, Ryle warned, distracted from their central obligation to proclaim the gospel. A busy ministry was not necessarily a fruitful ministry. In "Real Church Work" (1884), he observed that large numbers of clergy were investing their time and energies in church ceremonies, social reforms (like temperance and improved housing for the working classes), secular lectures, entertainments, guilds, and societies, and congratulating themselves: "What a great deal of Church-work there is in these days!" But amid the "incessant bustle and stir about matters of entirely secondary importance," many churches neglected the priority of evangelism and preaching to which the apostles had dedicated themselves. "It is quite certain," Ryle noted, "that musical

---
[12] Ryle, *Christian Leaders*, 17–18. For more recent analysis, see Jeffrey S. Chamberlain, "Parish Preaching in the Long Eighteenth Century," and Nigel Aston, "Rationalism, the Enlightenment, and Sermons," in *The Oxford Handbook of the British Sermon*, ed. Keith A. Francis and William Gibson (Oxford University Press, 2012), 47–62, 390–405.
[13] Ryle, *Christian Leaders*, 23–26.
[14] Ryle, *Christian Leaders*, 31, 50–56.
[15] Ryle, *Christian Leaders*, 408.

services, and church decoration, and concerts, and penny readings, and bazaars, and improved cookery, and the like, will not save souls."[16]

Yet Ryle's censures were not merely aimed at social reformers or Anglo-Catholics. He acknowledged that in the Victorian age there was a "vast quantity of religious machinery" created by evangelical networks—city missions, evangelical societies, annual conferences, numerous committees. Every well-oiled evangelical parish invested in them, alongside the regular round of classes for young men, groups for mothers, day schools for children, Sunday school outings, and so forth. The very success of the evangelical movement had given rise to a national and parochial infrastructure unimaginable to those in revival times like Henry Venn, who had arrived in 1759 as vicar of Huddersfield in Yorkshire with "nothing but his Bible, and his Master at his side." Therefore, Ryle explained, Venn was "forced to be pre-eminently a man of one thing, and a soldier with one weapon, a perpetual preacher of God's Word." In contrast, modern evangelicals had "lost sight of apostolic simplicity in our ministerial work.... It is hard to have many irons in the fire at once, and to keep them all hot. It is quite possible to make an idol of parochial machinery, and for the sake of it to slight the pulpit."[17]

This call to prioritize preaching was reiterated in Ryle's sermon to the Church Pastoral Aid Society (CPAS), founded in 1836, one of the many "home mission" agencies established by evangelicals in the nineteenth century.[18] In parallel with organizations like the Church Missionary Society, which sent missionaries to far-flung parts of the globe like Africa and India, the CPAS aimed to multiply gospel ministry closer to home among the many unreached people in England, principally by raising funds for missionary workers in local parishes. In May 1882, Ryle preached the CPAS annual sermon, taking as his text a question from the apostle Paul, "If the trumpet give an uncertain sound, who shall prepare himself to the battle?" (1 Cor. 14:8). His central application was the absolute priority of the preaching ministry as the God-ordained means "to arouse, to awaken, and to stir careless souls." Ryle feared that some Anglicans were seeking to exalt the priestly office (turning the clock back to the days of medieval Romanism

---

[16] J. C. Ryle, "Real Church Work," in *Principles for Churchmen: A Manual of Positive Statements on Doubtful or Disputed Points* (London, 1884), 282–83.
[17] Ryle, *Christian Leaders*, 269–70.
[18] On "home mission," see Martin Spence, "Evangelicals and Mission in the Atlantic North," in *The Routledge Research Companion to the History of Evangelicalism*, ed. Andrew Atherstone and David Ceri Jones (Routledge, 2018), 146–61.

or high church Laudianism), but he insisted that "the first, foremost, and principal work of the minister is to be a preacher of God's Word," and "in no sense is he a sacrificing priest."[19] The bishop lamented that too many ministers were obsessed by liturgical duties, exalting the Communion table so extravagantly that it overshadowed the pulpit, and neglecting their preparations for preaching. Too many congregations therefore had to endure "short, shallow, hastily-composed sermons, devoid alike of matter, power, fire, or effectiveness." The Lord's Supper, Ryle suggested, is mentioned in, at most, five books in the New Testament, whereas almost every page testifies to the value of preaching, the "chief instrument" used by the Holy Spirit to awaken sinners and establish saints. He agreed with the saying of old Hugh Latimer that "it is one of Satan's great aims to exalt ceremonies and put down preaching." "A contempt for sermons," Ryle warned, "is a pretty sure mark of a decline in spiritual religion." This was one of the chief lessons he took from church history, as he emphasized in a rousing peroration: "Do not forsake the old paths. Let nothing tempt you to believe that multiplication of forms and ceremonies, constant reading of liturgical services, or frequent communions, will ever do so much good to souls as the powerful, fiery, fervent preaching of God's Word." Ministers must therefore "blow the trumpet of the everlasting Gospel loud and long."[20]

Simplicity in Preaching

As a novice preacher in the 1840s without any homiletical training, Ryle made many mistakes. At first, he modeled himself on "the evangelical Chrysostom," Henry Melvill (1798–1871), who was famous among university congregations. But as curate of Exbury in Hampshire's New Forest, a tiny rural chapel, Ryle quickly discovered that his intellectual preaching was "miles over the heads" of the local farmers and their wives. Therefore, as he put it epigrammatically, "I crucified my style, and became plain John Ryle."[21] This was his lifelong motto. He sacrificed the classic rules of rhetoric and sermon composition in order to drive home the gospel message with clarity and simplicity.

To remedy the lack of training for preachers, a group of London clergymen in March 1874 launched the Church Homiletical Society, with the

---

[19] J. C. Ryle, *Soldiers and Trumpeters: A Word for the Times* (London, 1883), 12, 14.
[20] Ryle, *Soldiers and Trumpeters*, 16–19.
[21] Quoted in H. E. Fox, letter to the editor, *The Record*, November 16, 1916, 906.

backing of the archbishop of Canterbury. It aimed to deliver monthly lectures on preaching by senior ministers with significant pulpit experience, to establish regional preaching classes, to connect junior preachers with mentors for individual tuition, and to offer criticism of draft sermons submitted by post.[22] The society's journal, *The Clergyman's Magazine*, disseminated wisdom on preaching to parishes nationwide as well as to the mission field and North America. Ryle delivered the lecture in March 1876, in the Trophy Room at St Paul's Cathedral, and chose as his title "Simplicity in Preaching."[23] By then he had been preaching for thirty-four years to agricultural laborers in Hampshire and Suffolk, so he knew from personal experience the "enormous difficulty" of communicating the gospel in that context. He reckoned it easier in many ways to preach before undergraduates and professors at the Universities of Oxford and Cambridge, or barristers at the Temple Church and Lincoln's Inn, or members of Parliament, than before "an agricultural congregation on a fine hot afternoon in the month of August." According to one laborer, Sunday was the most enjoyable day of the week: "I sit comfortably in church, put up my legs, have nothing to think about, and just go to sleep."[24] Simplicity was essential if the preacher wanted to be understood.

Ryle offered five practical hints for simple sermons. First, the preacher must know clearly what he wants to communicate from the Bible text. If he is "in a fog," his congregation will be also. He must beware of obscure prophecies or fanciful subjects, and the temptation to preach continually on the seals, vials, and trumpets of the book of Revelation, or the hidden symbolism of Ezekiel's temple vision.[25] The preacher must handle texts straightforwardly, never "dragging out of them meanings which the Holy Ghost never intended to put into them."

> The sermon may seem very glittering and ingenious, and his people may go away saying, "What a clever parson we have got!" But if, on examination, they can neither find the sermon in the text, nor the text in the sermon, their minds are perplexed, and they begin to think the Bible is a deep book which cannot be understood.[26]

---

[22] Henry Lansdell, "The Church Homiletical Society," *Clergyman's Magazine* 2 (April 1876): 200–207.
[23] J. C. Ryle, *Simplicity in Preaching: A Few Short Hints on a Great Subject* (London, 1882); first published as "Simplicity in Preaching," *Clergyman's Magazine* 2 (April 1876): 240–54.
[24] Ryle, *Simplicity in Preaching*, 6–7.
[25] Ryle, *Simplicity in Preaching*, 13–15.
[26] Ryle, *Simplicity in Preaching*, 16.

Ryle always arranged his sermons (and the tracts that sprang from them) under subheadings, usually three in number, to help his congregation understand and remember. These divisions acted like "hooks and pegs and shelves in the mind," and he recommended C. H. Spurgeon's preaching in this regard as a model of simplicity. Preachers cannot be understood if their ideas are jumbled:

> What wise general would mix up artillery, infantry, and cavalry in one confused mass in the day of battle? What giver of a banquet or dinner would dream of putting on the table the whole of the viands at once, the soup, the fish, the entrées, the joints, the salads, the game, the sweets, the dessert, in one huge dish?

Simple sermons need a clear order and organization, so that the ideas follow one another "in beautiful regularity, like regiments marching past before the Queen on a review day in Windsor Park."[27]

Second, preachers should avoid "dictionary" words—words that are "abstract, or scientific, or pedantic, or complicated, or indefinite, or very long. They may seem very fine and sound very grand, but they are rarely of any use. The most powerful and forcible words, as a rule, are very short." That did not necessarily mean only using Saxon words of one syllable, but the preacher's language must be plain common English. Third, preachers should avoid complicated sentences and long paragraphs, because a sermon is not a book: "Beware of colons and semi-colons. Stick to commas and full stops, and take care to write as if you were asthmatical or short of breath."[28] Fourth, preachers should "get into the habit of talking plainly to the people," using direct speech personally applied: "I" and "you," not the vague, innocuous "we."[29] Fifth, preachers should use plenty of anecdotes and illustrations, like Jesus did in his parables. Ryle was sometimes known to take out his pocket watch in his Stradbroke pulpit to illustrate the glorious handiwork of the Creator, or to jangle a bunch of keys to emphasize that keys are needed only because human beings are deceitful.[30] Illustration should be kept within sensible limits, he advised. Preachers should not bake a "cake made almost entirely

---
[27] Ryle, *Simplicity in Preaching*, 19–21.
[28] Ryle, *Simplicity in Preaching*, 22–27.
[29] Ryle, *Simplicity in Preaching*, 30–33.
[30] Ryle, *Simplicity in Preaching*, 36–37.

of plums and containing hardly any flour. . . . Do not put on colour by spoonfuls, but with a brush."[31]

Ryle underlined that simplicity is no easy matter. It costs the preacher "pains and trouble" in diligent preparation and careful thought.[32] Lively delivery is also essential. It is no good to "bury your head in your bosom, and mumble over your manuscript in a dull, monotonous, droning way, like a bee in a bottle." But at the same time, there is no point in merely "letting off fireworks" in the pulpit: "'Beautiful' sermons, 'brilliant' sermons, 'clever' sermons, 'popular' sermons, are often sermons which have no effect on the congregation, and do not draw men to Jesus Christ." Of course, he concluded, preaching with simplicity is a waste of time "unless you preach the simple Gospel of Jesus Christ": "If Christ crucified has not His rightful place in your sermons, and sin is not exposed as it should be, and your people are not told plainly what they ought to be and do, YOUR PREACHING IS OF NO USE."[33]

Ryle drew out the same broad lesson from his heroes in Christian ministry. His introduction to the sermons of the famous Ipswich Puritan Samuel Ward (1577–1640) emphasized that his preaching was "always eminently simple." Ward was "not afraid to use familiar language such as all could understand—framing his sentences in such a way that an ignorant man could easily follow him—bold, direct, fiery, dramatic, and speaking as if he feared none but God."[34] The same was true of the giants of the Evangelical Revival, Ryle argued in *Christian Leaders*, a volume in which his own autobiography as a preacher was frequently echoed in the narrative of his heroes. For example, William Grimshaw (1708–1763), who led the revival at Haworth in Yorkshire, was "eminently a plain preacher. His first aim undoubtedly was to preach the whole truth as it is in Jesus; his second was to preach so as to be understood." Therefore, Grimshaw was willing "to crucify his natural taste" as a Cambridge-educated clergyman, even to be "thought a fool by intellectual men," provided he succeeded in "reaching the hearts and consciences of his hearers."[35] Likewise, John Berridge frequently preached to uneducated rural congregations in a style that might sound "coarse and vulgar and unrefined" to a university audience, but his "grand aim was to make his hearers understand."[36] Ryle celebrated the "extraordinary power"

---

[31] Ryle, *Simplicity in Preaching*, 39–40.
[32] Ryle, *Simplicity in Preaching*, 41.
[33] Ryle, *Simplicity in Preaching*, 46–47.
[34] J. C. Ryle, "Memoir of Samuel Ward," in *Sermons and Treatises by Samuel Ward* (Edinburgh, 1862), xv.
[35] Ryle, *Christian Leaders*, 115–16.
[36] Ryle, *Christian Leaders*, 238.

of Daniel Rowlands's preaching in Wales. Those sermons, often preached to thousands in the open air, were full of Jesus Christ, deep in Puritan theology, vividly expressed, and highly practical.[37] But they were also simple.

> The vast majority of sermon-hearers do not want fine words, close reasoning, deep philosophy, metaphysical abstractions, nice distinctions, elaborate composition, profound learning. They delight in plain language, simple ideas, forcible illustrations, direct appeals to heart and conscience, short sentences, fervent, loving earnestness of manner. He who possesses such qualifications will seldom preach to empty benches.[38]

James Hervey (1714–1758) had a very different ministry, chiefly as an author and apologist seeking to commend the gospel to polite eighteenth-century intellectuals. His most famous work, *Theron and Aspasio* (1755), taught the imputation of Christ's righteousness to sinners by means of dense and convoluted dialogues between his two central characters, full of literary and philosophical quotations. Ryle complained that Hervey wrote "in such a florid, high flown, luxuriant, bombastic, stilted fashion, that he almost takes your breath away. . . . The reader stands dumbfounded, and hardly knows whether he ought to laugh or to cry." Yet even Hervey appreciated that preachers must be easily and immediately understood, so his sermons were strikingly different from his treatises. In his Northamptonshire pulpit he was "eminently simple, perspicuous, pointed, and direct. . . . He deliberately left behind his flowers and feathers, his paint and his gilding, his fine words and long sentences, his classical allusions and elaborate arguments." Despite all his learning, Hervey's preaching was "plain enough to suit the humblest intellect."[39] These evangelical leaders, who left such a mark upon English Christianity in the days of the revival, were held up by Ryle in the 1860s as an excellent model for contemporary preachers.

Urgency in Preaching

Preachers must proclaim Christ not only with simplicity but also with passionate urgency, Ryle insisted. In a series of letters to *The Record* newspaper in 1869 on ways the church needed reformation, he again assailed the appalling standard of preaching in many Anglican pulpits. "How far a

---
[37] Ryle, *Christian Leaders*, 195–201.
[38] Ryle, *Christian Leaders*, 197.
[39] Ryle, *Christian Leaders*, 342, 347, 350.

man may travel before he hears a really striking sermon! How few clergymen command the attention of their congregation! How many forget that 'foolishness of preaching' is not foolish preaching!" He attacked the "stupid notion" being circulated among Victorian clergy that modern parishioners wanted ceremonial, not preaching, as a "mass of delusion" and a lame excuse for laziness in their sermon preparation.[40] Of course, evangelicals could be equally lazy, relying on the outward trappings of orthodoxy, he admitted. In August 1876 Ryle was heavily criticized in *The Rock* (an Anglican evangelical newspaper) for preaching at a church in Keswick wearing a surplice rather than the traditional preaching gown. In self-defense, Ryle robustly asserted, "If I were a hearer, I would far rather listen to a lively, searching, ringing Gospel sermon from a man in a surplice than to a dull, dreary, mumbling stupid homily from a man in a black gown."[41]

During the London Mission Week in February 1874, he emphasized the need for parish clergy to learn from the example of missioners in their style of preaching. Hundreds of London churches combined to organize evangelistic events across the capital, with special services for school children, hotel servants, cab drivers, police officers, soldiers, laborers, prostitutes, and many more. Evangelistic preaching went hand in hand with extensive house-to-house visiting across the metropolis.[42] Ryle hoped the London Mission Week would provoke the clergy to emulate these evangelists and thus result in "a thorough revival of the English pulpit," and a permanent forsaking of the "orthodox prosiness" and "dreary commonplaces" that characterized "the modern parson's sermon." He asked pointedly:

> Why, in the name of common-sense, should lively, fine, animated, rousing, stirring, interesting, heart-searching, conscience-pricking, mind-arresting, thought-suggesting, burning sermons, be confined to only one week in this year? Why should we not try to have them every Sunday in the year?

"It is my firm belief," Ryle proclaimed, "that if five out of six of our Church clergy would burn all their sermons tomorrow, and resolve to preach in a new style, it would be an immense blessing to the Church of England."[43]

---

[40] J. C. Ryle, letter to the editor, *The Record*, November 25, 1869.
[41] J. C. Ryle, letter to the editor, *The Rock*, August 1876.
[42] *The Standard*, January 14, 1874.
[43] J. C. Ryle, letter to the editor, *The Record*, February 17, 1874.

This call for ministers to burn their dull sermons was voiced again at the Church Congress held at Derby in October 1882, where Ryle gave a keynote address on evangelism, published in expanded form as *Can They Be Brought In?* (1883).[44] A recent survey of church attendance in the fifteen poorest parishes in Liverpool had shown that (leaving aside the Roman Catholic and Nonconformist populations) the Anglican diocese was reaching less than 7 percent of its urban mission field. The same picture was apparent in most other large English cities.[45] Ryle proposed some practical remedies to help the church reach these masses of people with the Christian message. First, they must multiply the number of gospel workers (lay and ordained) "whose chief weapon is the written word of God, the Bible," men and women willing to evangelize the lost "from street to street, and lane to lane, and alley to alley, and house to house, and room to room, and garret to garret, and cellar to cellar." They must not be like the clergyman who "never feels at ease unless he has a Prayer-book in his hand and a surplice on his back." They had to be evangelists with the gospel always on their lips, "full of zeal and love to souls."[46] Second, they must shake up the parochial system, with its rigid geographical boundaries, so that no one lived beyond the sound of the gospel in a parish ruled by an indolent or heretical incumbent. Third, Ryle insisted, the church needed "a great deal more direct lively preaching of the Gospel."[47] How did Whitefield attract such large crowds in the eighteenth century, or the American evangelist D. L. Moody (1837–1899) on his missions to Britain in 1873–1875? By proclaiming Christ with "fiery liveliness and directness of style."[48]

To the very end of his ministry, Ryle continued to agitate for a revival in the pulpit. Though he resigned his Liverpool bishopric in March 1900, at age eighty-three, passion for the public proclamation of the word of God continued to shape his vision. His final exhortation to his clergy, in his farewell letter after twenty years as their chief pastor, urged them again never to neglect their preaching and never to forget "that a lively, Christ-exalting minister will always have a Church-going people."[49] Preaching

---

[44] J. C. Ryle, "Evangelistic Work at Home," in *The Official Report of the Church Congress, Held at Derby* (London, 1882), 77–83; republished as Ryle, *Can They Be Brought In? Being Thoughts on the Absence from Church of the Working Classes* (London, 1883).
[45] Ryle, *Can They Be Brought In?*, 4–6.
[46] Ryle, *Can They Be Brought In?*, 17–18.
[47] Ryle, *Can They Be Brought In?*, 31.
[48] Ryle, *Can They Be Brought In?*, 35.
[49] J. C. Ryle to the clergy and laity of Liverpool diocese, February 1, 1900, *Liverpool Diocesan Calendar* (1900).

the Bible was central to Ryle's vocation and flowed into his tract writing, which disseminated his sermons to a much wider audience while retaining many of the original attention-grabbing dynamics. He never flagged in his conviction that lively proclamation of the gospel—whether from the pulpit or with the pen—is the God-ordained means of conversion and spiritual growth, essential to reviving the church and establishing healthy Christian disciples.

CHAPTER 10

SORROW AND AFFLICTION

Ryle's tract *Peace! Be Still!* (1853) focused on Jesus calming the storm on the Sea of Galilee (Mark 4). Ryle began by teaching forthrightly against a gospel of material prosperity. The disciples might have assumed that Jesus would "always grant them smooth journeys, fine weather, an easy course, and freedom from trouble and care," but in fact they found themselves in the midst of a great storm. In a similar way, Christians often have to endure anxieties and afflictions, Ryle emphasized, "having your share of sickness and pain, of sorrow and tears, of losses and crosses, of deaths and bereavements, of partings and separations, of vexations and disappointments." As a Christian minister, he was commissioned to offer eternal life and peace with God to any who would receive it. But he dared not offer "worldly prosperity as a part and parcel of the Gospel," because Christ never promised it. Christ's followers should expect not "health and wealth" but trial and tribulation, the "howling wind," and the raging storm.[1]

Misunderstanding on this crucial point, Ryle discerned, caused many Christians to abandon their faith when difficulties arrived. Trials were not only to be expected but also one specific means by which God carried out "the great work of sanctification" in the Christian's life.

> Trouble is often the only fire which will burn away the dross that clings to our hearts. Trouble is the pruning-knife which the great Husbandman employs in order to make us fruitful in good works. The harvest of the

[1] J. C. Ryle, *Peace! Be Still! A Page from Our Lord's History, Being Thoughts on Mark iv. 37–40* (Ipswich, 1853), 5–7.

Lord's field is seldom ripened by sunshine only. It must go through its days of wind, rain, and storm.

Therefore, Ryle urged his readers to "take the Lord on His own terms. Make up your mind to meet with your share of crosses and sorrows, and then you will not be surprised." Nevertheless, in the midst of these troubles, Christians could be confident that God "never makes any mistakes. Be sure that He does all things well. The winds may howl around you, and the waters swell. But fear not."[2]

By the time Ryle published *Peace! Be Still!* in the autumn of 1853, aged thirty-seven, he had already experienced significant personal trials and bereavements firsthand. The collapse of the family bank in 1841 was an early blow. It led to the enforced sale of Ryle's family home, Henbury Hall in Cheshire, to pay the creditors, a public humiliation that wrecked Ryle's social and financial prospects as a young man. More than three decades later, still living with the psychological scars, he explained, "My whole frame, body, mind, and spirit reeled, and was shaken to the foundation, under the blow of my father's ruin." He reflected that he had been "deeply wounded" by these events and might even have been driven to suicide, had he not been a Christian.[3]

Five years later, Ryle experienced another shock with the loss of one of his closest friends and supporters in his Suffolk parish, Georgina Tollemache of Helmingham Hall, wife of the local landowner. In his autobiography Ryle recalled that she "really delighted in my ministry" and was "the brightest example of a Christian woman I ever saw." Her sudden death in 1846, at age thirty-seven, after five hours of convulsions, was "an enormous loss" to Ryle.[4] She was interred in the Tollemache family vault in Helmingham church, and Ryle exclaimed in Latin, in the margins of the burial register, "eheu! quam dependa!" (alas! oh how depended upon!).[5]

Among Ryle's close family there were further sorrows. His first wife, Matilda, suffered from postpartum psychosis following the birth of their daughter in April 1847. She was slowly nursed back to health but then developed pulmonary disease and died in June 1848, after coughing up blood, aged just twenty-four.[6] Their daughter, Georgina, also suffered from

---

[2] Ryle, *Peace! Be Still!*, 7–8.
[3] *Bishop J. C. Ryle's Autobiography: The Early Years*, ed. Andrew Atherstone (Banner of Truth, 2016), 90–92.
[4] *J. C. Ryle's Autobiography*, 123–24.
[5] Andrew Atherstone, "Ryle's Funeral Tribute to Georgina Tollemache," in *J. C. Ryle's Autobiography*, 291.
[6] *J. C. Ryle's Autobiography*, 124–29.

serious mental illness, diagnosed as "mania," and spent most of her life confined to lunatic asylums.[7] Ryle and his second wife, Jessy, had further children, but one of them (an unnamed daughter) died at birth in January 1853—the same year that Ryle wrote *Peace! Be Still!* Jessy herself was plagued with illness throughout their ten-year marriage and died of kidney disease in 1860, aged thirty-eight, leaving Ryle a widower again, with five children between the ages of two and thirteen, and "altogether more disconsolate and helpless than ever."[8] Jessy's gravestone in Helmingham churchyard speaks of hope in Christ and bears several Bible texts, including "God shall wipe away all tears from their eyes" (Rev. 21:4). In *The Christian Leaders of the Last Century*, Ryle observed how the evangelical preacher Henry Venn was also left a widower with a young family, and Ryle commented: "There are anxieties in such cases which no one knows but he who has gone through them; anxieties which can crush the strongest spirit, and wear out the strongest constitution."[9] Later in life, he continued to experience painful bereavements. He buried his third wife, Henrietta, in 1889 after twenty-seven years of marriage, and his eight-year-old grandson, Roger Ryle, died without warning in 1897 while undergoing an operation to remove his adenoids.[10]

Ryle himself endured periods of serious illness. For example, in October 1872, on a visit from Suffolk to Yorkshire to speak at the Church Congress at Leeds, he was taken ill. He was nursed back to health by Henrietta, who recorded in the back of her Bible the chapters she read to her husband on his sickbed, including several penitential psalms, the account of the raising of Lazarus (John 11), and the encouragement that "whom the Lord loveth he chasteneth" (Heb. 12:6). She also noted the passages she read to him during his illness at Stradbroke in 1874, which lasted several weeks, and at Scarborough in 1878.[11] In the following decade, Ryle contributed a sermon to *The Record* newspaper on the malady of King Hezekiah (Isa. 38). He observed that sickness, even though painful, is sent by God for spiritual purposes: "It is a friendly letter from heaven. It is a knock at the door of conscience. It is the voice of the Saviour asking to be let in. Happy is he who opens the letter and reads it, who hears the knock and opens the door, who welcomes Christ to the sick room." Here Ryle spoke from personal experience. He urged his

---

[7] Andrew Atherstone, "Ryle's Last Will and Testament," in *J. C. Ryle's Autobiography*, 333–34.
[8] *J. C. Ryle's Autobiography*, 134.
[9] J. C. Ryle, *The Christian Leaders of the Last Century; or, England a Hundred Years Ago* (London, 1869), 280.
[10] Maurice H. Fitzgerald, *A Memoir of Herbert Edward Ryle* (Macmillan, 1928), 117–18.
[11] *J. C. Ryle's Autobiography*, xxvii.

hearers to approach sickness as "a blessing in disguise, a good and not an evil, a friend and not an enemy. No doubt we should all prefer to learn spiritual lessons in the school of ease and not under the rod. But rest assured that God knows better than we do how to teach us."[12]

Ryle often addressed these themes at fundraising events for hospitals and care homes. Two examples are examined here—preaching for a Nottingham hospital in 1858 and a Liverpool care home in 1885.

Nottingham General Hospital

In October 1858, Ryle preached the annual sermon for the Nottingham General Hospital before the mayor and corporation in St Mary's Church, Nottingham. It was an illustrious gathering, headed by nobleman Earl Manvers and five local members of Parliament, including the Speaker of the House of Commons.[13] For his Bible passage, Ryle chose Lazarus's terminal illness, an address published in tract form as *He Whom Thou Lovest Is Sick* (1859). He began by observing the prevalence of sickness: "The Englishman's house is called his castle. But there are no doors and bars which can keep out disease and death. . . . Who can count up the ailments by which our bodily frame may be assailed? Who ever visited a museum of morbid anatomy without a shudder?"[14] Anatomical museums flourished in mid-nineteenth-century Britain, attracting a public fascinated by their displays of dissected and diseased human organs.[15] New medical remedies and sanitary regulations might have extended average lifespans, Ryle acknowledged, but every person would eventually sicken and die, whether treated by allopathy (conventional medicine) or homeopathy (alternative medicine).[16]

Ryle suggested that only biblical Christianity could satisfactorily explain the prevalence of pain and disease in an otherwise remarkable world. Atheists denied creation by design, but Ryle insisted that their beliefs were demonstrably absurd in the face of anatomical science. He recommended taking an atheist to a surgical school to study the wonders of the human body, and the "matchless skill with which every joint, and vein, and valve, and muscle, and sinew, and nerve, and bone, and limb, has been formed,"

---

[12] J. C. Ryle, "Christ in the Sick Room," in *Christ and His People* (London, 1888), 144, 147.
[13] "General Hospital Seventy-Sixth Anniversary," *Nottinghamshire Guardian*, October 28, 1858, 8.
[14] J. C. Ryle, *He Whom Thou Lovest Is Sick: A Tract on Sickness, Being Thoughts on John xi. 3* (Ipswich, 1859), 5.
[15] Samuel Alberti, *Morbid Curiosities: Medical Museums in Nineteenth-Century Britain* (Oxford University Press, 2011).
[16] Ryle, *He Whom Thou Lovest Is Sick*, 6.

Sorrow and Affliction

surely the result of purposeful creation, not random chance. Deists, on the other hand, believed in a benign creator but denied the biblical doctrine of the fall. Their ideas were also easily proved false, Ryle argued, by a visit to the sick ward of a hospital. Show a deist a young child suffering from incurable cancer, or a dying mother in the final stages of an excruciating disease, and ask the deist for an explanation. Only the biblical account of creation and fall could explain these observable facts, Ryle maintained. God's perfect creation has been marred by sin, "like a handful of gravel in the midst of machinery," bringing pain and suffering in its wake. They are part of the curse that came into the world when Adam and Eve ate the forbidden fruit. "There would have been no sickness if there had been no fall. There would have been no disease, if there had been no sin."[17]

Next, Ryle considered the relationship of sickness to divine providence. Skeptics often challenged the Christian worldview: "Can God be a God of love, when He allows pain? Can God be a God of mercy, when He permits disease?" Ryle admitted that these questions applied as much to other aspects of creation's disorder, like earthquakes and hurricanes, or to the recent "horrible massacres" of British men, women, and children at Delhi and Cawnpore during the Indian Rebellion of 1857. But he reasoned that pain is often necessary for a greater good, as when submitting to a dangerous surgical operation for the sake of future health, or when loving parents sent their young sons away to a Victorian boarding school, amid many tears, knowing that it would ultimately benefit them. In a similar way, Ryle argued, God allows pain and disease to benefit humanity. "Sickness is a good. It is a blessing quite as much as a curse," he said. "It is a rough schoolmaster, I grant. But it is a real friend to man's soul."[18]

These spiritual benefits are numerous, Ryle reckoned. Sickness reminds the sufferer to live in the light of eternity and to think seriously about God. It exposes the "emptiness and hollowness" of material things. "The man of business finds that money alone is not everything the heart requires. The woman of the world finds that costly apparel, and novel-reading, and the reports of balls and operas, are miserable comforters in a sick room." Sickness humbles everyone to the same level. "In the sight of the coffin, and the grave, it is not easy to be proud." It also thoroughly tests the sick person's religious foundations in the same way that winter storms

---
[17] Ryle, *He Whom Thou Lovest Is Sick*, 7–8.
[18] Ryle, *He Whom Thou Lovest Is Sick*, 10–11.

reveal the defects in a poorly built house. "Many a creed looks well on the smooth waters of health, which turns out utterly unsound and useless on the rough waves of the sick bed."[19]

For these reasons, Ryle described sickness as "God's day of visitation" and as "one of the greatest aids to the minister of the gospel," because it increases the impact of sermons and spiritual counsel, and often leads to conversions. He called sickness "God's witness" and "the soul's adviser." "So long as we have a world wherein there is sin, it is a mercy that it is a world wherein there is sickness."[20] As always, Ryle's peroration in his Nottingham sermon was a call to conversion and to heartfelt faith in Christ. "Of all gambling in the world, there is none so reckless as that of the man who lives unprepared to meet God, and yet puts off repentance. . . . Flee to the only Saviour this very day, and cry mightily to Him to save your soul." "The time is short," Ryle urged. "A few more sicknesses, and all will be over. . . . Heaven is becoming every year more full, and earth more empty. The friends ahead are becoming more numerous than the friends astern."[21]

Liverpool Home of Rest

One local example of the burgeoning Christian philanthropy of late-Victorian Britain was the "Turner Memorial Home of Rest for Chronic Sufferers," opened in the Dingle district of Liverpool in 1884. It was erected and endowed by Anne Turner in memory of her husband, Charles Turner (1803–1875), a wealthy Liverpool businessman, shipowner, and member of Parliament. Designed by the prominent Gothic revival architect Alfred Waterhouse (most famous for designing the Natural History Museum in London), it was located on six acres of land overlooking the River Mersey, with eleven wards, accommodating fifty-one male patients. Residents had to be members of the Church of England and suffering from incurable disease, though cancer and geriatric patients were excluded.[22] There was a similar "House of Rest" in the city, founded in 1869 by social reformer Josephine Butler, for women patients suffering from chronic illnesses, known from 1885 as the Liverpool Home for Incurables.

---

[19] Ryle, *He Whom Thou Lovest Is Sick*, 11–12.
[20] Ryle, *He Whom Thou Lovest Is Sick*, 13–14.
[21] Ryle, *He Whom Thou Lovest Is Sick*, 19, 23.
[22] "The Turner Memorial Home," *Liverpool Weekly Courier*, August 5, 1882, 4; "The Turner Memorial Home," *Lancaster Gazette*, October 24, 1885, 8.

Ryle preached at the dedication of the Turner Memorial Home chapel in October 1885. He chose as his Bible text the final words of the elderly King David, as the king reviewed the many vicissitudes of his life and looked forward to the coming of God's eternal kingdom, the dawning of a new day, "a morning without clouds" (2 Sam. 23:4). Ryle himself was approaching his seventieth birthday and drew lessons from the many sorrows of David's family life. He described trials as "spiritual medicines" and as one of the ways God "sanctifies and purifies His believing people." The bishop acknowledged that some people have "a larger cup of sorrows to drink than others," but few can escape trouble for long. Therefore, Christians should pray to be able to say with King David, "My times are in thy hand" (Ps. 31:15), adding, "let it be when Thou wilt, where Thou wilt, and how Thou wilt."[23]

Ryle urged his care home hearers in the midst of suffering to remember the Holy Trinity's "everlasting covenant" with humanity. "There is unspeakable consolation in the thought that the salvation of our souls has been provided for from all eternity, and is not a mere affair of yesterday. Our names have long been in the Lamb's book of life." Comfort amid trials and spiritual power to keeping fighting in the Christian life "were all arranged for us from endless ages, and long before we were born." Although Christians might often struggle and groan and weep, God is always providing for them, even if they cannot see it at the time. "There is no luck or chance in anything that happens to us. The least events in our life are parts of an everlasting scheme or plan in which God has foreseen and arranged everything for the good of our souls." Ryle insisted that this doctrine is entirely different from fatalism and is, instead, a "refreshing cordial" for the Christian faced with trial and bereavement. God's providence will finally be explained on the resurrection morning.[24]

Sanctified Affliction

This teaching permeated Ryle's other tracts. "Suffering is the diet of the Lord's family," he wrote in *Are You an Heir?* (1852). "Suffering is a part of the process by which the sons of God are sanctified. . . . A suffering Saviour generally has suffering disciples."[25] *Do You Want a Friend?*, Ryle's

---
[23] J. C. Ryle, *The Morning Without Clouds: Being Thoughts on 2 Samuel xxiii. 4, 5* (London, 1885), 6-7, 9.
[24] Ryle, *The Morning Without Clouds*, 11-12.
[25] J. C. Ryle, *Are You An Heir? A Question for Everybody* (Ipswich, 1852), 21.

Christmas tract for 1855, asserted that Jesus gives Christians just as much sickness and sorrow as their souls require. "He mixes their bitterest cups like a wise physician, and takes care that they have not a drop too little or too much."[26] In *Do We Grow?* (1864), Ryle argued that trial and affliction are keys to maturing in holiness, whereas constant prosperity is often "injurious to a believer's soul." Encumbered by sickness and anxiety, the Christian can say: "This also is for my profit, that I may be a partaker of God's holiness. It is sent in love. I am in God's best school. Correction is instruction. This is meant to make me grow."[27] Likewise, in *The Garden Inclosed* (1869), Ryle observed that some flowers smell particularly sweet when their petals are crushed, just as grace often shines through heavy affliction. He spoke especially of a young Christian woman to whom he had once ministered. She had been bedridden for six years, living in poverty in a cold garret, with a spinal complaint, "helpless, motionless, cut off from everything that could make this world enjoyable," but "ever rejoicing."[28] Ryle called her "one of the happiest people I ever saw. . . . She was happy because Christ was with her."[29]

These themes also appeared frequently in Ryle's *Expository Thoughts on the Gospels*, especially when he was discussing Jesus's encounters with sick people and their relatives. Ryle emphasized that affliction can be a blessing if it drives people to Christ. For example, he suggested that the paralyzed man at Capernaum would never have been brought to Christ by his friends, or heard pronouncement of his sins forgiven, if he had not been incapacitated (Mark 2). He would probably have "lived and died in ignorance, and never seen Christ at all. . . . That palsy was indeed a blessing. Who can tell but it was the beginning of eternal life to his soul?"[30] Likewise, the nobleman (John 4) and the Canaanite woman (Matt. 15) would never have gone to Christ if their children had not been suffering. "Health is a good thing," Ryle observed, "but sickness is far better, if it leads us to God. Prosperity is a great mercy; but adversity is a greater one, if it brings us to Christ."[31] "Every sickness and sorrow is the voice of God speaking to us," he reiterated.[32] Affliction teaches the Christian "many precious lessons" he or she would

---
[26] J. C. Ryle, *Do You Want a Friend? A Question for Christmas* (Ipswich, 1855), 10.
[27] J. C. Ryle, *Do We Grow? Being Thoughts on Growth in Grace, 2 Peter iii. 18* (London, 1864), 28.
[28] J. C. Ryle, *The Garden Inclosed: A Parable for All Who Love Flowers* (London, 1869), 24–25.
[29] J. C. Ryle, *Are You Happy? A Question for 1856* (Ipswich, 1856), 24.
[30] J. C. Ryle, *Expository Thoughts on the Gospels, for Family and Private Use: St Mark* (Ipswich, 1857), 28.
[31] J. C. Ryle, *Expository Thoughts on the Gospels, for Family and Private Use: St Matthew* (Ipswich, 1856), 180.
[32] J. C. Ryle, *Expository Thoughts on the Gospels, for Family and Private Use: St John*, vol. 1 (London, 1865), 269.

never learn otherwise. For example, it is often on a sickbed or in bereavement that someone discovers the value of Bible passages read many times before.[33] "There are no lessons so useful as those learned in the school of affliction," Ryle noted. "There is no commentary that opens up the Bible so much as sickness and sorrow." He therefore viewed "sanctified disease" as a spiritual boon.[34]

Ryle's appreciation of suffering was closely linked to his understanding of divine providence. "Nothing whatever, whether great or small, can happen to a believer, without God's ordering and permission," he asserted.[35] Everything that befalls the Christian was "foreknown" and "forearranged" by Christ. "There is no such thing as luck, chance, or accident, in the journey of our life. Everything from beginning to end is foreseen—arranged by One who is too wise to err, and too loving to do us harm."[36] Christians are not to be "cold, unfeeling statues," like the Stoic philosophers, nor "idle fatalists," like some contemporary Muslim theologians.[37] They should make prudent financial provision for the future and should use every available means to combat illness, including seeking the best medical advice. Nevertheless, they can rest assured that God is overruling all events for their good, Ryle proclaimed. "The very hairs on their heads are all numbered. Sorrow, and sickness, and poverty, and persecution, can never touch them unless God sees fit. . . . They are immortal, till their work is done."[38]

Cattle Plague and Cholera

Ryle taught that affliction sometimes takes the form of national calamity. During the mid-1860s, a cattle plague (the deadly rinderpest virus) swept across Britain, leading to economic disaster for agricultural communities. There were severe outbreaks on farms in Suffolk, local to Ryle. Christian preachers sought to interpret the contagion theologically, and it called forth dozens of sermons and tracts urging national repentance, such as Edward Harman's *The Cattle Plague: Its Warnings and Its Lessons*, William Clarke's *The Cattle Plague: A Judgment from God for the Sins of the Nation*,

---

[33] Ryle, *St Mark*, 83, 314.
[34] Ryle, *St John*, 1:255–56.
[35] J. C. Ryle, *Expository Thoughts on the Gospels, for Family and Private Use: St Luke*, vol. 2 (Ipswich, 1859), 61.
[36] J. C. Ryle, *Expository Thoughts on the Gospels, for Family and Private Use: St John*, vol. 3 (London, 1873), 511.
[37] Ryle, *St Luke*, 2:138.
[38] J. C. Ryle, *Expository Thoughts on the Gospels, for Family and Private Use: St John*, vol. 2 (London, 1869), 32, 258.

Charles Holland's *The Hand of the Lord upon Our Cattle*, Newton Smart's *The Cattle Plague: A Divine Visitation*, and Bishop Samuel Waldegrave's *The Cattle Plague: A Warning Voice to Britain from the King of Nations*, all published in 1865–1866.[39] Ryle added his voice during this national emergency with his tract *This Is the Finger of God!*, issued in March 1866. He was glad that members of Parliament, scientists, physicians, and farmers were seeking solutions from political, medical, and agricultural perspectives. New laws and remedies were needed to contain the disease and slow the rate of infection. But Ryle made explicit that he spoke as a minister of Christ, approaching the calamity from a biblical perspective.[40]

Concerning the origins of the disease, Ryle gave a direct reply: "I answer unhesitatingly that it comes from God. He who orders all things in heaven and earth—He by whose wise providence everything is directed, and without whom nothing can happen—He it is who has sent this scourge upon us. *It is the finger of God.*" This was the theological verdict of Pharaoh's magicians during the plague of lice (Ex. 8:19), and Ryle wished that "all Englishmen were as wise as these Egyptians!" "I cannot understand," he continued, "how anyone can be called a believer of the Bible who denies God's providence over this world." War, famine, flood, tempest, and disease were all instruments in God's hands. To say that the cattle plague originated in the plains of Russia or was the return of an old disease was to evade the question. To offer merely naturalistic explanations was to think like "an atheist," Ryle proclaimed.[41]

Some suggested that God was too loving to send a plague upon the nation, but Ryle replied that every wise and loving parent chastises his or her children. "There is love even in this fell scourge which is now upon us. The cattle plague is the finger of a wise and loving God." Ryle called it "a message from heaven" designed to awaken Britain to its "great national sins," in the same way that God dealt in the Old Testament with cities like Babylon and Nineveh. He named seven sins as particularly prevalent in British society in the 1860s—desire for wealth, love of amusement, desecration of

---

[39] Matthew Cragoe, "'The Hand of the Lord Is upon the Cattle': Religious Reactions to the Cattle Plague, 1865–67," in *An Age of Equipoise? Reassessing Mid-Victorian Britain*, ed. Martin Hewitt (Ashgate, 2000), 190–206; Stephen Matthews, "Explanations for the Outbreak of Cattle Plague in Cheshire in 1865–1866: 'Fear the Wrath of the Lord,'" *Northern History* 43, no. 1 (2006): 117–35; Joseph Hardwick, "Cows, Communities, and Religious Responses to the 1865–66 British Rinderpest Outbreak," *Journal of Religious History* 48, no. 2 (2024): 153–71.

[40] J. C. Ryle, *This Is the Finger of God! (Exodus viii. 19): Being Thoughts on the "Cattle Plague"* (London, 1866), 4, 12.

[41] Ryle, *This Is the Finger of God!*, 3–6.

Sorrow and Affliction 157

the Sabbath, drunkenness, sexual impurity, friendship to Roman Catholicism, and rejection of the Bible. With regard to alcohol, for example, Ryle lamented:

> The quantity of intoxicating drink needlessly consumed every year in England is something frightful. The number of public-houses, gin-palaces, and beer-shops in our large towns is a standing proof that we are an intemperate people. There are more people, every Sunday night, in some London parishes, in gin-shops, than there are in churches and chapels. We are worse in this respect than either France or Italy.

He believed that these seven national sins were "crying to God against England," and that the cattle plague had been sent as a divine punishment to persuade them to repent.[42]

Ryle approached other national calamities in a similar way. Asiatic cholera was a dangerous scourge of British towns and cities in the mid-nineteenth century. The first major outbreak in 1831–1832, starting in Sunderland, led to the deaths of over thirty-two thousand people. There were further virulent epidemics in 1848–1849, 1853–1854, and 1866, often in places of deprivation, driven by poor sanitation.[43] Ryle's tract *Are You Forgiven?*, written in December 1849, tapped into public alarm at the second outbreak to focus his readers' attention on their own mortality: "We have lately seen the pestilence slaying its thousands and tens of thousands of our countrymen. The strongest have been carried off in a few hours. The cleverest physicians have found their skill entirely unavailing.... Our turn may come next. Our graves may soon be ready for us."[44]

During the fourth cholera outbreak, Ryle composed an entire tract on the subject—*The Hand of the Lord!* (1866)—borrowing a phrase used by King David when plague had come upon the nation of Israel, resulting in seventy thousand funerals in three days (2 Sam. 24:14). Although cholera had recently been identified as a waterborne disease by the epidemiologist John Snow (1813–1858), his theories were not yet widely accepted, and many questions remained unanswered about its cause and transmission. Ryle's analysis reflected the limited medical knowledge of the day: "Cholera is a most *mysterious* visitation. Why it comes in some years and not

---
[42] Ryle, *This Is the Finger of God!*, 7–8, 10–11.
[43] Amanda J. Thomas, *Cholera: The Victorian Plague* (Pen and Sword, 2015).
[44] J. C. Ryle, *Are You Forgiven? A Question for 1850* (Ipswich, 1849), 3.

in others—why it breaks out in one place and not in another—why it is so much more virulent in one parish than it is in another—all these are questions that nobody can answer." However, cholera's fatal consequences were well known. "Think of a thousand sudden deaths in a single week in a city like London. How many helpless widows and orphans it throws on the world! . . . Paupers and peers, doctors and patients, all are alike liable to be attacked."[45]

Despite his occupation as a clergyman, Ryle was not afraid to offer his readers practical sanitary advice, observing that God himself gave rules for cleanliness and good health in the book of Deuteronomy. Yet Ryle's detailed instructions belonged more to the domain of a medical practitioner than to that of a preacher, unlike anything in his other tracts: "Wage war against all bad smells and heaps of dirt, as you would against a poisonous serpent. . . . Forbid green apples, unripe plums, and cheap stale fish to come within your doors. . . . Have a bottle of some simple cholera medicine always in the house."[46] This advice has led twenty-first-century readers to accuse Ryle of inconsistency by the logic that if cholera is God's will, then to evade cholera is to evade God's will.[47] Yet Ryle himself saw no contradiction. He also urged practical support for cholera victims, and financial donations to the London Hospital and to charities like the Metropolitan District Visiting Society and the Mansion House Cholera Relief Fund.[48]

Nevertheless, the heart of Ryle's tract was theological and evangelistic. He insisted that cholera, like every other disease, was a "direct visitation from God." He was therefore not satisfied with scientific explanations like poor drainage, water supply, sanitation, and diet. These might be "second causes," Ryle agreed, but the first cause was God's providence, and therefore he urged his readers to take comfort: "The cholera is an enemy that can do no more than God is pleased to allow." Although cholera sufferers might receive no help from the actions of government and local parish vestries, or from failed medical treatments in overcrowded hospitals, they had no reason to despair. God in his mercy was "directing, managing, and controlling everything around us" and would remove the cholera as soon as its work of "chastisement" was complete.[49]

---

[45] J. C. Ryle, *The Hand of the Lord! Being Thoughts on Cholera* (London, 1866), 4–5.
[46] Ryle, *The Hand of the Lord!*, 13.
[47] Lucy Bending, *Representation of Bodily Pain in Late Nineteenth-Century English Culture* (Clarendon, 2000), 21.
[48] Ryle, *The Hand of the Lord!*, 14.
[49] Ryle, *The Hand of the Lord!*, 7–8.

Sorrow and Affliction

Building on this theology of suffering, Ryle argued that although cholera was painful and distressing, people should not complain, because it was good for the English "body politic." "There are national sins which are calling loudly for amendment, and crying against us before God. Who can tell but cholera is sent to impress these things on our minds?" The latest virulent outbreak, Ryle suggested, was God's way of reminding people that they had souls as well as bodies and must prepare for eternity. Too many Victorians, he warned, were absorbed in the race for financial riches and political power, "living as if they had never to die." But at the "brink of the grave" these pursuits were seen in their true proportions. Ryle also interpreted cholera as God's way of drawing particular attention to the spiritual needs of overcrowded urban districts, because they usually suffered worst from the disease. These districts were famous for "Sabbath-breaking, drunkenness, infidelity, blasphemy, fornication, and the like." "There are hundreds of streets in the east and south of London," Ryle announced, "where you might write up with perfect truth, 'No God here!' Yet these are precisely the kind of places where cholera, when it breaks out carries off its victims by hundreds." He therefore viewed the epidemic as a lesson "that heaps of spiritual and moral filth are just as dangerous to a nation as heaps of material dirt."[50]

Ryle suggested that the reason calamities had fallen upon Britain in such quick succession since the 1840s—the Irish potato famine, the Crimean War, the Indian Rebellion, the cotton famine, the cattle plague, and cholera—was that Britain had failed to repent: "One rod after another has been laid on our backs, and yet we have not humbled ourselves and learned righteousness!" Urgent action was needed. They must all prepare to die, because cholera often attacked suddenly and without warning. "In the face of the deadly disease around you, never be ashamed of seeking safety for your soul. Arise this day and begin to pray. Repent, believe, and be saved."[51] As always, evangelism was Ryle's primary motivation in all his tracts, which were deeply concerned for the spiritual welfare of his hearers and readers. He recognized sorrow and affliction, whether individual or national, as opportunities for gospel summons.

---

[50] Ryle, *The Hand of the Lord!*, 9–11.
[51] Ryle, *The Hand of the Lord!*, 11, 13.

CHAPTER II

FACING ETERNITY

Death was ubiquitous in Victorian society. The prevalence of sudden tragedy, bereavement, and grief generated its own rituals and ceremonies surrounding the deathbed, funerals, mourning, and memorialization. Christian didactic and devotional literature, including obituaries and evangelistic biographies, promoted the ideal of a "good death" and offered advice in the *ars moriendi* (the art of dying).[1] Ryle was part of this flourishing industry. His writings on the Christian life consistently emphasized the need to prepare carefully for death and for what comes afterward.

In Ryle's *Expository Thoughts on the Gospels*, for example, he observed that the gravestones in every English churchyard indicated that only a small proportion of the population lived to be fifty years old, and many never reached adulthood at all. This had been the case throughout human history, he argued. Alluding to Abel in Genesis 4, he noted: "The first grave that ever was dug on this earth, was that of a young man. The first person who ever died, was not a father but a son." Therefore, it is essential to be ready for death: "He that is wise, will never reckon confidently on long life.... The strongest and fairest are often cut down and hurried away in a few hours, while the old and feeble linger on for many years." It is vital "to put nothing off which concerns eternity" and to be prepared "to depart at any moment."[2]

---

[1] Pat Jalland, *Death in the Victorian Family* (Oxford University Press, 1996); Mary Riso, *The Narrative of a Good Death: The Evangelical Deathbed in Victorian England* (Ashgate, 2015); Judith Flanders, *Rites of Passage: Death and Mourning in Victorian Britain* (Picador, 2024).
[2] J. C. Ryle, *Expository Thoughts on the Gospels, for Family and Private Use: St John*, vol. 1 (London, 1865), 254–55.

This motif recurred frequently in Ryle's tracts. *What Is Your Hope?*, written in December 1856, began: "Another year in our short lives is drawing to a close. The sand is running quickly out of the glass. We are drifting on toward death, judgment, and eternity. A few more winters and we shall be gone."[3] He suggested to his readers that the trees from which their coffins would be constructed may already have been cut down; the winding-sheets in which their corpses would be wrapped may already have been woven; the spades with which their graves would be dug may already have been made.[4] Likewise, in *Where Are Your Sins?* (1858), Ryle asked where everyone had gone—the landlords and the laborers, the children "who played in the sunshine as if they would never be old," and the elderly "who leaned on their sticks and gossipped about the days when they were young." "They are all dead, dead, dead! Strong, and beautiful, and active, as they once were, they are all dust and ashes now. Mighty and important as they all thought their business, it all came to an end. And we are travelling the same way! A few more years and we also shall be lying in our graves!"[5] "A new year is coming in sight," he wrote a few months later. "We see its January very near us, but who shall see its December?"[6]

Several of Ryle's Christmas tracts began in a similar way. *Shall You Be Saved? A Christmas Question* (1852) wished his readers a merry Christmas with their families, but observed: "Yet a little while, and your fireside will know you no more. You will be lying in a narrow, silent home. And then, consider—shall you be saved?"[7] *Come! A Christmas Invitation* (1859) urged spiritual reflection amid the seasonal mirth: "There are some missing at Christmas parties this winter, who a year ago were alive and well. . . . Reader, how long have you yourself to live? Will another Christmas find you alive?"[8]

The rapid approach of eternity was a key motivation of Ryle's evangelistic urgency. *Do We Grow?* (1864) chimed in: "Years are slipping away and time is flying. Graveyards are filling up and families are thinning. Death and judgment are getting nearer to us all. And yet you live like one asleep about your soul! What madness! What folly! What suicide can be worse than this? Reader, awake before it be too late." He reiterated: "A few

---

[3] J. C. Ryle, *What Is Your Hope? A Question for 1857* (Ipswich, 1856), 3.
[4] Ryle, *What Is Your Hope?*, 20.
[5] J. C. Ryle, *Where Are Your Sins? A Question for Everybody* (Ipswich, 1858), 10.
[6] J. C. Ryle, *Do You Confess? A Question for 1859* (Ipswich, 1858), 18.
[7] J. C. Ryle, *Shall You Be Saved? A Christmas Question* (Ipswich, 1852), 3.
[8] J. C. Ryle, *Come! A Christmas Invitation: Being Thoughts on Matt. xi. 28* (Ipswich, 1859), 3–4.

more summers, a few more winters, a few more sicknesses, a few more sorrows, a few more weddings, a few more funerals, a few more meetings, and a few more partings, and then—what? Why the grass will be growing over our graves!"[9]

Immortality

Ryle impressed upon his readers that that death is followed by resurrection and judgment. "All is not over when the last breath is drawn and your body becomes a lump of cold clay. No! all is not over! The realities of existence then begin." Every man, woman, and child would be called from their graves to the "great assize," and the "ears that would not obey the church-going bell shall be obliged to obey that summons."[10] This message dominated Ryle's address at the first series of special Sunday evening services for the "working classes," at London's Exeter Hall in June 1857. The platform party included several prominent evangelical parliamentarians, notably the Earl of Shaftesbury, figurehead of this evangelistic initiative.[11] The hall was crammed, with every seat and passageway occupied, and those left outside on the Strand, unable to gain admittance, were dispersed by the police.[12] Ryle's Bible text was Mark 8:36: "For what shall it profit a man, if he shall gain the whole world, and lose his own soul?" It was a question, he told the gathered masses, that should "ring in your ears like a trumpet-blast."[13]

"We live in an age when the multitude are increasingly absorbed in earthly things," Ryle began, "in railways, and docks, and commerce, and trade, and banks, and shops, and cotton, and corn, and iron, and gold." These temporal concerns captivated the Victorian imagination, but Ryle urged his audience to prepare instead for eternity—for what comes after "the doctor's last visit has been paid . . . the coffin is screwed down," and "ashes to ashes and dust to dust" had been pronounced over their grave.[14] In a series of vivid illustrations, Ryle contrasted the incomparable value of the human soul with earthly glories. He remarked how any horse that won the Derby at Epsom Downs or the St Leger Stakes at Doncaster—two of

---
[9] J. C. Ryle, *Do We Grow? Being Thoughts on Growth in Grace, 2 Peter iii. 18* (London, 1864), 23, 29.
[10] Ryle, *Where Are Your Sins?*, 11.
[11] "The Fifth of the Exeter Hall Special Sunday Evening Services," *Morning Chronicle*, June 22, 1857, 6.
[12] "The Exeter Hall Services," *The Nonconformist*, June 24, 1857, 482.
[13] J. C. Ryle, *Your Soul! Being Thoughts on Mark viii. 36, 37* (Ipswich, 1857), 3.
[14] Ryle, *Your Soul!*, 4.

the great "classics" of the flat racing season—was lavished with attention. Vast sums of money hinged on its victories, and painters and engravers captured its image for posterity. Indeed, in early June 1857, just three weeks before Ryle's address, the filly Blink Bonny was catapulted to national fame after winning the Epsom Derby, although there was a riot in September that year when she failed to win the St Leger and her jockey was accused of deliberately throwing the race on the orders of one of the bookmakers. The carnival racing atmosphere and the Blink Bonny scandal were immortalized in *The Lazy Tour* (1857), a short story cowritten by Charles Dickens and Wilkie Collins, who were both in the St Leger crowd.[15] "Yet," Ryle declared, "the weakest infant in a working man's family, is far more important in God's sight than that horse. The spirit of the beast goeth downwards; but that infant has an immortal soul."[16]

Next, he turned to the Manchester Art Treasures Exhibition, then in full swing, where paintings by Rubens, Titian, and other old masters were admired by rapturous crowds. "But there is no immortality about these things. The earth, and all its works, shall be burned up. The little babe that cries in a garret, as the excursion train whirls past, shall outlive all those pictures for it has a soul which shall never die." Ryle also imagined a future century when ancient constructions like the Egyptian pyramids and the Athenian Parthenon would have crumbled to dust alongside impressive royal residences like Windsor Castle and the Palais des Tuileries in Paris. "But the soul of the humblest labourer is of far more enduring stuff. It shall survive the crash of an expiring universe, and live on to all eternity."[17] The Tuileries was gutted in an arson attack by the Paris Commune in 1871 and demolished in 1883, so in the later compilation version of his Exeter Hall address, Ryle replaced it with Westminster Abbey, another long-standing but ultimately temporary structure.[18]

As a Christian minister, Ryle attended many deathbeds. He observed that the solemnity of death "strips off the tinsel and pretence," forcing the dying person to consider the value of his or her soul. "The man who can tell good stories, and sing good songs to merry companions, turns very grave when he begins to feel that life is leaving his body. The boasting infidel

---
[15] Jamie Wise, "Horse Racing in Nineteenth-Century Literature" (MA thesis, University of Chester, 2013), 58–60.
[16] Ryle, *Your Soul!*, 6.
[17] Ryle, *Your Soul!*, 6.
[18] J. C. Ryle, "Our Souls!," in *Old Paths: Plain Statements on Some of the Weightier Matters of Christianity, from the Standpoint of an Evangelical Churchman* (London, 1877), 44.

at such a season has often cast aside his infidelity." Indeed, Ryle argued that the "vaunted philosophy" of famous Enlightenment deists like Voltaire (1694–1778) and Thomas Paine (1737–1809) "breaks down when the grave is in sight."[19] He therefore urged his audience to recognize that their soul was a treasure of eternal value and to let that reality shape their ambitions. The discovery of gold in California in 1848 and New South Wales in 1851 led to the first "gold rushes" of the Victorian age, as masses of people traveled thousands of miles, chasing the dream of sudden riches.[20] Ryle told his working-class hearers that they might possess all these piles of newly discovered gold, or even be "the owner of half a county" back home in England, like the richest aristocrat; but despite "all your money or broad acres, you will carry nothing with you when you die. A few feet of earth will suffice to cover that body of yours when life is over. And then, if your soul be lost, you will find yourself a pauper to all eternity."[21]

Continuing the theme of poverty and riches, Ryle warned of a coming day "when banknotes shall be worth no more than wastepaper, and gold and diamonds shall be as the dust of the streets—when the palace of the peer and the cottage of the peasant shall both alike fall to the ground—when stocks and funds shall be all unsaleable." On that judgment day, "soul-loss will then be seen to be the greatest of losses, and soul-gain the greatest of gains. . . . Once lost, no loss can compare with the loss of the soul."[22] Ryle therefore saw it as his Christian duty to awaken people to the reality of their predicament without Christ. He likened their "imminent peril" to an emigrant attempting to sail across the Atlantic Ocean, from England to America, in a leaky ship without compass, water, or provisions—or to a young child attempting to carry the irreplaceable Koh-i-Noor diamond, a recent addition to the crown jewels, from the Tower of London to Bristol without being robbed. Such foolishness was bound to end in disaster. Varying the image again, Ryle urged: "The stream of life can never stand still. Whether you are sleeping or waking, you are floating down that stream. You are coming nearer and nearer to the rapids. You will soon pass over the falls, and if you die without a decided faith, be cast away to all eternity."[23]

---

[19] Ryle, *Your Soul!*, 11.
[20] George Fetherling, *The Gold Crusades: A Social History of Gold Rushes, 1849–1929* (University of Toronto Press, 1997); Mark A. Eifler, *The California Gold Rush: The Stampede That Changed the World* (Routledge, 2016).
[21] Ryle, *Your Soul!*, 10–11.
[22] Ryle, *Your Soul!*, 13.
[23] Ryle, *Your Soul!*, 7–8.

As usual, Ryle ended his Exeter Hall address with an evangelistic summons. To drive home his appeal, he turned again to contemporary events absorbing public attention. In mid-June 1857, the Crystal Palace (relocated from Hyde Park to Sydenham, in south London) hosted its first great "Handel Festival." It was a musical phenomenon with a mass choir of two thousand singers and a giant orchestra with three hundred strings, nine flutes, nine oboes, nine clarinets, nine bassoons, nine trombones, twelve horns, twelve trumpets, and nine drums. The organ, weighing twenty tons, with 4,568 pipes, was the largest in Britain. The festival was attended by Queen Victoria and Prince Albert, and the audience swelled to eighteen thousand people on the last day. It was said that the "Hallelujah" chorus, from Handel's *Messiah*, could be heard half a mile away.[24] With this freshly in the mind of his congregation, Ryle proclaimed:

> But what was all that burst of harmony in the Hallelujah Chorus to the outburst of joy which is heard in heaven when a soul turns from darkness to light? What was it all but a mere whisper compared to the joy of angels over one sinner taught to see the folly of sin, and to seek Christ? Oh! come and add to that joy without delay. . . . Oh! come to Christ, and your soul shall live.[25]

Also in the news was the first investiture ceremony of the Victoria Cross, due to take place in Hyde Park just a few days after Ryle's sermon, for sixty-two heroic veterans of the Crimean War.[26] Ryle praised these gallant soldiers and their bravery but noted that they could enjoy their medals for only a few years before they too would die. "But the crown which Christ gives never fades," the preacher declared. "The rewards of Christ's soldiers are for evermore. Their home is eternal. Their glory never comes to an end."[27]

The Reality of Hell

Competing visions of death and eternity dominated Victorian literature, art, and theology. The doctrine of hell, in particular, caused pastoral anxieties and troubled consciences. It was therefore refashioned by preachers

---

[24] Michael Musgrave, "The Handel Festivals, 1857–1926," in *The Musical Life of the Crystal Palace* (Cambridge University Press, 1995), 35–37.
[25] Ryle, *Your Soul!*, 18–19.
[26] Melvin Charles Smith, *Awarded for Valour: A History of the Victoria Cross and the Evolution of British Heroism* (Palgrave Macmillan, 2008); James W. Bancroft, *The Victoria Crosses of the Crimean War: The Men Behind the Medals* (Frontline, 2017), 2.
[27] Ryle, *Your Soul!*, 20.

and poets to embrace alternative ideas such as universalism, annihilationism (or "conditional immortality"), and postmortem repentance.[28] Ryle often broached the topic directly and took a conservative approach, which he viewed as the only scriptural option. At Exeter Hall, he announced, "I am one of those old-fashioned ministers, who believe the *whole* Bible—and everything that it contains." He condemned the new doctrines as "smooth-spoken theology," and affirmed, "I believe that there is a real hell." Rather than keep silent, Ryle insisted that it was an act of Christian compassion, and also his ministerial duty, to speak about hell. "I see danger ahead, and I would fain warn every man to flee from the wrath to come. I see peril of shipwreck, and I would light a beacon and entreat every man to seek the harbour of safety."[29]

Ryle expounded the reality of hell at length in *Wheat or Chaff?* (1851). Echoing John the Baptist, he declared that when Jesus Christ returns in judgment, he will "burn up the chaff with unquenchable fire" (Matt. 3:12). Ryle interpreted this to mean the punishment of unbelievers in eternal, conscious torment. "There is no pain like that of burning," he observed. "Put your finger in the candle for a moment if you doubt this and try." He encouraged his congregation to look into the mouth of a blast furnace at an iron foundry and imagine what it would be like to be inside. Furthermore, Ryle maintained that this painful punishment will never end. "Millions of ages shall pass away, and the fire into which the chaff is cast shall still burn on. That fire shall never burn low and become dim. The fuel of that fire shall never waste away and be consumed." He lamented that within the Victorian church and wider English society erroneous views of hell were taking root. One practical consequence was the "utter apathy" of contemporary Christians for holy living and urgent evangelism.[30]

Ultimately, Ryle saw this as a matter of biblical authority. His determination to teach the doctrine of hell was closely linked to his doctrine of Scripture:

> Do you believe the Bible? Then depend upon it, *hell is real and true*. It is as true as heaven—as true as justification by faith—as true as the fact

---

[28] Geoffrey Rowell, *Hell and the Victorians: A Study of the Nineteenth-Century Theological Controversies Concerning Eternal Punishment and the Future Life* (Clarendon, 1974); Michael Wheeler, *Heaven, Hell, and the Victorians* (Cambridge University Press, 1994).
[29] Ryle, *Your Soul!*, 7, 10.
[30] J. C. Ryle, *Wheat or Chaff? A Question for 1851* (Ipswich, 1851), 22–23.

that Christ died upon the cross—as true as the Dead Sea. There is not a fact or doctrine which you may not lawfully doubt if you doubt hell. Disbelieve hell, and you unscrew, unsettle, and unpin everything in Scripture.[31]

Furthermore, Ryle argued that this question concerned the very nature of God as revealed in Scripture. To preach heaven without hell was a form of idolatry, he suggested, because it was equivalent to manufacturing a god to suit modern Victorian sensibilities, "a God who is all mercy, but not just—a God who is all love, but not holy." He protested:

> Such a God is an idol of your own, as real as Jupiter or Juggernaut—as true an idol as any snake or crocodile in an Egyptian temple—as true an idol as was ever moulded out of brass or clay. The hands of your own fancy and sentimentality have made Him. He is not the God of the Bible, and beside the God of the Bible there is no God at all.

Ryle rebuked his hearers for trying to squeeze Scripture into their own "fanciful theories," or making selections from it to suit their tastes, "refusing, like a spoilt child, whatever you think bitter—seizing, like a spoilt child, whatever you think sweet." This was no better, he remarked, than the attitude of King Jehoiakim, who cut out objectionable parts of Scripture with his penknife and destroyed them in the fire (Jer. 36). "What does it amount to but telling God, that you, a poor short-lived worm, know what is good for you better than He. It will not do. It will not do. You must take the Bible as it is. You must read it, and believe it all."[32]

Ryle observed that in the New Testament those with the most to say about hell were Jesus, the compassionate Savior, and John, the apostle of love. They should be the clergyman's model. Although many Victorian commentators in the 1850s were suggesting it was "bad taste" to mention the subject, Ryle refused to "soothe men with constant lullaby of peace." "The devil rejoices when Christians are silent about hell," he insisted.[33] Likewise, in *Lot's Wife* (1855), Ryle asserted, "No man can honestly read the four Gospels and fail to see that he who would follow the example of Christ, *must* speak of hell." Although Ryle was mocked for this old-fashioned "brimstone theology," he was determined not to depart from

---

[31] Ryle, *Wheat or Chaff?*, 24.
[32] Ryle, *Wheat or Chaff?*, 26–27.
[33] Ryle, *Wheat or Chaff?*, 24, 26.

"the old paths of apostolic Christianity." He reasoned: "The watchman who keeps silence, when he sees a fire, is guilty of gross neglect. The doctor who tells us we are getting well when we are dying is a false friend. And the minister who keeps back hell from his people in his sermons is neither a faithful nor a charitable man." Therefore, Ryle warned his readers to avoid fashionable preachers who muzzled these gospel truths. Such ministry may seem pleasant, "but it is far more likely to lull you to sleep than to lead you to Christ.... It may be popular, but it is not scriptural. It may amuse and gratify, but it will not save."[34]

In the same month that he wrote *Lot's Wife*, Ryle penned *Strive!* (1855), based on the command of Jesus in Luke 13:24: "Strive to enter in at the strait gate: for many, I say unto you, will seek to enter in, and shall not be able." Ryle warned that one day the door to heaven will be shut, and it will then be impossible to turn to God. "The day of grace will be over. The gate of salvation will be bolted and barred. It will be *too late!*" On that day, banknotes will be "as useless as rags," and silks, satins, velvets, and laces will be no substitute for "the robe of Christ's righteousness." People will no longer be able to deny eternal realities. On that day, Ryle declared mournfully, every faithful gospel minister, though mocked and scorned now, will be publicly vindicated.[35] Therefore, he urged his unconverted readers to acknowledge their mortality and put their faith in Christ without delay:

> A few more years at most and you are gone. Your place in the world will soon be filled up. Your house will be occupied by another. The sun will go on shining. The grass and daisies will soon grow thick over your grave. Your body will be food for worms. And your soul will be lost to all eternity.

At the same time, Ryle exhorted his Christian readers to take seriously their responsibilities in evangelism. "Happy indeed is that Church, whose members not only desire to reach heaven themselves, but desire also to take others with them!" He calculated that if every believer brought one person to Christ each year, the whole human race would be converted within twenty years.[36] Gospel proclamation, Ryle celebrated, is the God-given means of helping sinners to change their destinies from the miseries of hell to the

---
[34] J. C. Ryle, *Lot's Wife: Being Thoughts on Luke xvii. 32* (Ipswich, 1855), 19, 22–25.
[35] J. C. Ryle, *Strive! Being Thoughts on Luke xiii. 23* (Ipswich, 1855), 21–24.
[36] Ryle, *Strive!*, 26, 29.

joys of heaven. *Never Perish* (1855), written just three months after *Lot's Wife* and *Strive!*, hammered home the point. Ryle warned unbelievers that they were "literally hanging over the brink of the bottomless pit," and he pleaded: "Sudden death to the saint is sudden glory; but sudden death to the unconverted sinner, is sudden hell. Oh! search and see what is the state of your soul!"[37]

In subsequent decades, Ryle continued this line of teaching. In December 1877, he was invited to contribute the fourth sermon to an Advent series at Peterborough Cathedral on life, death, judgment, and eternity—a variation on the traditional "four last things": death, judgment, heaven, and hell. Ryle argued that if heaven is eternal, then hell must be also, and that errors concerning eternity usually stemmed from distorted views of God. For example, some theologians focused exclusively on God's mercy, love, and compassion, while ignoring God's holiness, purity, justice, and hatred of sin. "Let us beware of falling into this delusion," Ryle warned. "It is a growing evil in these latter days."[38]

That same Advent season, Church of England clergyman Frederic Farrar (1831–1903) preached a controversial sermon series at Westminster Abbey, published as *Eternal Hope* (1878), which challenged traditional conceptions of hell, especially eternal punishment.[39] In reply, Ryle rejoiced, like Farrar, in God's "amazing mercifulness" and acknowledged that there were many mysteries concerning the origin of evil, God's allowance of cruelty and sickness, the death of infants, and the future prospects of the "heathen" in China, India, and Africa who had never heard the Christian gospel. These, he said, were "great knots which I am unable to untie, and depths which I have no line to fathom." Nevertheless, he recognized a "mass of Scripture evidence" in support of eternal punishment and that, by ignoring it, Farrar might as well throw the Bible away altogether.[40] Ryle, now aged sixty-two, quoted at length from *Wheat or Chaff?* (written when he was just thirty-four), observing that over the intervening years he had "stood by many graves, shed many tears, carried many crosses, spoken with many Christians, and read many books." But now, older and wiser, he still found no reason to alter his teaching.[41]

---

[37] J. C. Ryle, *Never Perish: Being Thoughts on Final Perseverance* (Ipswich, 1855), 31.
[38] J. C. Ryle, *Eternity! Being Thoughts on 2 Cor. iv. 18* (London, 1878), 12.
[39] Frederic W. Farrar, *Eternal Hope: Five Sermons Preached in Westminster Abbey, November and December, 1877* (London, 1878). See, further, Geoffrey Rowell, "Eternal Hope," in *Hell and the Victorians*, 139–52.
[40] Ryle, *Eternity!*, 22, 24–26.
[41] Ryle, *Eternity!*, 29.

The Hope of Heaven

Ryle's conviction about the reality of judgment went hand-in-hand with a strong emphasis on the joys of heaven. His first wife, Matilda, was buried in 1848 in her family vault at Nonington parish church in Kent. The following year, Ryle published *Christ and the Two Thieves* (1849), which included a meditation on being with Christ "in paradise" (Luke 23:43). "Some of us know by bitter experience," Ryle lamented, that the days after the death of a loved one "are the slowest, saddest, heaviest weeks in all our lives."

> But, blessed be God, the souls of departed saints are free from the very moment their last breath is drawn. While we are weeping, and the coffin preparing, and the mourning being provided, and the last painful arrangement being made, the spirits of our beloved ones are enjoying the presence of Christ.

They have passed through the valley of death to the place where sorrow, strife, and sin are abolished. "Surely we should not wish them back again," Ryle reasoned. "We should not weep for them, but for ourselves."[42]

In confirmation of this doctrine, Ryle quoted from the burial liturgy in the Book of Common Prayer, which had been read at Matilda's funeral: "We give thee hearty thanks, for that it hath pleased thee to deliver this our sister out of the miseries of this sinful world."[43] He also quoted a striking letter from *The Life of the Late Rev. Henry Venn* (1834), in which Venn announced the death of his second wife, Catherine. In words that resonated with Ryle's own experience, Venn wrote to a friend in 1792: "I have some of the best news to impart. One beloved by you has accomplished her warfare, has received an answer to her prayers, and everlasting joy rests upon her head. My dear wife, the source of my best earthly comfort for twenty years, departed on Tuesday."[44] Ryle, though, had been married for only three years, not twenty like the Venns. Preaching to himself, perhaps, he exhorted those who were grieving the death of a Christian to take comfort from the scriptural promise that their loved one was with Jesus in paradise and now "in the best of hands." To Christian readers facing their own death he gave this encouragement: "Then see from these verses how near you

---

[42] J. C. Ryle, *Christ and the Two Thieves: Being Thoughts on Luke xxiii. 39–43* (Ipswich, 1849), 21–22.
[43] Burial of the Dead (1662), in *The Book of Common Prayer: The Texts of 1549, 1559, and 1662*, ed. Brian Cummings (Oxford University Press, 2011), 456.
[44] Ryle, *Christ and the Two Thieves*, 22; quoting *The Life and a Selection from the Letters of the Late Rev. Henry Venn, M.A.*, ed. Henry Venn (grandson) (London, 1834), 500.

are to home. A few more days of labour and sorrow, and the King of kings shall send for you; and in a moment your warfare shall be at an end, and all shall be peace."[45]

Pastorally, Ryle applied this teaching to those who felt bereft. He observed, for example, that Christmas family gatherings were often painful occasions, especially for the older generation, because the joyful festivities reminded them of the loss of loved ones. *Our Gathering Together!*, Ryle's Christmas tract for 1868, asked:

> Do tears rise unbidden in your eyes, when you mark the empty places round the fireside? Do grave thoughts come sweeping over your mind, even in the midst of your children's mirth, when you recollect the dear old faces and much loved voices of some that sleep in the churchyard? . . . Do you feel lonely and desolate as every December comes round?

Ryle encouraged his readers with the assurance that separated Christians will be permanently reunited in heaven, around the throne of God. "Those whom you laid in the grave with many tears are in good keeping. You will yet see them again with joy. . . . The lonely time will soon be past and over. You will have company enough by and by."[46] This consolation was inscribed by Ryle in 1889 on the gravestone of his third wife, Henrietta, in Childwall churchyard, on the outskirts of Liverpool. It states that she "rests in hope, waiting for the coming of our Lord Jesus Christ and our gathering together unto him." On that day, Ryle emphasized in *Our Gathering Together!*, there will be no more partings or goodbyes. "The youngest babe that ever drew breath shall not be overlooked or forgotten," he wrote, perhaps thinking of his own daughter who died at birth in 1853. "We shall once more see our beloved friends and relatives who fell asleep in Christ, and left us in sorrow and tears—better, brighter, more beautiful, more pleasant than ever we found them on earth."[47] Yet this great gathering in heaven will be only for Christ's followers. Therefore, woven through Ryle's tract was a warning: "Reader, take care that you are not left behind."[48]

In one of his earliest public lectures, delivered at St Clement's Church, Ipswich, on New Year's Day 1849—six months after he was bereaved of his first wife—Ryle highlighted the doctrine of assurance as a particular com-

---

[45] Ryle, *Christ and the Two Thieves*, 24.
[46] J. C. Ryle, *Our Gathering Together! A Tract for Christmas, Being Thoughts on 2 Thes ii. 1* (London, 1868), 15.
[47] Ryle, *Our Gathering Together!*, 10–11.
[48] Ryle, *Our Gathering Together!*, 8.

Facing Eternity

fort at the hour of death. It enables the Christian to say not merely "I hope and trust" all will be well in the end but "I know and feel" it.[49] He pointed again to the Book of Common Prayer and its liturgy for the visitation of the sick, which describes Almighty God as "a most strong tower to all them that put their trust in him" and prays that the sick person would "know and feel" that health and salvation are found only in "the name of our Lord Jesus Christ."[50] Ryle often reminded his readers that what they needed most on their deathbeds were the "old foundation truths" of salvation by grace alone through faith in Christ. "These are the old friends to which our souls will turn at last in the hour of our departure. These are the ancient doctrines on which we shall lean back our aching heads, when life is ebbing away and death is in sight." When all human props are stripped away, "new-fangled notions" of theology will be useless. "Nothing will do us good then but the blood of Christ."[51]

When death loomed near, Ryle encouraged Christians to remind themselves of this reality: "Nothing can break my union with Christ." Illness and frailty, he said, may make someone feel "like an old useless log, a weariness to others, and a burden to thyself. But thy soul is safe. Jesus is never tired of caring for thy soul." Thus Ryle celebrated:

> Doctors may have given over their labours. Friends may be unable to minister to thy wants. Sight may depart. Hearing may depart. Memory may be almost gone. But the loving-kindness of God shall not depart. Once in Christ thou shalt never be forsaken. . . . Reader, may this be your portion in life and death! And may it be mine![52]

Furthermore, rejoicing in the doctrine of God's providential care, Ryle taught that the very hour of a Christian's death is God's choosing. In his *Expository Thoughts on the Gospels*, he explained: "Till the hour comes for dying no Christian will die. When the hour comes nothing can prevent his death."[53] Therefore, Christians should not be "over-anxious" about the future, even while they use medicines and make prudent plans. The happy person, Ryle concluded, is the one who can affirm: "I shall live on earth till my work is done, and not a moment longer. I shall be taken when I am ripe

---

[49] J. C. Ryle, *Assurance* (Ipswich, 1849), 36.
[50] Visitation of the Sick (1662), in Cummings, *The Book of Common Prayer*, 447.
[51] Ryle, *Where Are Your Sins?*, 30.
[52] Ryle, *Never Perish*, 34–35.
[53] J. C. Ryle, *Expository Thoughts on the Gospels, for Family and Private Use: St John*, vol. 2 (London, 1869), 97.

for heaven, and not a minute before. All the powers of the world cannot take away my life, till God permits. All the physicians on earth cannot preserve it, when God calls me away."[54]

Ryle's Deathbed

Ryle often meditated on the joys of communion with Christ and its implications as he faced eternity. For example, he wrote in 1852, in full health, aged thirty-six: "Blessed prospect indeed! I am a dying man in a dying world! All before me is dark! The world to come is a harbour unknown! But Christ is there, and that is enough."[55] Likewise, preaching in Nottingham in 1858, he remarked that "bare union" with Christ is not enough. He urged the congregation to seek "heartfelt, experimental *communion* with Him."

> The day may come when after a long fight with disease, we shall feel that medicine can do no more, and that nothing remains but to die. Friends will be standing by, unable to help us. Hearing, eye-sight, even the power of praying, will be fast failing us. The world and its shadows will be melting beneath our feet. Eternity, with its realities, will be looming large before our minds. What shall support us in that trying hour? What shall enable us to feel, "I fear no evil"? Nothing, nothing can do it but close communion with Christ.[56]

This was the attitude Ryle sought to cultivate as he approached his own death. He observed that many Christians wrongly regarded energetic action as the only way to glorify Christ and saw death as merely "a painful termination of usefulness." But Ryle insisted that it is equally possible to glorify God on a deathbed, through patient endurance. He urged his readers to be prepared for death at any moment, and he wanted to be found "like a sentinel at his post . . . with a heart packed up and ready to go."[57]

Ryle pursued Christian ministry as long as he was physically able. On his seventieth birthday, in 1886, he announced in Liverpool that "although he could not run as fast, jump over a five bar gate, pull a boat, or play cricket, he could still do something. . . . His labours were a joy to him and

---

[54] J. C. Ryle, *Expository Thoughts on the Gospels, for Family and Private Use: St Luke*, vol. 2 (Ipswich, 1859), 139.
[55] J. C. Ryle, *Are You an Heir? A Question for Everybody* (Ipswich, 1852), 28.
[56] J. C. Ryle, *He Whom Thou Lovest Is Sick: A Tract on Sickness, Being Thoughts on John xi. 3* (Ipswich, 1859), 22–23.
[57] J. C. Ryle, *Expository Thoughts on the Gospels, for Family and Private Use: St John*, vol. 3 (London, 1873), 512–13.

the greatest pleasure he had for the few remaining years of his life was to preach the Everlasting Gospel throughout the diocese."[58] He continued in an active ministry of public evangelism and had hoped "to die in harness," as he told his diocese in a farewell letter, but old age and ill health forced him to resign his bishopric in March 1900.[59] In weakness, he returned to Suffolk, to the seaside town of Lowestoft, thirty miles from his old parish of Stradbroke. There he died of a stroke in June, aged eighty-four.

Ryle's body was returned to Liverpool for burial next to his third wife. One of his Bibles, which he had used constantly for more than half a century, was placed in his coffin, clasped in his folded hands.[60] His gravestone in Childwall churchyard is inscribed with two Bible texts. First, the apostle Paul's dying testimony, which ably summarized Ryle's own public witness and pursuit of holiness: "I have fought a good fight, I have finished my course, I have kept the faith" (2 Tim. 4:7). Underneath is Ryle's conversion text, from his days as an Oxford undergraduate: "By grace are ye saved through faith" (Eph. 2:8). Taken together, these two texts express the heartbeat of Ryle's ministry and encapsulate many of the great themes of his tracts on the Christian life.

---

[58] Quoted in Ian D. Farley, *J. C. Ryle, First Bishop of Liverpool: A Study of Mission Amongst the Masses* (Paternoster, 2000), 121.
[59] J. C. Ryle to the clergy and laity of Liverpool diocese, February 1, 1900, *Liverpool Diocesan Calendar* (1900).
[60] "The Late Bishop Ryle: Funeral at Childwall," *Liverpool Mercury*, June 15, 1900, 9.

FURTHER READING

Primary Texts

Many of Ryle's writings, including his most popular compilation volumes, remain in print with the Banner of Truth Trust:

Charges and Addresses
Christian Leaders of the Eighteenth Century
Expository Thoughts on the Gospels (7 vols.)
Holiness
Knots Untied
Light from Old Times
Old Paths
Practical Religion
The Upper Room

For a compilation of five Christmas tracts, see J. C. Ryle, *Christmas Thoughts*, ed. Andrew Atherstone (Banner of Truth, 2022).

For further important source texts, see *Bishop J. C. Ryle's Autobiography: The Early Years*, ed. Andrew Atherstone (Banner of Truth, 2016), and *Bishop J. C. Ryle's Letters: The Later Years*, ed. Andrew Atherstone (Banner of Truth, forthcoming).

Biographical Studies

Atherstone, Andrew. "J. C. Ryle and Evangelical Churchmanship." In *Making Evangelical History: Faith, Scholarship and the Evangelical Past,* edited by Andrew Atherstone and David Ceri Jones. Routledge, 2019.

Bebbington, David. "J. C. Ryle." In *The Heart of Faith*, edited by Andrew Atherstone. Lutterworth, 2008.

Farley, Ian D. *J. C. Ryle, First Bishop of Liverpool: A Study in Mission Amongst the Masses*. Paternoster, 2000.

Gatiss, Lee, ed. *Stand Firm and Fight On: J. C. Ryle and the Future for Anglican Evangelicals*. Lost Coin, 2016. Collected essays from *The Churchman* journal, by Andrew Atherstone, Alan Munden, Vaughan Roberts, Peter Toon, and others.

Loane, Marcus. *Makers of Our Heritage: A Study of Four Evangelical Leaders*. Hodder and Stoughton, 1967.

Munden, Alan. *Travel with Bishop J. C. Ryle: Prince of Tract Writers*. Day One, 2012.

Murray, Iain H. *J. C. Ryle: Prepared to Stand Alone*. Banner of Truth, 2016.

Rogers, Bennett W. *A Tender Lion: The Life, Ministry, and Message of J. C. Ryle*. Reformation Heritage, 2019.

Russell, Eric. *That Man of Granite with the Heart of a Child: A New Biography of J. C. Ryle*. Christian Focus, 2001.

Toon, Peter, and Michael Smout. *John Charles Ryle, Evangelical Bishop*. Reiner, 1976.

Wellings, Martin. "J. C. Ryle's 'First Words.'" In *Evangelicalism in the Church of England, c. 1790–c. 1900*, edited by Mark Smith and Stephen Taylor. Boydell, 2004.

GENERAL INDEX

About Sin! (tract), 22–23
Aeschylus, 25
affliction, and sanctification, 153–55
agnosticism, 18–19, 98
agricultural illustrations, 86
Albert, Prince, 48, 166
Alford, Henry, 122
Alfred the Great, 33
Anglo-Catholics, 138
Anna Ivanovna, Empress, 44
annihilationism, 167
antinomianism, 36, 58, 87
Apostles' Creed, 80, 124
Are We Overcoming? (tract), 104
Are We Sanctified? (tract), 54–55, 109, 112–14, 116
Are You an Heir? (tract), 44–45, 153
Are You Converted? (tract), 46, 87
Are You Fighting? (tract), 101–4, 107
Are You Forgiven? (tract), 21, 157
Are You Free? (tract), 32
Are You Holy? (tract), 109
Arminians, 61
armor of God, 115
Arnauld, Antoine, 83
ars moriendi, 161
Art Treasures Exhibition. *See* Manchester Art Treasures Exhibition
ascetism, 113
assurance, 172–73

Athanasian Creed, 80
atheists, 31, 44, 150
atonement, 27–29, 62–64
Augustine, 46, 64
Avesta, 31

backsliding, 66, 118
ballroom dancing, 93
banknotes, 120
baptism, 87, 105
Battle of Waterloo (1815), 101
Baxter, Richard, 63, 75, 136
Belcher, Edward, 83
Bell, John, 104
Bengel, Johann Albrecht, 122
Berridge, John, 52, 142
Bible, 9
　as anchor and authority, 20
　apparent mistakes in, 17
　centrality of, 146
　on hell, 167–68
　infallibility of, 10–11
　inspiration of, 14–18
Bible education, 11–14
Bible reading, 120–23
birdlime, 25
Blackstone, William, 12
Blaikie, W. G., 98
Blink Bonny scandal, 164
body, in Christian theology, 97

179

Book of Common Prayer, 22, 45, 71, 75, 119, 124
  burial liturgy, 105, 171
  ordination liturgy, 133
  visitation of the sick, 173
  wedding liturgy, 111
Book of Mormon, 13
book prayers, 119
Brace, C. L., 98
Bradford, John, 59
Brewster, David, 12
"Brigade of Guards," 104
Bright, John, 12
"brimstone theology," 168
British and Foreign Bible Society, 121
British Association for the Advancement of Science, 18, 97
British Empire, 2, 101, 105
British Medical Association, 97
British Reformation Society, 9
broad church movement, 2
Brooks, Thomas, 109
Buckland, William, 12
Bunyan, John, 79, 114
Burgess, Anthony, 21
Burgon, John, 16
Burke, Thomas, 24

Calvin, John, 64, 68
Calvinists, on election, 58–59
Cambridge University, 2
Can They Be Brought In? (tract), 145
card-playing, 93
Carey, William, 82
Carfax Church (Oxford), 40
Carroll, Lewis, 2
cattle plague, 155–56, 159
Cavendish, Frederick, 24
ceremonialism, 78, 130, 139, 144
Chalmers, Thomas, 12, 16
Champollion, Jean-François, 28
Charges and Addresses (book), 7
charity, 30, 32, 94–97

Cheshire Yeomanry, 101
cholera, 157–58, 159
Christ and the Two Thieves (tract), 171
Christianity, good for the world, 97–99
Christian Leaders of the Last Century (book), 51–52, 136–38, 142, 149
Christian life
  founded on Scripture, 7, 9, 20
  framed by Thirty-Nine Articles, 85
  growth in, 108–9
  as warfare, 102–5, 107–11
Christian maturity, 123
Christocentrism, of Ryle, 30
Christopher, Alfred, 40, 51
church, not infallible, 10
Church Association, 7, 21, 80
Church Congress movement, 7
Church Homiletical Society, 139–40
"Churchianity," 75
church membership, 33, 87
Church Missionary Society, 138
Church of England, 7, 39
  training in preaching, 135
Church of Ireland, 2
Church Pastoral Aid Society, 105, 138
church reform, 7
Clarke, William, 155
classics, 12
Clergyman's Magazine, The, 140
Colenso, John, 20
Collins, Wilkie, 164
Colonial Church and School Society, 81
Come! A Christmas Invitation (tract), 162
Come Out! (tract), 90–92
comfort, amid trials, 153
communion with Christ, 174
conditional immortality, 167
conversion, 39–55, 80, 81, 87, 107
cotton famine, 159
counterfeit faith, 74–76

creation, disorder of, 151
cricket, 92
Crimean War, 25–26, 101, 104, 105, 159, 166
Cross, The (tract), 27–29
cross of Christ, 28
crown of glory, 104
crucifixion, 28–29
Crystal Palace, 1, 43, 48, 166

Daily Prayer Union, 50
Darwin, Charles, 2, 20
Davenant, John, 64, 68
death, readiness for, 161–63
Decalogue, 124
deists, 30, 151, 165
democracy, 32
demonic possession, 52
De Quincey, Thomas, 36
Derbyshire General Infirmary, 95–96
de Rougé, Emmanuel, 28
Dickens, Charles, 2, 81, 164
dictation (theory of inspiration), 15
"dictionary" words, 141
discipleship, 79–82, 83, 86, 91
Disraeli, Benjamin, 3, 32
"Dissentianity," 75
divine sovereignty, and human responsibility, 65
double predestination, 64
Do We Grow? (tract), 108–9, 154, 162
Do You Believe? (tract), 66, 80–81
Do You Love Christ? (tract), 76, 80, 87
Do You Pray? (tract), 117–20
Do You Want a Friend? (tract), 153–54
Duke of Marlborough, 104
Duke of Wellington, 103, 104

Earl of Shaftesbury, 163
earnestness, over doctrine, 107
Edouart, Augustin Gaspard, 35
educational standards, 11
Edwards, Jonathan, 71
Egypt, 28

election, 57–58
Eliot, George, 2
Ellicott, Charles, 122
Elliott, Charlotte, 37
English Reformers, 10
Enlightenment, 165
enthusiasm, 47
eternal punishment, 170
Eton College, 3, 12, 85, 92
evangelicals
    missional and reformist activities of, 2–3
    networks, 138
evangelism, responsibilities in, 169
Exeter Hall (London) addresses, 34, 163, 166
experiential religion, 80–81
experimental Christianity, 77, 114
Expository Thoughts on the Gospels (book), 16–17, 18, 60, 63, 66–67, 117, 120–21, 122, 154, 161, 173
external religiosity, 113

faith, 33, 34, 87
    and character, 111
    and works, 85
false peace, 26–27
false worship, 130
family prayer, 117
fanaticism, 47
Faraday, Michael, 12
Farrar, Frederic, 170
fatalism, 153
fiction, 95
finger of God, 156
Fletcher, John, 137
formalism, 76–79, 113
Form or Heart? (tract), 76
forsaking sin, 36
"four-point" Calvinism, 63
franchise, extension of, 32, 33, 55, 57
Franco-Prussian War, 101, 105
Franklin, John, 82–83

freedom, 32
fruits of faith, 85–90, 94–95
fundraising bazaars, 96

gambling, 94
Garden Inclosed, The (tract), 47–48, 154
Gaussen, Louis, 16
Gilgamesh epic, 18
Gladstone, William, 57
God
   as Creator, 45
   as Father, 45
   love for all humanity, 62
godliness, 77, 88
   and prayer, 117–18
   pursuit of, 125
golden chain of salvation, 30
gold rushes, 165
good death, 161
good Samaritan, 96
Goodwin, Thomas, 48, 75
good works, 85
Graham, Billy, 37
graveyards, 162–63
"Great Ejection" (1662), 77
Great Exhibition (Crystal Palace), 43–44, 48
"Great Tom" (London bell), 36
Grimshaw, William, 142
Gurnall, William, 110

Haldane, Robert, 16
Hall, Thomas, 77
"Hallelujah" chorus, 166
Hand of the Lord!, The (tract), 157–59
Harman, Edward, 155
Have You a Priest? (tract), 120
Have You Charity? (tract), 94–95
Have You Peace? (tract), 26–27, 101
Have You the Spirit? (tract), 86
heart religion, 71–83
heaven, 171–73
hell, 166–70
Helmingham, 3–4, 73, 124, 125, 126

Henry, Matthew, 122
Herschel, John, 12
Herschel, William, 12
Hervey, James, 141
He Whom Thou Lovest Is Sick (tract), 150–52
higher Christian life, 106
HMS Victory, 14
Hogarth, William, 52
holiness, 109–10, 111
Holiness (book), 88, 106–8
holiness movement, 106–7, 108
Holland, Charles, 156
Holy Spirit, 111, 122
   and conversion, 46–47, 49, 50
   indwelling of, 86–87
Hooper, John, 68, 125
Horace, 12
horse racing, 92–93
How Do You Worship? (tract), 129–30
How Readest Thou? (tract), 15
human impotence, 60
Hunt, Edward, 6
Hunt, William, 6
hyper-Calvinism, 62–64, 65
hypocrisy, 75

iconography, 115
idolatry, 115
"imputed sanctification," 112
Indian Rebellion, 101, 159
industrialization, 1
indwelling sin, 109
intellectualism, 79–81
Irish potato famine, 159
Is It Real? (tract), 52–53, 74–76
Is Thy Heart Right? (tract), 72–74

"jellyfish Christianity," 107
Jesus Christ
   compassion of, 67
   love of, 64
   suffering of, 83, 153
Jewel, John, 16, 68

General Index

Jones, Griffith, 41
Judas Iscariot, 75
judgment day, 93, 163, 165
Judson, Adoniram, 82
"Just As I Am" (hymn), 37, 106
justification, 27, 108
    and good works, 85
    and sanctification, 111–12

Keep It Holy! (tract), 124–28
Keswick Convention, 106–7
Knots Untied (tract), 23, 127

Latimer, Hugh, 68, 135–36, 139
Laud, William, 136
Laudianism, 139
Lawrence, John, 105
Layard, Austen Henry, 17, 127
laziness, 121
Lee, William, 16
legalism, 36
Lepsius, Karl Richard, 28
liberalism, 31
licentiousness, 58
Lightfoot, J. B., 122
lingering, 89
Liverpool, 4, 11, 101, 145
Liverpool Home for Incurables, 152
Living or Dead? (tract), 41–43, 85–86
Lloyd-Jones, Martyn, 7
London Mission Week, 144
London Zoo, 37
Lord's Day Observance Society, 124
Lord's Prayer, 124
Lot, 88–89
Lot's Wife (tract), 71–72, 90, 168, 170
love, of neighbor, 94–97
Luther, Martin, 46

Macaulay, Lord, 12, 81
Manchester Art Treasures Exhibit, 48–49, 164
Mansion House Cholera Relief Fund, 158

Manton, Thomas, 21, 75, 106
Martyn, Henry, 82
Marx, Karl, 123
matrimony, not a means of conversion, 89
McCaul, Alexander, 16
M'Cheyne, Robert Murray, 79
McNeile, Hugh, 48
means of grace, 61–62, 115–17, 128
Melvill, Henry, 139
mental health, 94
Metropolitan District Visiting Society, 158
military metaphors, 101
Milton, John, 13
miracles, 15
moderation, 94
modern technology, 72
monasticism, 91, 113
Moody, D. L., 145
More, Hannah, 3
"more than conquerors," 103
Morgan, Edward, 41
Mormonism, 31
Morrison, Robert, 82

Napoleon, 25
Napoleonic Wars, 101, 103
national calamities, 155–59
National Lord's Day Rest Association, 124
national sins, 159
National Sunday League, 123–24
Nelson, Admiral, 14
"Neologians," 18
Never Perish (tract), 50–51, 68–69, 170
new birth, 50
Newman, John Henry, 2
Newton, Isaac, 12
Newton, John, 3, 46, 50, 71
New Zealand, 42
Nicene Creed, 80
nominal Christians, 102

Nonconformity, 7, 75
None of His! (tract), 48–50, 87
Nottingham General Hospital, 150

Only One Way (tract), 30–31
opium, 36
orthodoxy, 80
Our Gathering Together! (tract), 172
Owen, John (Puritan), 21, 63, 75, 114
Owen, John (Victorian clergyman), 41
Oxford University, 2, 12, 79, 92

Paine, Thomas, 44, 165
Paley, William, 20, 34
Palmerston, Lord, 3
particular redemption, 62–63
Peace! Be Still! (tract), 147–48
peace with God, 25–27, 108
Pearson, John, 34
perfection, 106
perseverance of the saints, 66–69
Peter Lombard, 79
Pharisees, 18, 78
philanthropy, 96–97
plenary verbal inspiration, 15
Pope, Alexander, 32, 49
popery, 130
postmortem repentance, 167
poverty and riches, 165
Practical Religion (book), 94, 116
prayer, 117–20
preaching, 133–46
  training for, 135, 139
  urgency in, 143–46
predestination, 58
prevenient grace, 61
private judgment, 9–10
private prayer, 117–20
providence, and suffering, 151–52
public prayer, 117
public worship, 128–31
purgatory, 44
Puritans, 22, 35, 71, 109

Qur'an, 13, 31

Racovian Catechism, 31
recreation, 92–94
Reformation, 85, 98, 135
regeneration, 40
Regeneration (tract), 42
religious pluralism, 31
Remember Lot (tract), 88–89, 125–26
repentance, 35–37, 54, 159
reprobation, 64
resurrection, 163
revival, and biblical preaching, 135
revivals, 50–55
Richmond, Legh, 13
ritualism, 2, 75
Robert the Bruce, 33
Roman Catholicism, 7, 18, 47, 119, 121, 135, 138, 157
romantic novels, 95
Rosetta Stone, 28
Rowlands, Daniel, 40–41, 143
Russian ice palace, 44
Rutherford, Samuel, 111
Ryle, Georgina (daughter), 148–49
Ryle, Henrietta (third wife), 149, 172
Ryle, J. C.
  as author, 4, 6
  as bishop of Liverpool, 4
  burial of, 175
  collapse of his family's bank, 148
  conversion of, 3, 39–40
  death of, 174–75
  education of, 12
  illnesses of, 149–50
  military experience of, 101
  ordination of, 9, 133
  as popularizer, 113
  sermons of, 4–5
  tracts of, 4–6
Ryle, Jessy (second wife), 149
Ryle, Matilda (first wife), 148, 171
Ryle, Roger (grandson), 149

Sabbath, 123–28
sacramentalism, 129–30
sacraments, 87
sacrificialism, 130
Sadducees, 18
sanctification, 55, 105–14, 116
    through trials, 147–48, 152, 153–55
sanitary advice, 157–58
Scott, Thomas, 46, 122
Scotus, John Duns, 79
Scripture. *See* Bible
Scupoli, Lorenzo, 114
Second Reform Act (1867), 32
secularization, 2
selfish indifference, 96
Selwyn, George, 42
sensuous worship, 113
separation from the world, 90–91
sermon delivery, 142–43
Sermon on the Mount, 111
sermons, simplicity in, 140–41
Shaftesbury, Lord, 3, 34
Shakespeare, William, 13, 92
Shall You Be Saved? (tract), 162
Shastras, 13
shipwrecks of faith, 66–67
Sibbes, Richard, 106
sick, care of, 97
sickness, and providence, 151–52
Simeon, Charles, 3
Simon Magus, 75
"Simplicity in Preaching" (tract), 140–42
sin
    fighting against, 103
    sinfulness of, 21–23
sincerity, 31
sinless perfection, 112
skepticism, 18–19, 80, 98, 99
slavery in America, 33
Smart, Newton, 156
Smith, George, 18
Smith, Hannah Whithall, 106, 107
Smith, Joseph, 31

Smith, Robert Pearsall, 106, 107
Snow, John, 157
social reforms, 137–38
Society for Irish Church Missions, 119
Socrates, 98
Soldiers and Trumpeters (tract), 105
Sophocles, 25
sovereign grace, 40, 60–61, 65–66, 69
spiritual freedom, 33–34
spiritual laziness, 111
spiritual maturity, 117
spiritual warfare, 89, 102–5, 107, 110
sports, 92, 93–94
Spurgeon, Charles Haddon, 2, 141
St Ann's Church (Manchester), 48
St Clement's Church (Ipswich), 29
Stephenson, Robert, 14
stony heart, 72–74
Stowell, Hugh, 48
Stradbroke, 3, 115
Strive! (tract), 115–16, 169, 170
suffering, 151–55, 159
Suffolk, 3–4
Sugden, Edward, 12
Sumner, John Bird, 3
Sunday, 123–28, 140
surplice, 144
Swedenborg, Emanuel, 31
Synod of Dort (1618–1619), 62–63, 64

Taylor, Jeremy, 114
Tell, William, 33
theaters, 93
theological liberalism, 2
Thirty-Nine Articles of Religion, 10,
    22, 30, 39, 58, 61, 68–69, 75, 85
This Is the Finger of God! (tract), 156–57
Thomas á Kempis, 114
Thomas Aquinas, 79
Thompson, Elizabeth, 105
Tollemache, Georgina, 148
Tollemache, Lionel, 73
total depravity, 24

Tractarianism, 2, 75
tracts, of Ryle, 4–6
traditionalism, 18
Traill, Robert, 75, 111
trials, 147–48, 153
Tried by Its Fruits (tract), 98
True Priest, The (tract), 119–20
truth telling, 30
Turner, Anne and Charles, 152
Turner Memorial Home of Rest for Chronic Sufferers (Liverpool), 152–53

unbelief, 18–19
union with Christ, not broken with death, 173
universal salvation, 62, 167

Vedas, 31
Venn, Henry, 92, 138, 171
Victoria, Queen, 1, 13, 35, 101, 105, 166
Victoria Cross, 166
Victorian age, 1–3, 96, 138, 163, 165, 168
　formalism in, 78–79
　evangelicalism in, 105
　revivalism in, 52
　unbelief in, 18–19
Victorian theologians, 16
Voltaire, 44, 165

Waldegrave, Samuel, 156
Wallbridge, Elizabeth, 13
Ward, Samuel, 142
War of the Spanish Succession, 104

Washington, George, 33
Watch (tract), 118
Waterhouse, Alfred, 152
Watson, Thomas, 21
Wesley, John, 137
Westminster Abbey, 164
What Does It Cost? (tract), 53, 107
What Is the Church? (tract), 130
What Is Wanted? (tract), 134–35
What Is Your Hope? (tract), 81, 162
Wheat or Chaff? (tract), 43–44, 67, 167, 170
Where Are Your Sins? (tract), 21, 29, 34, 162
Whitefield, George, 51, 137
Whitgift, John, 68
Whose Word Is This? (tract), 15
Wilberforce, William, 3
Williams, Henry, 82
Woodiwiss, Abraham, 95–96
Wordsworth, Christopher, 16
working classes, 34
worldliness, 88–94, 126, 136
Worldly Conformity (tract), 90
World War I, 102

Young, Thomas, 28
Young Men's Christian Association, 136
Young Men's Society for Aiding Missions at Home and Abroad, 135
Your Election! (tract), 57–59, 67

zeal, 81–83
Zoroastrianism, 31

SCRIPTURE INDEX

Genesis
book of   16
19:16   88
19:26   88

Exodus
8:19   156
20   16
20:8   124

Leviticus
book of   22

Deuteronomy
book of   158

1 Samuel
21:1   17

2 Samuel
6:14   93
23:4   153
24:14   157

1 Chronicles
book of   16

2 Chronicles
book of   16

Ezra
1:9   16

Psalms
31:15   153

Ecclesiastes
3:4   93

Isaiah
38   149

Jeremiah
36   168

Ezekiel
11:19   72

Matthew
3:12   167
11:26   60
15   154
27:9   17

Mark
2   154
2:26   17
4   147
7:13   18
7:33   117
8:36   163
10:9   111
16:15   65

Luke
2:2   17
10   78
10:26   11
10:37   96

13:3	35	14:8	138
13:24	169		
14:28	107	**2 Corinthians**	
18:35	62	6:14	89
23:43	171	6:17	90
24:45	122		
		Galatians	
John		6:14	27
1:29	63		
3:16	62	**Ephesians**	
4	154	2	40
6:37	61	2:1	41
6:39	66	2:8	175
6:44	60	6:14–17	115
8:36	32		
10:28	68	**1 Thessalonians**	
11	149	5:21	10
12:47	63		
15:16	60	**1 Timothy**	
17	16	2:4	64
20:24	129	6:12	102
		2 Timothy	
Acts		3:16	14
book of	16	4:7	175
4:12	30	4:13	16
16:31	45		
		Hebrews	
Romans		12:6	149
1	25		
5:1	26	**1 Peter**	
7	109, 112	5:4	104
8	16	5:8	37
8:9	48		
8:37	103	**2 Peter**	
9:15	62	1:21	14
10:20	62	3:9	64
16:12	13		
		Revelation	
1 Corinthians		book of	140
13:2	94	21:4	149

WISDOM FROM THE PAST
FOR LIFE IN THE PRESENT

Theologians on the Christian Life

AUGUSTINE by GERALD BRAY	**BAVINCK** by JOHN BOLT	**BONHOEFFER** by STEPHEN J. NICHOLS	**CALVIN** by MICHAEL HORTON	**EDWARDS** by DANE C. ORTLUND	
GRIMKÉ by ANDREW J. MARTIN	**LEWIS** by JOE RIGNEY	**LLOYD-JONES** by JASON MEYER	**LUTHER** by CARL R. TRUEMAN	**NEWTON** by TONY REINKE	
OWEN by MATTHEW BARRETT & MICHAEL A. G. HAYKIN	**PACKER** by SAM STORMS	**RYLE** by ANDREW ATHERSTONE	**SCHAEFFER** by WILLIAM EDGAR	**SPURGEON** by MICHAEL REEVES	
STOTT by TIM CHESTER	**WARFIELD** by FRED G. ZASPEL	**WESLEY** by FRED SANDERS	**WHITEFIELD** by TOM SCHWANDA & IAN MADDOCK		

The Theologians on the Christian Life series provides accessible introductions to the great teachers on the Christian life, exploring their personal lives and writings, especially as they pertain to the walk of faith.

For more information, visit **crossway.org**.